Frameworks for Cultural and Racial Diversity:
Teaching and Learning for Practitioners

Dorothy Chave Herberg

Department of Social Work
York University

Canadian Scholars' Press Inc.   Toronto   1993

Frameworks for Cultural and Racial Diversity:
Teaching and Learning for Practitioners

First published in 1993 by
Canadian Scholars' Press Inc.
180 Bloor Street West, Suite 801
Toronto, Ontario
M5S 2V6

Canadian Cataloguing in Publication Data

Includes bibliographical references.
ISBN 978-1-55130-022-1

1. Discrimination in employment. 2. Minorities -
Employment. 3. Pluralism (Social science). 4. Race
relations - Philosophy. I. Title.

HD4903.H47   1993   648.3'041   C93-093647-7

Printed and bound in Canada

Acknowledgements

It is with more than gratitude that I remember the hundreds of students in the School of Social Work at York University who have taken part in the evolution of these frameworks. Through almost two decades, students in my classes have produced Acculturative Frames on themselves and their families, taken part in non-verbal simulations and examined their own values through the Ethnic Root Behaviour Pattern exercise. I feel a deep connection and partnership with them, and, in fact, still remember many of their frames and patterns.

I would also like to thank the many community and hospital workers who have participated through workshops in the contexting scheme, non-verbal simulations and other training activities. Through them I got a glimpse of agency and hospital work that enabled me to understand a little of what the cross-cultural issues were like for them in professional life.

So many others have been part of my development. I would like particularly to remember the Multicultural Workers' Network. Especially, Anne Marie Nosal Singh who as the President of the Alumni of the Faculty of Social Work in 1976 pioneered the organization of a multiculturalism conference for alumni social workers that resulted in the Network. Here I met Diana Abraham who, with Carl James, has gently tried, over the years, to teach an Anglo about race and racism. Also in the Network, it is a pleasure to acknowledge Eva Allmen and Esther Blum who have been supportive friends over the years; their careful response to the models in the book have been vital to my understanding. In particular, I would like to acknowledge the idea of Benchmark transparencies (in Chapters 7 and 8) from Esther and her University of Winnipeg Social Work students.

From my earlier life as a graduate student at the University of British Columbia, I would like to recognize the support of Cyril Belshaw, Harry Hawthorne and Kaspar Naegele. At the University of Michigan, I remember with affection Robert Cooley Angel who encouraged a new Canadian student who was far from home, and Lou Ferman who supported my graduate research project through the U.S. Dept. of Labor. Of course, over years, Henry Meyer and Eugene Litwak were enormously influential for me in the Doctoral Programme in Social Work and Sociology and I hope that they can see a little of what they were trying to achieve in that programme in this book.

So many other people in and close to the social work community have helped me. Margaret Norquay, who was an early pioneer in this subject, has been a close critic and staunch friend over many years. Earlier and recent drafts were read by her and those careful comments helped me greatly to see the material in better perspective. To other members of the small group, known as CIIEPS, the Committee for Intercultural and Interracial Education in Professional Schools, I have been especially indebted: May Yoshida, Roberta Marcus, Saroj Chowla, Marion Bogo, Michael Cormier, Diana Gendron.

Although acknowledged in the Introduction of the Book, I am very grateful to Mildred Sikkema and Agnes Niyekawa-Howard, Edward T. Hall, and Daphne McGoldrick, all pioneering authors whose written works have profoundly helped me understand the task that was before me.

A very sustaining person from the early days in my writing was Marilyn DeFlorio, who typed many versions of what are now chapters in this book.

Finally, to my husband, Edward, who has been a loving and tireless advisor and editor through many revisions of this book and who has patiently helped me iron out knots in my thinking, I can only say, that without him, this book would not have been written. Also, thanks to my daughter, Naomi, for her support and care, even when a Mother was not always available.

TABLE OF CONTENTS

Section 2
VALUES IN BEHAVIOUR: THE NON-VERBAL MODES

Section 3
TRACING BACK TO VALUE ORIGINS
WITH THE ACCULTURATIVE FRAMEWORK

Introduction

CONCEPTUAL AND EMPIRICAL ORIGINS

This is a book for human service workers on how to apply social science knowledge about cultural and racial sensitivity on an ongoing, moment-to-moment basis in their professional practice. It is rooted in a specific philosophical approach, builds on findings from basic social science theory and is indebted to earlier applied cultural studies. It is based on an holistic approach, because the real world of experience is whole; it does not depend on labelling people by their ethnicity but by considering the cultural attributes that must be present in any real experience.

The ideas come out of my own education in social work, sociology and anthropology; and my twenty-five years experience as a teacher in Schools of Social Work and participant-trainer in workshops in the community. The need for this book has been apparent to me because, throughout my experience as a teacher in this field, I have found no works on how practitioners are to integrate social science knowledge into their daily practice.

To begin, this book is rooted in the philosophical principle of Canadian life guaranteed under the Charter of Rights and Freedoms: that everyone living in Canada has an equal place in our society. This approach is based on the relation that, although the facts of our emergence as a nation are not in dispute, many people have **acted** as if Canadians, especially the Charter groups, have always been here, owned the land, have undisputed rights to occupancy. Further, those ethnicities that are said to have been here "first" have an absolute right to cultural hegemony. That aboriginal peoples had been here for thousands of years was ignored. The Multiculturalism Policy of 1971, however, transformed that principle into a more egalitarian one. Since then, the vision of Canada has widened to include groups that have come to Canada more recently. Because of the Charter and the 1988 Multiculturalism Act, the most recent shift is a focus on anti-racism education and the structural shifts that a non-racist Canada will require. (Thomas and Novogrodsky, 1983)

In this book the aim is to enfold everyone, including Native and Non-Native Peoples, into the scope of the country, find a way to talk about everyone evenhandedly and all at once in the same picture. This is not easy to do and not everyone will want to be included, but at least the possibility of doing so should be in our minds because literally anyone can walk into our office and require service.

Given a philosophical base, this book is built on findings from earlier studies that point the way to more harmonious and satisfying intercultural and interracial relations. Three of these that have stimulated me and directed my thinking are commented on: One of the most important research projects for intercultural work, which took place over fifteen years ago in Hawaii at the School of Social Work, is the first source. In a field project, overseen by the International Association of Social Workers, social work students were placed in a Guamanian village to learn about the process of attaining "biculturality," a term used then to refer to cross cultural sensitivity. These students, interacting with the Guamanian villagers, reported experiencing many important alterations:

- mutual growth in respect for each other

- changed attitudes and outlooks about themselves and others

- recognition of how much there is to learn about other people, and pleasure in contemplating that learning

- re-examination of their own values that they had earlier taken for granted

- willingness to take risks in getting to know new people

- greater comfort with not knowing all the answers

- willingness to divest themselves of feelings of superiority over others

- a beginning understanding that basic principles permeate action and that these can be conceptualized and understood.

These comments from students in that project operationalize several aspects of cultural sensitivity. The important methodological advance in the project involved the principle that **understanding others was based on one's cultural growth and self-understanding.** Contrary to "common sense," cultural sensitivity is not based on cognitive learning about a culturally different people — in this case, the Guamanians — it was not necessary to label people by their ethnicity and learn that ethnic culture. In fact, the learning about others occurred by learning about their own selves as they behaved in a foreign environment. The process whereby this sensitivity was learned is the subject of the 1977 book by Mildred Sikkema and Agnes M. Niyekawa-Howard, *Cross-cultural Learning and Self-Growth*. Aspects of this project are summarized here in Chapter 1.

Another vital conceptual source upon which this book depends is that of "contexting," an analytical process developed by Edward T. Hall in *Beyond Culture* (1976a, 1976b). Contexting is described in Chapters 3 and 4 and is the first of several "frameworks" presented in the book. "Contexting" covers cultural values in a way that applies to everyone. Hall's ideas make it practical to think of identifying cultural values in the ongoing practice of human service work.

The next major set of concepts, for which I am very indebted to others, has to do with non-verbal behaviour. There are six non-verbal modes thatI have learned about, using simulations during classroom teachings and community workshops. Years ago, I attended the Second International Conference on Non-verbal Behaviour organized in Toronto by Aaron Wolfgang (1984). The state-of-the-art addresses on these different modes and additional supporting papers then were valuable additions to knowledge about these modes for developing cultural sensitivity. These ideas form the second "framework" in the book, Chapters 5 and 6.

The third "framework" of the book is the Acculturative Framework that I have been developing in classroom teaching and in community consultations. It is a strategy for organizing the components of ethnic identity with the fewest possible number of variables. In Chapters 7, 8, and 9 as in all the others, the situation of the practitioner is always in view; the need for practical, "portable" models that can be internalized and integrated with other knowledge comprises a vitally important aspect of making cultural sensitivity training realizable and reliable.

These three very different kinds of work form the foundation for this book because, though quite distinct, the concepts are all interrelated. Together they indicate what is needed to start cultural sensitivity training where the outcome is awareness of the cultures operating in the setting.

My own work on Ethnic Root Behaviour Patterns, which appears in Chapter 9, is an exercise developed especially for people who have little awareness of their connection to an ethnicity. My data, extracted from frequently conducted exercises into ethnic root patterns, indicate that the culture of origin perseveres powerfully through generations and that most people, even those many generations Canadian-born, can discover a connection with their cultural past and identify "basic assumptions" or values of their own that influence their daily ideas and actions.

Practice Theory

The models or frameworks in this book begin to create "practice theory," a systematic way of applying knowledge in the practice of serving clients. These models draw on some of the most central and well-established theories in sociology and anthropology. The ideas themselves then are not in question but, rather, to whom do they apply and to what extent, in any given situation. The task of enquiry for the service provider becomes the extent to which these ideas apply in a given practice situation.

To assist in their usefulness in the real world of practice, there has been considerable work to reduce the number of variables in the models so that there can be a clear image of the main processes involved and so that they can be "portable" — i.e., easily remembered and easily carried into the practice situation. The frameworks covered here carry only 21 variables altogether, a feasible number for the helper to remember. Because the models are constructed simply, they are easy to recall in the practice situation. Deciding which variables to emphasize was not an easy process because there is little or no data possible for variables that apply at a very abstract level. I have made these decisions from impressions I gathered over years of teaching, informal discussion with other teachers, and from reports and studies that bear on the subject.

What emerged is that it is indeed possible to reduce this complex arena to concepts that are "metapatterns," concepts that are simple, abstract and non-contextual. Metapatterns can open up thinking on a subject, but do not provide precise details; an enormous number of topics can be subsumed under such a concept. These concepts act as catalysts to understanding a subject and suggest where to look for meanings; they are guideposts or handholds that are easily recalled when it is necessary to find one's way in new places. These kind of concepts are responsive to the constantly changing scene of practice. Gregory Bateson's work (1979) has been helpful; the idea of "the pattern that connects" (Bateson,1979: 11) is what lies behind the process of simplifying the conceptual arena.

THE CENTRAL PURPOSE OF THIS BOOK

All of these introductory remarks are preparatory to the central purpose of this book. In one sentence: **the end result sought is developing a sensitivity to racial and cultural diversity to make human services work more beneficial.** Both collegial relations, and relations between service providers and service receivers need to be improved. Amelioration of the climate for anti-racism training to be conducted, as well as ways to achieve equity in employment are also objectives of this sensitivity training. I believe that the objectives in this book form the solid foundation of self-confidence, better communication and knowledge of differences that is needed to move forward to effect structural change.

Stated in the language of cultural sensitivity training, the issue can be put thus: **If people are not aware of their own basic cultural values, then it is all too easy to impose those values on others.** In the workplace itself, without this awareness, colleagues can be evaluated in a biased way and clients-patients being served can be quite negatively assessed and served. Although cultural sensitivity by itself will probably not lead to structural change, it can (1) reveal what changes are needed and (2) point to the attitudinal changes necessary to make those structural changes possible. The attitudinal changes that this book aims for include: feeling more positively about (liking) a specific ethnocultural group of people; feeling more comfortable that changes to assist a group are legitimate and beneficial; feeling less threatened by the demands of ethnocultural groups; feeling freer to discuss subjects like prejudice and racism that previously the worker considered as taboo; being more understanding of the values maintained by another group; feeling more comfortable about not knowing all the answers; and becoming more conscious about the parameters of one's own ethnocultural identity.

DIFFICULTIES IN TEACHING/LEARNING CULTURAL SENSITIVITY

There are two main difficulties in trying to communicate about or learn cultural sensitivity, both involving the substantive and conceptual; the substantive one relates to terminology, and the conceptual aspect is the lack of concrete needs in this area.

Terminology

It seems to be almost impossible to use terms that will please everyone. In fact, the changing consciousness reflected in using new terms is an intellectual "journey" in itself, not just for each person but for the entire field of cultural and racial sensitivity training. For example, in the United States, the term "Negro" was discarded in favour of "Black." The movement underlying this name change was the increasing confidence and pride by people of African ancestry in being "Black." The term "Black" brings with it those same qualities and has been used almost exclusively now in Canada. However, there are some now who prefer the term "Afro-Canadian" because it points to the region of origin as other ethnic labels do, and is thus more parallel to other groups. Similarly, Native Peoples have moved away from the term "Indian," and especially "Eskimo," because of the association of that term with the historic error made by European explorers on landing in North America believing they had reached the Indian sub-continent. The term "Native Peoples," and now, more frequently, "First Nations," or "Aboriginal Peoples" reflects the pride felt by Canadian aboriginal people in their ancient connection to this continent. The term "Indian People" is also used because there are historical connections to it that some people wish to keep. Another terminological development is for the term "people of colour" to be used if national ancestry is unclear or complicated.

The terminology in the field of cultural sensitivity has also undergone many changes. At first the Canadian term "multiculturalism" was used to cover almost any thing or activity associated with things ethnic. Exactly what was being referred to, though, was vague. Other countries started activity in this field and other terms — "cross-cultural," "intercultural," "ethnocultural," and "transcultural" — all became appropriate synonyms, some of which came about because authors tried to distinguish different aspects of the work. In this book, I use the term "multicultural work" to mean work carried out by people in a nation whose members are diverse not only because of different streams of new immigration but also because these other terms do not encapsulate the increasing heterogeneity in ethnoculture, race, and religion of Canada's people.

Connected to the problems in using the term multicultural is the word "culture." The heart of the concept culture is "pattern," which carries the idea of something abstracted from the "real" world of the senses. Thus, it also carries the idea that who is doing the abstracting is vitally important to understanding what has been abstracted. Probably no word has accrued to itself more ideas that are only tangentially connected. Words linked with culture, like "ethno-culture," sometimes become the whole concept. For example, if programme funders encapsulate the idea of culture in the term ethnoculture, then funding for cultural issues is interpreted as ethnocultural issues only; this error may mean that interest in another aspect of culture such as "women's culture" is not legitimate.

Another word that is in the middle of a storm of controversy is "race." Some would like to jump over the issues it raises by saying that there is only one race, the "human race." It would be nice to be able to elide this difficult dimension in this way; however, the facts are incontrovertible that many, in

North America at least, find racial differences a deeply emotional issue. We must face these issues and struggle with the term with all its attendant problems in order to reach a more equitable condition.

Another problematic area of terminology is that for referring to people in the human service field. I want to talk to people providing a wide range of services; I use the terms "practitioner," "service provider," "professional worker" as generic terms including social worker, physician, nurse, teacher, lawyer, etc.

One way around terminology problems, wherever they exist, is to use other people's own words to talk about the issues in which they are interested. This takes more flexibility but in the long run it may be more effective. I have learned that when one comes upon an issue in an oblique way or in ways that do not feel "right," much time is wasted finding a common ground on which to work. People care very deeply about how they appear in print. In the writing of this book, much care has gone into trying to be respectful to those who might read it. However, when words are found that seem to get in the way of communication, the reader is asked to try to find other ways of expressing what is there to be discussed. We should all be trying to communicate that others' own words and ways of expression have power and legitimacy.

A "Soft" Field

Cultural sensitivity training has its detractors, calling this activity "soft," because being "sensitive" to someone may not really change very much in the power differential between dominant and subordinate ethnocultural-racial groups. The alleged "softness" refers to the difficulty in measuring change experienced in sensitivity. Since "culture," in the first place, is an abstraction, and insubstantive, changes in it are hard to empirically ascertain with any certitude and precision.

Notwithstanding, it is urgent and absolutely essential that the process of cultural and racial sensitivity be taken very seriously. The Canadian Charter of Rights and Freedoms, Section 15 (1) states:

Equality Rights

15.(1) Every individual is equal before and under the law and has the right to the equal protection and equal benefit of the law with out discrimination and, in particular, without discrimination based on race, national or ethnic origin, colour, religion, sex, age, or mental or physical disability.

These Equality Rights are being developed in procedural ways that apply across the nation, to all sectors of work and service. In business and professional work of all types, management people are obligated to operationalize the idea of equity in their work place. Partly because this task is quite immense and partly because the techniques of improving cultural sensitivity are as yet underdeveloped, the process of moving organizations towards greater equity is slow and problematic. This book provides important perspectives on how this difficult task can be accomplished.

Through the three models, I draw out the ethnic identity of everyone and provide a metapattern framework for considering value conflict or value changes for each person. We must each focus on ourselves or else, unknowingly, we impose on others. The harvest from our work will be greater harmony and understanding among diverse colleagues, and our work extended not only to harmony with the others' value assumptions but also to produce the greatest possible benefits for clients/patients and others with whom we work and whom we serve.

ORGANIZATION OF THE BOOK

In Chapters 1 and 2, I set the stage by outlining the nature of the multicultural method and the "political" stance of the book: towards being "one people" in Canada — a diverse people but one characterized by a developing appreciation of those differences.

Chapters 3 and 4 carry the description of "Contexting" and provide exemplars of how the dimensions of contexting apply in the workplace. The underlying strategy is that as we can identify the values that are extant around about us we can then evaluate what is being communicated, and identify the ways in which our values are changing and what value conflict may emerge.

Chapters 5 and 6 are on the six non-verbal modes, the building blocks in communication. Chapters 7, 8, and 9 draw out the ethnic identity of each person as the Acculturative Framework is described and applied for the Immigrant and later generations. Chapter 10 takes all these elements in the book to analyse the issue of Race in cultural sensitivity training.

Suggestions for Using the Book

Because of the conceptual and ideological nature of the content, and goals, certain stylistic variations are present in the text. One variation that occurs is in the orientation of the reader. Sometimes it seems as if the reader is a "teacher" and sometimes a "student." This dual orientation has always been important to me and, at times, one or the other gains ascendency in the writing. I believe that anyone who learns cultural and racial sensitivity is always in one or other mode — sometimes a teacher, sometimes a learner. We constantly learn from each other or from being the teacher for others; this is the proper orientation for multicultural work. As you read the text, it is necessary to adjust to this dual orientation.

Another orientation is that many of my examples come out of social work education and practice, and to some extent, interdisciplinary health care, since most of my "real" world experience comes out of Schools of Social Work, social agencies and hospitals. However, I believe that most of the "practice theory" I develop is applicable to any situation where human service is provided.

To get the most out of the book, it is probably necessary to memorize the 21 variables because there is an interplay between them. Fortunately, this should not be at all difficult. The Benchmarks in Chapters 7, 8, and 9, especially, need to be remembered. The variables in Chapter 9 are not "new" variables; they are also Ethnic Identity variables like the last of the variables covered in Chapter 8.

Apart from these variables, there is, from time-to-time, mention of special studies or important sectors of knowledge that are available to the teacher/learner that can only be noted in this book, but are easily available through an academic library. In this sense, the book is both a textbook and a source of resources on the subject of cultural and racial sensitivity training. It is not possible to touch on all that could be useful, but I have attempted to exemplify how other sources of knowledge could be brought into the learning experience. Hopefully the learner/teacher will feel free to range as widely as possible in order to develop this field of study for themselves. Each person as "teacher" has their own special fields of knowledge that are useful to others.

One type of knowledge that is introduced is that about body awareness. At times exercises are introduced to remind ourselves about the demanding nature of multicultural work, and that values are "built into" our nervous system and muscles; that we can learn about ourselves from our behaviour and that we can become stressed from the heavy requirements of the work.

Although these ethno-cultural variables are introduced in three separate conceptual schemes, they can be put together like beads in a necklace. One can enter the culture of a person by starting with any one of the variables.

Finally, this book answers some essential questions related to culture in a practice setting: where does a person's culture come from; how does culture change; how do I feel about others' and my own cultures; how do I talk about cultural patterning; and what do norms and values look and feel like.

I will always appreciate feedback from readers. A return card is enclosed in each book for comment and easy return.

Chapter
1

Towards Sharing One Country

The term "multicultural work" is used in this book to refer to the content of
the work **within** a country, done by and for the benefit of its own peoples.
This distinction is made because cross-cultural work done across national
boundaries, as, for example, when a business transaction is conducted over-
seas, will have a different emphasis than that conducted within a country,
and though some of the same concerns, in cross-cultural communication,
can occur within a country, instrumental needs of business will take priority
across nations. However, there are issues of national values and identity that
must be considered within a country.

There is, of course, a conscious awareness that those serving or being
served in multicultural work, have different ethno-cultural or racial backgrounds and identities. However, it is not the client/patient/customer only
who is of interest, but everyone on both sides of the professional relationship who is part of the service system, that must be considered. Multicultural
work, therefore, can include not only the work by helping human service
professionals, but also that work done by store clerks, bureaucrats and factory workers, who find that the cross-cultural interface with other people is
an important factor in their work and that they, also, have an interest in
national goals about equity.

Canadians are a diverse people, and we are getting used to the idea
that our ancestors came not just from Europe but from all other parts of the
world. This insight has only recently been widely acknowledged, that people
of all races have contributed to the development of the country. We are
learning to acknowledge that there are aboriginal peoples and immigrant
peoples. We have talked about our varying heritages, but more to celebrate
the traditional "songs and dances." But, this level of validation about our
contributions to Canadian life is not enough, because many major contribu-
tors, aboriginal and immigrant, have been left out of our recorded history
because of their race. It is a strange irony that the "visible minority" became
"invisible" when history was written. We have much repairing to do to see
that everyone is appropriately included in the reconstruction of our history,
and the daily living of collective life today.

Sometimes, people prefer to say simply, "We are Canadian." Why then should we draw out the cultural identity of everyone, if we appear to prefer just "to be Canadian"? The main reason is to increase the accuracy of our perceptions about who we are and to respect our differences. Through recognizing diverse properties and needs, we can attain harmony between the parts, between those who share this country. Much of this book explicates this idea. To get underneath the issues that divide us, in particular the reasons for some peoples being so excluded, we need to conceptualize those divisive forces. For example, a quick look at our use of terms will show that we dichotomize ourselves into sub-populations: Native/non-Native, immigrant/Canadian-born, white/non-white, "ethnic"/Charter group and so forth. In this way, we always imply that some people are included and others are excluded.

In the case of the non-white immigrant category, there is no possibility of race becoming less visible; racial identity remains regardless of the passage of time or of the personal identity changes that take place. The only way race differences can become less "visible" is if we carefully inspect how our reactions persist even when we may not wish them to. For instance, how do we gain control of our reactions to the visual stimuli of racial differences, so we can redefine where race should go in our list of priorities? Should the media react to public conflict by always noting the race/colour of the participants? Or, should we also note that many of the participants are unemployed, or lacking an education to meet their abilities, or have been abused as children, or frequently harassed and slurred? Accurate reporting of an event could include more of the issues involved than the participants' colour of skin. If we truly want to be fair and equitable to all its Canadians, much restructuring needs to be done. And some of this includes the way we think through the issues that confront us on the job. These changes must come, but they can be accomplished more smoothly if we understand the process of change. (Considerable development of this idea, therefore, is throughout this book).

In addition to issues of different people sharing a country, placing people in excluded categories is not a good condition for healthy adjustment. It is not desirable in any professional work for some colleagues or clients/patients to be relegated to an "out" category. In multicultural work, there are no "outs," but diversity is recognized to the extent it is appropriate for rendering services. In multicultural work there are no labelling distinctions to keep people from full membership; our service behaviour and vocabulary acknowledge diversity, but without stigmatizing anyone by some exclusionary category or derogatory implication. Rather our multicultural methods will expand qualitatively and quantitatively to accommodate a greater range of cultural backgrounds among both providers and consumers of service. In the process, everyone will be served better.

As an introduction to several further ideas about the multicultural method, in this chapter and in the next, four important concepts are briefly explored: culture, ethnicity, proxemics and race.

Culture

"Culture" has many definitions but the ones we need to pay attention to are those that will pertain to issues of action that underly the helping activity. These action issues include communication and identity, mutuality (described later) and practicality. One of the most important facets of the concept, "culture," refers to the **patterned** nature of behaviour, beliefs, values, customs and institutions. Pattern, it should be pointed out, cannot be seen directly; there is an abstracting process that must be done before the pattern appears. This abstracting, which is an instantaneous and automatic process, is done by the observer and in helping work the observer is the professional helper.

Abstracting is the most human characteristic and is thus not normally noticed unless some deliberate activity is undertaken to draw it to one's attention in the process of communication. The product of the abstracting may be an observation, consciously or unconsciously done, that certain behaviours are different from one's own. Further, these differences will be negatively or positively evaluated. Where one's own patterns are not noticed by oneself, they are often obvious to someone not of your culture. It sometimes is hard to believe, from within a particular culture, that those with other values and patterns are not as aware of their "strange" patterns as you are. This tendency to see culture as obvious in the other person but not in oneself underlies some of our problems in multicultural work and training. It seems as though one has only to learn about those **other** strange patterns. Hence, we falsely believe problems can be solved by workshops on "The Italians" or "The West Indians." What has to gain our attention is our own "abstracting process." As we put ourselves into the picture, the basis of conflict or negative feelings lies in an interaction between our own values and those of others, not just in the "other." Part of multicultural training is, therefore, a raised awareness of ourselves and a willingness to look at our own expectations and how to react when they are not met. Part of this training has to do with how to react to racial differences, in particular how our culture has raised "race" into a major category when it should be some minor point of dissimilarity.

Ethnicity

"Ethnicity" is also an abstraction. It refers to the specific aspect of culture of an individual or group that derives from another national cultural heritage. In the case of immigrant Canadians, which technically includes all of us except Natives Peoples, the culture of another country was brought into Canada in the minds and hearts of immigrants and remains a dynamic element in their and their children's lives, even if conscious awareness of cultural differentness has dissipated. These cultural residues often have become invisible to ourselves.

Ethnoculture is a blend of the old culture and new host culture adapted to a specific environment, therefore, a Canadian phenomenon. The old culture persists in Canada, unaffected by changes in the national culture of the country of origin from which it derived. Thus Canadian ethno-cultures may seem "old-fashioned," to those who came later to Canada from the same nation. For those returning to the homeland in later years, the changed "old country" is unfamiliar and often disturbing and unpleasant. Thus **a Canadian ethnoculture is a unique cultural product of a time and place**. For example, an Italo-Canadian community in Toronto deriving from the 1950s wave of immigration, is unlike the evolving culture in Italy; it is unlike later waves of Italian immigration anywhere in Canada; and it is unlike its counterparts in the U.S. or elsewhere.

Multicultural work takes into account ethno-cultural communities and ethno-specific components in the cultural repertoire of individuals and families. (In a later chapter, these ethnocultural components are shown to persist for generations in a residual form in the behaviour of individuals.) It is the connecting link of ethnicity that provides a clue as to how our diversity can lead towards unity as a Canadian people.

All groups in Canada including the French, English and Native Peoples can be viewed equally as ethnocultural groups. In the case of Native Peoples, their culture was changed, not by immigration, but by an invasion and forced contact and control by Europeans who took over their ancestral lands. It should be noted, however, that for aboriginal peoples the term "ethnic" is flatly rejected if the term connotes that their place as "first" nations is not affirmed.

It should be noted, as well, that ethnicity is used in a "neutral" way in this book. It is argued here that it is not the place of professionals to either advocate the development of ethnic groups or their eradication. Rather, they are seen as part of reality and one having vivid effect on all Canadians. If we simply "start where people are," we must acknowledge the presence of ethnic groups and understand the kind of effects they have.

Proxemics

The term "proxemics"' was coined by Edward T. Hall to refer to the way social space is used to express cultural values (Hall, 1969: 1). Social space can refer to the micro-environment around each person or can refer to something as extensive as the land mass of a nation. Hall considers this range of ideas in his book *Hidden Dimensions* (1969). However, for people who are in helping or service jobs, it is likely that micro-environments will be more relevant; thus it is that micro-environments are more likely to be referred to in this book.

It is clear that Hall has been greatly influenced by American anthropologists of his era; the work of Boas and his students have shaped his ideas about culture. These early theorists discovered the integral nature of culture and communication; that the structure of language and culture are deeply and mutually affected. They taught that the rules from one family of languages cannot be applied to another; that each one must be analysed on its own. It is the work of the linguist to reveal the patterns and describe them. The socio-linguist, John Gumperz, has teased out the aspects of culture that are in the words themselves and in the non-verbal aspects of speaking those words. Seeing language as both a verbal system and a non-verbal one is one of many ways that proxemics is introduced in this book.

One other very important effect from the proxemic view of culture is the relation of language to thought and perception. Underlying all of the applied work on culture is the knowledge that our perceptions are programmed by the language we speak just as a computer is programmed. Like the computer, our minds will register and understand external reality in terms of the programme. Thus there is a necessity to become more aware of and knowledgeable about the way our minds are conditioned. The chapters on non-verbal modes attempt to put forward variables that will lead us into this perspective.

Race

It is ironic that at the point in time when more people are willing to acknowledge the negative effects of racism, we are also aware of race as a very unscientific "mental construct." The United Nations has over the years made various statements about race and pronouncements about how it should be regarded (Montagu, 1961). How do we strongly acknowledge racism's existence and yet not perpetrate an idea that has no scientific foundation?

THE NATURE OF MULTICULTURAL WORK

We talk about multicultural work because we want to operationalize our values about human services. Human service work should assist individuals to help themselves; should be competently done in a fair, evenhanded way; and should be done to the best extent possible, with positive feelings. However, how do we help people to help themselves if their values, goals and behaviour are unfamiliar to us? How do we communicate positive feelings if we dislike the person being served because of cultural and racial factors? In order to achieve the goal, we can divide up the job of operationalizing our values into several parts. Eventually, the parts are put back together in an integrated whole that would constitute the multicultural method. The best place to start, however, is with ourselves.

Here is another paradox: it has been repeatedly proved that "the first step toward understanding another culture is becoming aware of one's own cultural habits and values so that they will not interfere with learning those of the new culture" (Sikkema, 1977: 6). In Chapter 2, the physio-social processes of perception are discussed. These processes underly the basic precept of understanding the self first. The results that can eventually follow are ones that allow the human service worker more fully to achieve the quality of desired behaviour, at both the direct service and the policy levels.

The changes that can occur from fuller understanding of oneself include greater appreciation of the self and its value structure as well as greater comprehension of what one does **not** value or know in the context of expressing emotions and emotional acceptance. Prejudices and stereotypes can become known, and improved feelings about others will result. This changed psychological state makes it easier to learn about other cultures because the invisible internal barriers to such learning are diminished. This kind of "self-growth," to use Sikkema's term, takes time to occur; also, people vary in their ability to change.

PERSONAL CHARACTERISTICS

The characteristics that are encouraged in multicultural work are those of risk-taking, divergent thinking, toleration of ambiguity, flexibility (Sikkema, 1977: 10-16), and introspective growth. It is not so much that people are picked for these qualities (although some few people might be contraindicated if their personalities are too rigid to change), as that the conditions must be created to allow these potentials to develop in people. It is assumed that most can grow in these ways. Moreover, these qualities are necessary for new ways of thinking and feeling and, eventually, acting.

A final consideration here concerns the learning and working environment in which these qualities can develop. The environment should be open, trustworthy and learner-controlled. Creativeness rather than rote learning should be rewarded. Good adult learning situations require participation of the learners in developing goals, teaching that is experiential as well as didactic, methods that are wide-ranging in context and expressive of feeling (McLean, 1983). This is especially important in multicultural work.

Risk-Taking

Multicultural work constantly presents delights and anxieties related to change. It is easier to remain in situations where we can behave automatically and never have to worry about how to dress, what to think or say, how to act. Where situations are ambiguous or unknown, we have to take a risk that our clothing may not be appropriate, that what we say could offend someone and that our behaviour will be perceived as incorrect. Maslow (1956) suggested that we have two sets of forces within us. One set clings to safety out of fear of taking chances, while the other set of forces impels us forward to confidence and wholeness in facing the external world. Thus, we each encounter a never-ending set of choices between the delights and anxieties of safety and growth. When the delights of growth and change outweigh the anxieties, we grow and change.

But Maslow's way of conceptualizing risk-taking suggests that it is not just strength or nature of character that will determine growth, but that the environment can make risk-taking a delightful or fearful event. Thus, if we can make risk-taking a positive experience, or at least reduce its fearsomeness, then we will more often engage in risk-taking behaviour. The learning environment that we create for multicultural learning is, therefore, crucial.

Divergent Thinking

The second characteristic, divergent thinking, is a term first identified by Guildford (1959). He posited a factor in the intellect called convergent and divergent thinking. In convergent thinking, facts lead to one logical conclusion; in divergent thinking, a fact or starting point can go in different directions: there is no one correct answer, rather, alternatives are available (Guildford, 1959). More succinctly, Getzels and Jackson (1962: 13, 14), contrasted the two modes: "The convergent mode tends toward retaining the known, learning the pre-determined and conserving what is," while the divergent mode "tends toward revising the known, exploring the undetermined and constructing what might be." Multicultural work in Canada clearly needs people who can think "divergently." The fashioning of new methods and programs requires creative thinking and a willingness to keep opening up the possibilities of new ways to work. This mode of thinking is probably also unlikely to be elitist in orientation because it becomes obvious that in opening up possibilities, no one person or profession has all the answers.

Toleration of Ambiguity

The ability to tolerate ambiguity is an important aspect of both risk-taking behaviour and divergent thinking, for there is less that is known and pre-determined. The cues about what is "right" and "proper" are less clear. In fact, in multicultural work it may be unclear for years if a course of action is actually for the best, because differing values will be introduced into helping systems and all the systemic repercussions cannot be anticipated. For example, if a modern health care system permits the practice of folk medicine techniques in its roster of services, it is unknown how old and new techniques fit together, how practitioners of old and new methods will work together, how much better-served patients will be. The situation could be ambiguous for some time.

If ambiguity is tolerated, practitioners, administrators, policy makers and volunteers will find day-to-day work is less automatic; there are more alternatives to consider and outcomes cannot be judged in a fixed and fully anticipated way. There are anxieties in all this, but as Maslow said, there are also delights. There are the prospects of better helping a wider range of people and operationalizing our values to a greater degree. There are also pleasures in the unfolding and understanding of other ethnocultural ways.

Mental Flexibility

Mental flexibility is an ability to see the world through different perceptual lenses. Pierre Casse (1979) spoke of the mental flexibility to "construct new realities." In his book, *Training for the Cross-Cultural Mind*, he included exercises that can test and develop this ability. He has reproduced several well-known exercises that many may have met at one time in introductory psychology courses. For example, there is a picture designed by the American psychologist, E.G. Boring. The picture is of **two** women, but the lines to depict the two people are one and the same. If only certain of the lines are selectively perceived, the picture appears to be that of an "old" woman, but if other lines in the drawing are "noticed" then the picture is that of a stylish young woman. The observer can watch him/herself construct reality by mentally flipping from what is perceived as the "old" woman to the "young" woman and back to the "old" woman.

Such an exercise, done the first time, gives a small indication of the ability to quickly perceive different realities. By practising the exercise, one can improve the ability and at the same time one's awareness is drawn to the nature of one's **own** mind. That is how our minds perceive reality. It is sometimes hard to move from one way of seeing reality to another, but our ability to be flexible and openminded can yield a rich repertoire of cultural ideas and behavioural patterns. Having such a repertoire is valuable in multicultural work.

Introspection and Self-Awareness

A further correlate of good multicultural work is the ability to be introspective — to know oneself. Part of introspection is learning how to explore one's thoughts and feelings and be aware of one's own verbal and non-verbal behaviour. Since much emphasis is placed on experiential learning, one needs to be able to incorporate the results of experiential knowledge into the "professional self" and new programmes. In fact, useful knowledge may come from many sources. Almost all the academic disciplines — sociology, anthropology, psychology, political science, the humanities, communications, history — have knowledge that can be incorporated as multicultural knowledge. In addition, one's colleagues and others in the community, whether in ethno-specific agencies or in any other walk of life, can provide information specifically related to a particular group at a particular time of adjustment. An introspective and reflective mode is needed to consciously incorporate such new ideas into one's ideas and practice.

Body Awareness

The multicultural method is one where one has to be able to do at least two things at once: you must be able to pay attention to yourself as well as to the people whom you serve and the situation in which you are working, both "parts" must be given attention. You must know what you are feeling in any situation so you can monitor your evaluations of the new situation to make sure that the values and norms from your own system are not used unthinkingly to evaluate another. You must be able to move in harmony with another culture but, at the same time, take care not to do damage to yourself.

Body awareness is of great help in this aspect of the multicultural method. In yoga, one of the main foundations of the many body awareness techniques used widely today, it is necessary to pay attention to more than one activity at once. For example, during the execution of a posture, the attention must be directed to several matters while the body is put into a particular position; there is the breathing, which must be done in the correct way, the body must be in correct alignment, joints or muscles must be moved and stretched in the optimum manner so as either not to over stretch or under stretch that part of the body that is being exercised (in which case very little benefit would occur). In addition to these positive actions, there is the complementary one of allowing all uninvolved parts of the body to remain absolutely relaxed. In some cases the last activity may be the most difficult. In any case, there are several actions to be taken simultaneously. The concentration required to do this takes a great amount of body awareness and generates an ability to move from one point of concentration to another very rapidly. The resulting effects are not only increased flexibility in the muscles but also greater serenity of mind and reduced stress. It is hypothesized that this ability to be able to pay attention to several things at once that is learned in a technique like yoga, can be transferred to other activities and in particular to helping activities done in a cross-cultural situation. The rationale for this would be that it is the same body that learns body awareness that also communicates non-verbally with gaze, social distance, timing and pacing etc., and that those skills can be transferred from the muscles used for yoga to those used in communication. Chapters 5 and 6 will give more details about this need for managing more than one thing at a time.

MAKING THE "MOSAIC" MOVE

At the beginning of this chapter, the major objective to achieve non-assimilative unity as one Canadian people was introduced. As individuals change to become more open to new cultural forms and are willing to consider new programmes and methods, there needs to be a direction for this new activity. The idea of unity is very abstract and bound to be controversial in application. However, we need over-arching images or symbols, as general guides. In this book, an attempt is made to use images as strategy and content for objectives.

There have not been many images on which we as Canadians converge. Beavers, maple leaves and Mounties are not much help to the practitioner. The idea of cultural "mosaic" has been helpful to distinguish us from the American idea of cultural absorption. But, if we are to make the mosaic concept useful for practitioners, the mosaic must start to "flow." The symbol or image of a "river" is a good example. Rivers dominate the Canadian landscape and could symbolize unity from diversity: many tributaries make a river; rivers are varied in colour, depth and pacing; they go through varied territory; and yet even in the diversity of a river, it is clearly all one body of water. In this book, the river image is simplified to a moving line or belt which is the basic image in the Acculturative Framework (Chapters 7, 8, and 9). Chapter 2 prepares the way for the Contexted Values and other multicultural concepts.

The Multicultural Method

A SOCIETY IN CHANGE

Canada is a society in transition, in a world in transition. Of the many changes that are occurring, those considered here are ones that would improve communication and reduce power differentials between Canadian peoples of different racial, religious or ethnic backgrounds. In the human service fields, entire delivery systems must be modified to achieve equal access to and reception of services by all ethnoracial communities. There are many barriers to effecting these changes. One has to do with understanding what peoples of different backgrounds need that is not currently available, in order to be well served; Another is people's emotional reactions when their stereotypical thinking must be changed, or when their power must be shared with those who seem different from themselves.

There are so many loci for change all at once: train the police; change curricula in professional schools; institute in-service education for all staff; develop employment and pay equity plans for hiring and promotion; involve new ethnoracial sectors of the population in the decision-making of organizations; sensitize service staff to the culture and language needs of consumers in our hospitals and agencies, and of students in our schools; assure complete respect for all people in stores, offices and wherever else you find Canadians. The aim in each case is always the same: better services to all ethnoracial groups and equity for service providers. For many, the truly multicultural society must be one that is working towards all these goals.

Change, then, becomes a complex and formidable undertaking if every change is viewed as separate and unique. However, there are common underlying themes, thus providing a beginning for a generic approach. In the human services, moving towards an explicitly multicultural stance can reduce duplicative efforts and be the basis for a common understanding across the helping professions and other human service workers.

CHARACTERISTICS OF A MULTICULTURAL METHOD

Both Canada and the U.S. are multicultural nations experiencing increasing diversity. In the United States, there finally is a growing awareness that the long-standing policy of "Anglo-conformity" has been more empirical reality than ethnoracial pluralism. Although cultural conformity permitted a sense of peoplehood to emerge amongst Americans over the last two centuries, diversity in ethnocultural values was discouraged; nevertheless, ethnic differences have remained, even if attenuated, compared to Canada. Today, American mental health specialists and social workers are beginning to take the fact of ethnocultural values into account in their work (McGoldrick et al., 1982; Green, 1982; Parry, 1990). There is a beginning willingness in America to see what is really there.

While Canada has used the ideology of cultural pluralism for over 125 years, we have not had a strong sense of being one people, rather, the opposite. We are also regionally identified, but even within regions we do not articulate strong across-cultural bonds or a willingness to reduce consideration of race as a categorical division. We have not yet developed a clear Canadian way of adapting to our diversity in a way that equalizes all groups: either we do not talk about the diversity or else we use American language to talk about differences, e.g., often all "non-whites" are called "Black" as they have been called in the U.S. when in reality we in Canada have many racial groups more numerically balanced than in America; or we speak about "minority groups" as is done in the U.S. when, in fact, no longer in Canada is any ethnic group a numerical majority. Also, ethnic, racial and religious groups have retained their identity to a much greater degree here than in America, and contributed more to Canada's evolution.

Thus, there is very basic work to be done prior to developing an agreed-on multicultural method. We have to keep our focus on ourselves and not borrow ideas inappropriately from other countries. We need to consciously resist using American concepts unless we can show they apply to us. But what issues would we want to address in a Canadian method, to have our best wishes fulfilled?

In accordance with federal and provincial multicultural legislation and policies we need a method that includes everyone — Native Peoples, French, British, and all of the "Other Groups," that today comprise nearly half of all Canadians. The method needs to be action-oriented — one that is centred in the practitioner role and permits that practitioner to enter their clients' many different cultural frames of reference. At the same time, the practitioner must also be able to confront their own stereotypical thinking. This kind of self-growth, as mentioned in Chapter 1, requires experiential learning modes to enable reflective observation of one's own ideas and acts, and to develop the inductive thinking needed for an active exploration of new realities. Similarities, or over-arching concepts, are used here to create a unified approach. Because practitioners face a plethora of problems in their daily work, the method is systematic and provides concrete ways of organizing information, while yet reflecting the real, processual world.

Inclusivity

There is a strong tendency in Canadian social life to use exclusionary language. Our regional and ethnoracial biases make this a common basis for including some and excluding others, e.g., "Westerners," "Easterners," "Central Canadians," "Indians," "Anglo-Saxons," "Quebecers," and so forth, are terms that, while including some, exclude many and even most.

Terms such as "ethnic" or "immigrant" often are used to refer to **other** people and exclude ourselves. Until recently, many mainstream service agencies usually did not see themselves as serving "ethnics or immigrants." Sometimes conferences are held at which some groups are automatically excluded. In one recent conference on ethnicity and mental health, Native Peoples were not expected to be included. When the question was put to conference organizers, the response was, "Oh no, they belong somewhere else." It is not that those professional people consciously and actively wanted to exclude Native Peoples; they are often very aware of injustices done to them and their need for service. Rather, people are normatively categorized as being of a certain "type" and there is an automatic or unthinking exclusion.

When people are relegated to a category, they become cloaked in stereotypical traits. If you live in Ontario, "Westerners" become a certain type of people; if you live in Alberta, Ontarians become "Eastern Canadians" and, thereby, a certain type of people. That in actual fact Canadians share about the same range of problems and are about the same kind of people, is not reflected in this exclusionary thinking. The same kind of stereotypical cloaking occurs when people are categorized as "ethnic," or "non-white." Reducing the use of exclusionary categories as a normative way of talking about ourselves and consciously trying to be inclusive in our thinking, would be a unifying principle. Thus, inclusivity is a central dimension in the multicultural method.

Mutuality

Mutuality, also called "laterality" (Draguns, 1976: 5), draws attention to the twin importance that both giver and receiver are in a transaction. Both are affected and changed by a transaction. Part of the change has to do with individuals having a comparative experience from which they can become aware of their own cultural uniqueness. Some of this dimension was discussed under "culture" in the last chapter. Another aspect of mutuality is that there is a "boundary maintenance" effect in intercultural relationships. This becomes especially critical when there is a power differential between the parties interacting. James W.Green (1982: 9-27) talks at length about this under the topic of the "transactional approach" under American conditions. Some of his ideas are useful in the Canadian context.

For Green, the transactional approach avoids seeing ethnicities as bundles of distinctive traits, but rather as the way people who are communicating maintain their sense of cultural distinctiveness. Further, it is the "boundary maintenance" effect of intercultural relationships that becomes salient for helping professionals. "To understand ethnicity, therefore, one must examine the values, signs and behavioural styles through which individuals signal their identity in cross-cultural encounters" (Green, 1982: 12). This way of looking at ethnicities, then, is very different from the idea of seeing ethnicities as bundles of specific traits that one memorizes.

Thus, whether drawing on millennia of boundary maintenance experiences, such as Native Peoples have had, or a relatively short experience, such as Asian refugees, the service worker's interaction will be imbued with political and cultural symbolic meanings. For example, Watson (1981: 457) pointed to the long-term effect for Native Peoples of transactional phenomena: "All Indians are in an important sense creatures of Euro-Canadian Society, and are to be understood primarily in terms of massive adjustment to the Euro-Canadian administrative structure, participation in a cash and welfare economy and the pervasive presence of Euro-Canadian technology." Here, as an example of extreme power differences, Indians became defined by the needs of European explorers and subject to their very dominant perceptions. To this day, Native Peoples have the task of divesting themselves of these destructive meanings and replacing them with ideas of their own choosing.

Asian refugees have only recently started their cross-cultural experiences in Canada. First, there were sponsor relationships to manoeuvre, and perceptions of the refugees as strange and persecuted people, mixed with earlier perceptions of Asians as docile and inscrutable, members of large extended families, people who would do any kind of work, or people taking jobs away from Canadians. As they become settled in Canadian life they also must define their own way of being seen.

The transactional approach suggests that ethnic boundaries are social phenomena, not bundles of categorical traits. This means then that group boundaries and personal identity membership can be altered. For Native Peoples, as long as the relationship remained controlled by a Euro-Canadian government, the amount of change that was possible was very limited because of the ideas and actions of the people with whom their transactions occurred. Coercive power, stereotyping, insensitivity to cultural meanings reduced their ability to handle Natives' identity. Fortunately, this relationship is changing as public opinion makes it harder for governments and others to relate to Native groups as they did in the past.

At the other extreme, English-Canadians maintain their position of power and manage to keep an identity they themselves regard as superior to Native Peoples and often others. The norms that keep ethnicity from being discussed protect the British plurality. If their way of doing things cannot be debated, then there is a good likelihood they can maintain dominance.

Interdisciplinary Knowledge Application

A multicultural method needs many kinds of knowledge. It should, therefore, be a multidisciplinary and interdisciplinary approach. However, the research enterprises that produce knowledge have generally not addressed the complexity of practice phenomena (Rosen, 1981) and, even less, have addressed the complexity of multicultural practice conditions.

First, research findings are typically stated in probabilistic terms; the uncertainties created in an action framework are increased when the conditions are multicultural. Another source of great uncertainty for practitioners is the problem of the "fit" of a selected principle or standard of measurement to a multicultural setting. One always wonders if the standard has hidden cultural biases that would make it inappropriate in a particular setting. One question often asked by practitioners is, "how do you know if a trait exhibited by a client is cultural (therefore legitimate) or psychological (and therefore open to intervention by the practitioner)?"

Second, because the world of knowledge about ethno-cultural matters is potentially so large, a very wide range of disciplines should be drawn upon. Whole bodies of knowledge about, and deriving from each country — the arts, literature, music, history, religion, politics, rural and urban life and so on — could become relevant to understand some precursor of a client's situation or goals. In addition to knowledge of countries of origin, there is the rapidly growing field of Canadian ethnic studies, about the experience and adjustment of ethnicities in Canada. Of course this knowledge also is presented in probabilistic terms and is often merely descriptive rather than related to practice issues.

Since these fields of knowledge do not translate easily into practice-based concepts or theories, one way for them to be useful to practitioners is to view them as ways of increasing one's repertoire of ideas for understanding practice situations. For example, Danziger's early study of elementary school youth, involving Italian boys in Toronto (Danziger, 1971), suggested a practitioner should become aware of the changing attitudes towards education of first generation parents. His finding about attitudes shifting towards greater interest in education is helpful, but this finding, presented as a probabilistic generalization, cannot immediately be applied to any specific Italian family but it can remain a valid question in the mind of the practitioner. Obviously, practitioners would like to have comparable inter-ethnic studies, concerning changing attitudes to many other issues, such as extended family connections, the status of wives and daughters, the role of husband and father, discipline of children, independence of children and so forth. However, the availability of such information remains scanty.

Academic studies could be also useful to practitioners by providing measurement instruments, such as the schedule of questions used to operationalize the study variables. For example, practitioners may not be sure how to elicit information about attitudes to education. The schedule of questions used in the Danziger study could provide a base for developing practice-related questions useful to the service-providers.

There can be additional desirable spin-off effects: again, using this educational example, the practitioner might perceive more clearly how a particular family understands the Canadian educational process and use this information to assist school personnel to work more effectively with the family. Another service delivery system thus would move towards more cultural sensitivity.

Provision of a Frame of Reference

We are all used to the projections of different points of view. Both the electronic and print media spend much effort portraying the lives and points of view of different peoples. We evaluate the competence of these media productions to project the inner meanings and realities of the lives they portray. This process is based on that most human ability of "taking the role of the other" (Mead, 1934), or of "stepping into someone else's shoes." Taken for granted in families and friendships, this is a basic process in any human interaction needing co-operation and understanding, and is important in counselling, health services, education, in most police work, and anywhere else that human services are rendered.

Wherever it occurs, the purpose for attempting to enter another's frame of reference is to establish the meanings a given situation has for that person. The frame of reference is composed of everything that person has experienced, but, luckily, not everything need be known to grasp sufficient understanding of the subjective meaning to carry out some action. The action may have to do with pain, disease, moral behaviour, nutrition, alcohol consumption, drunken comportment, parenting, learning, and deviant behaviour or one of a myriad of other things. All topics can be understood differently by different people. In multicultural work, of course, there is the added component of ethno-cultural differences that mediate these personal meanings. (The Acculturative Framework explicitly takes into account the effect of culture changes on these meanings: Chapters 7, 8 and 9).

Since a multicultural method must also take account of the "observer," in this case the service workers, their frame of reference is also important. How far apart or close together these practitioner-client frames of reference are will effect communication. If the respective frames of reference are far apart, as may happen in multicultural work, then special consideration must be given to ways of bridging the distance. The Framework presented in Chapters 7, 8, and 9 is a systematic way of understanding different frames of reference and the contexting model in Chapters 3 and 4 outlines how far apart are the cultural values of each.

How much detail is needed to define a frame of reference? The degree of detail depends on the purpose for which the knowledge is to be used and the ability of the worker to take in, absorb and understand the detail available. Probably a less experienced person will be able to handle less detail than an experienced person. Fortunately, workers develop a skill of knowing how much they can handle and of what to elicit.

Entering another's frame of reference cannot readily be accomplished without the cooperation and help of the client/patient recipient. Gaining the client's help, two problems are solved: the amount and kind of detail forthcoming will be largely determined by the client and the subjective meanings of the information will be clarified. The practitioner participating in the process of receiving information can actively enter the frame of reference of that person. If meanings are unclear, the interviewer can ask questions. Thus, there is mutual learning as the client perceives what is not understood by the interviewer.

In experiential learning, the learner momentarily enters the frame of reference of someone he/she is **not** and glimpses that person's subjective reality. For example, the meanings of a particular racist experience may be understood in a simulation in which the role player is slurred or stereotyped. The ability to apply concepts about culture and culture change to that experience helps to integrate that understanding into one's knowledge base.

Objectification

Closely related to entering a frame of reference is the ability to "talk about oneself as an object" or to objectify oneself. We frequently "talk about" ourselves, our lifestyle, our friends, our job, etc.

Examples of self-objectification are: "I am the kind of person who likes to socialize" or "I am the kind of person who must have a lot of privacy and time to myself" or "I am finally becoming more assertive about my own rights," statements that reflect seeing the self as an object that can be described or changed. One should have a sense of ownership and consciousness about one's self, because it is this "self" that is taken into the workplace and finds expression there. For example, the person who needs privacy will probably need to be more private on the job may want the door of the office shut or may be less available to others for informal discussions about work issues or may sit by him/herself in the cafeteria. This can be regarded as a matter of personal style and the organization should be able to accommodate people whose style is to be gregarious or to be private. However where these personal ways of behaving become a problem to the organization then the person will be expected to be able to examine that behaviour in an objective way. Actually self-objectification is a common middle-class behaviour; in fact, it is considered sophisticated to be able to analyse oneself and, if done with elan and wit, the person accrues prestige from this. The *New Yorker* magazine, for one, has myriad cartoons that satirize this tendency. In therapy, it is generally expected that the patient will come to view him/herself as an object that is undergoing change.

However, people vary considerably in their ability to perceive themselves this way. There is some evidence that people from urban, modern technological systems are more likely or able to objectify themselves than people from traditional groups. "High context" people, those with a strong sense of themselves as born to and belonging to a lifelong network of kin and reciprocal associations, may not objectify themselves as much because the rich context of their life is firmly established and relatively unchanging. Consequently, there is no need to create a context in each transaction; it is immanent in the situation. Such people will have had less practice with viewing the self as an object that one directs or changes. It is not that high context people cannot do this objectification, but that they may need to understand the need for it.

In contrast, some people from low-context backgrounds and especially those with strong performance values, may scrutinize themselves to the point of seldom relaxing the process of self-objectification. From a mental health point of view, it probably is better to ease such self-pressure. More details on high and low contexts are presented in Chapters 3 and 4.

Finally, entering another person's frame of reference and the ability to objectify the self as something that one consciously analyses, directs or changes are concepts that are essential to the multicultural method. As the service worker helps clients to impart information and perceives the cultural dimension of that information, he/she enters clients' frames of reference. In the process, it is also possible to perceive if clients can objectify themselves in the situation. For example, a statement such as "I don't like Canadian life" shows lower ability to self-objectify than, I haven't been in Canada long enough to understand Canadian life." In the latter case, there is perception of the self as potentially undergoing change.

Acknowledging Differences

In a multicultural country, differences between people and groups can either be acknowledged and given room to be expressed, or such differences can be played down in the interest of national unity and personal adaptation. Sometimes the first strategy is appropriate and sometimes the second. However, it often seems that we focus on what should be ignored and deny the things that need to be acknowledged.

Solving this conundrum must start with self-knowledge. We need honest, clear answers to ourselves about how we feel about different ethnicities and races. If we feel dislike, resentment and discomfort toward some, the chances are we will do the "wrong" thing: wrong for the client and in terms of a service ideal. How does this work?

If there is dislike or discomfort about someone of another race or ethnic background, there is a strong chance, in Canada, that those feelings will be denied and blocked out; they will not get a chance to be sorted out. The dislike or discomfort, or even fear, are usually based on stereotypes. These may have come from explicit early home training, from the idea that those who are not members of one's own group are not as worthy of respect, or may have come from television, magazines, newspapers, textbooks, literary works of all kinds, "street talk" and so forth. Because there are strong norms in this country not to talk about racial or ethnic differences and how one feels about them, a person may not be fully aware of the range of feelings and ideas he/she actually harbours.

It is hard to learn about something if there is a limited vocabulary and there is an absence of thought about it, or if the subject is not a legitimated topic for discussion. In this climate, it is easy for vague stereotypical ideas to persist and traditional ways of behaving to continue, unchallenged. Thus, a person's race may become a focus in some situations but denied in others. The climate of denial or unawareness does not permit exploration to ascertain if those involved agree with the way it is handled. For example, sometimes a person is alluded to by their race, e.g., "that Indian over there" or "that Black" when the people involved do not feel their race is relevant to the situation. In other cases, a person's race is denied, e.g., one colleague said to another, "You are not Black, you are just coffee-coloured" as though this made the two people alike and the issue of racial differences did not need to be addressed.

If there was complete comfort, in the first instance race might be appropriately ignored, whereas in the second instance, the two colleagues could feel free to discuss how each felt about the differences. For instance, the two might consider why does a light-skinned Black wish to acknowledge being Black when he/she could pass without it?

The first step in acknowledging differences is to recognize that feelings of dislike or fear are present. It requires good self-objectification skills to be honest, especially with ourselves. For service providing people, this kind of self-examination is a responsibility. It is difficult for supervisors or colleagues to identify and manage this kind of hidden self-knowledge. And, it can take a long time for these feelings to be acknowledged and to reduce the barrier to communication that they represent. A group experience, guided by a sensitive group leader, in which participants discuss these feelings, enhances the growth process involved. Other ways of developing self-growth are detailed later in this book.

With self-knowledge, one can proceed to learn more about race and ethnicity. Our own observations, now more complete and reliable because our emotions are not blocking out important information, can be a good basis for beginning to know when and which differences should be acknowledged or ignored and in what circumstances.

One important set of observations will be about how others regard their **own** ethnicity or race. Some people appear to be quite unaware of their own race or ethno-culture. The most marked unawareness, of course, is within the majority Caucasian group. Caucasian or "white" people tend not to be aware they **have** a race! However, if race is important in this society, then everyone needs to be aware of their race. Such an awareness is especially important in cross-racial interactions and is basic to a more evenhanded, inclusive approach.

Some people tend to deny their race or ethnicity. They will staunchly state that these issues are not important in Canada. This stance may also involve a denial mechanism and should be treated as sensitively as any other denial. Other people feel quite militantly about racial identity, these including the White Supremicist groups, who have an ideology unacceptable in Canada. Those in other racial groups may band together, on the basis of race, to militantly counteract the negative racial behaviour they experience. The Acculturative Framework acknowledges these differences in identity.

As professionals, it is generally not for us to tell others how they should handle their own racial identity (although we may advise on how to react to discrimination). Our job is to keep our own emotions clear and honest so that our best helping behaviour and competence can be brought to bear in any situation. Only in this way can our ability to acknowledge differences appropriately, improve. In Chapter 10, the issue of race is explored.

Specific or Generalized: Emic or Etic

The terms emic and etic are becoming widely used in multicultural work. The term **"emic" means culturally specific**: data are viewed in terms unique to a particular culture. **"Etic" means culturally generalized**: categories that are universal in their applicability. Of course, in a multicultural method, both approaches are needed (Draguns, 1976: 2; Green, 1982: 72-74). In Spiegel's work he moves from Kluckhohn's etic model to an application of it to specific groups in the United States. A summary of Spiegel's work is found in McGoldrick's book, (McGoldrick et al., 1982: 31-51), a book used to identify emic examples for understanding the continua of the Contexting model, Chapters 3 and 4.

However, the position I take here is that the **"etic"** side of this dualism needs special development for work within our Canadian multicultural society. The models employed in this book — Contexting and the Acculturative Framework — are "etic" ones. By using concepts that apply to everyone, exclusionary language, referred to earlier, is avoided; the "Canadianness" of everyone is emphasized. A practitioner can avoid "ethnic labelling" techniques, which can too easily lead to simplistic stereotyping of a specific ethnic group. Instead, one can focus on patterns of behaviour that are relevant to Canadian social life as a whole. For example, concepts about the degree of hierarchy or gender segregation (See Chapter 3), can be applied to the family or community or any ethnic group.

The client, of course, will use his/her own **emic** or ethnocultural ideas about problems. In this way, the practitioner can tune in to the degree of acculturation of a particular client and use the specific language and ideas of that person to enter that person's frame of reference. The practitioner can move between etic and emic language to understand the client more completely. For example, while the traditional Ukrainian costume and distinctively-patterned Easter egg can be understood emically only within the particular frame of reference of being a Ukrainian-Canadian, they are etically appreciated as indicators of ethnocultural pride and cultural identity. Both levels of analysis enhance the practitioner's understanding.

The "Real" Processual World

Practitioners require a time perspective. We need concepts that include a processual dimension. Since "culture" is the main dimension in this book, it is essential to keep cultural change, through short and long periods of time, in centre attention. Present values come out of the past; ethnoculture is rooted in some previously experienced national culture. Chapters 7, 8, 9 deal explicitly with these processes.

It should never be necessary to deny the past, but it should be recognized that people have a "right" to do so. It is probably more healthy, in the long run, to accept and acknowledge the past. However, people who have escaped extremely traumatic conditions, understandably, may deny it. Other people, too, may want to forget past pain and let "bygones be bygones"; let the present bury the past. For others, in contrast, there is a conscious return to the past (Hansen's principle, Hansen 1962; Isajiw, 1981) by some Canadians as they search for new meanings in life through a return to their ancestors' ethnic roots.

In multicultural service work, the method must include a systematic examination of relevant past events. This does not mean dwelling on the past, but understanding the sources of present attitudes and values. These ideas from the past are often highly valued by clients and "are the most important resources of human beings in their struggles to protect and advance their own welfare" (Green, 1982: 12). They are the very content we are trying to understand when we enter another's frame of reference.

At another level of analysis, an overview of all Canadians would see today's Canadian families in time-depth, whether going back a few or many years, and that all come from some **where**. Even Canada's Native Peoples can look at their history in terms of migrations and powerful cultural contacts that changed them. We need an inspirational image to capture the time flow dimension of our identity. Images are important; thus an image of a vast river with numerous tributaries, can embody our diversity and our unity.

Identifying Value Frames Through Contexting

CONTEXTING

The next two chapters discuss the concept "contexting," a term coined by Edward T. Hall many years ago.

This concept is useful to practitioners because it describes value frames that cover whole cultural groups, members of which can be in interaction with each other for the purpose of professional service.

By understanding one's own value frame, which may be invisible to oneself, and the frames of other people, some professional objectives may become more possible: good rapport between practitioner and client; a better understanding of how decision-making can take place, of how authority is understood; and a more realistic view of what the goals of professional activity can be.

For high context cultures, social life is coterminous with the network of kinship relationships. Messages are embedded in the network and do not need to be articulated. In contrast, low context culture, which characterizes most of professional activity in Western countries, does not rely on personal kinship but rather on professional credentials, individually earned, and the context of each relationship must be defined, a skill which low context people start to learn quite early in life.

The ten dimensions along which high and low context cultures vary are developed in Chapters 3 and 4.

Chapter
3

Values: Emotional Heartland —
Five Contexted Values

INTRODUCTION TO CONTEXTING, A PRIME CONCEPT
FOR THE MULTICULTURAL METHOD

Since this book is about a **multicultural** approach to human service work, the main concepts will be about **values**, the central element of culture. Later chapters will discuss values in behaviour and where values come from. The next two chapters present a scheme for a vocabulary about values in service settings. The values that concern us in this scheme are those that might be considered to frame the actions of those who are interacting; they are major value forces in their lives but are often so taken for granted that they are invisible. When they are very different, value clashes can occur. In the next few pages, is a discussion about the issues raised in the last chapter about the multicultural method and a values schema. Contexting itself is described in detail after that.

When applying value concepts, it is understood that, like "culture," values are always an abstraction from something "real"; on the other side of every cultural "coin" is a real, structural dimension. For example, the word "hierarchy" can refer to the value that says hierarchical arrangements are right and proper but also point to actual social arrangements that have a hierarchical form. In this schema, for example, the traditional family has a high regard for hierarchical arrangements, but because these values are so ordinary to them, the values can be considered to be invisible to them and frame their actions.

It is important in any schema of values for practice situations that the unique history of each person/family/group is taken into account. The chapters on the Acculturative Framework (Chapters 7, 8, and 9) lead the reader through a way of thinking about any unique history of values. In this chapter, it is assumed that individuals have unique histories that have led to the current framework of values governing their behaviour; this unique framework evolves from family, community, and national sources of values.

Since no scheme can capture all these varied sources, generalizations have to be made. The abstract scheme presented rests fully on a social science knowledge base about these values and how they have evolved, and it is understood that those who use it have had some social science education.

Another assumption that is made is that value concepts for practice situations need to be quickly usable for the busy and varied practice situations most workers are in. It is important in many cases to be able to develop rapport quickly and begin assessing situations at first contact. The model introduced here is simple and highly abstract, in order to apply in a wide variety of settings; as noted earlier, this is an "etic" method. The number of dimensions in ethno-cultures has been reduced by combining common elements under a simple rubric. For example, the term "hierarchy" covers a wide range of relationships with power differentials — gender, class and race -and especially such as are found in descriptions of family life (see McGoldrick et al., 1982: 116-118). The term becomes a "handhold" or a checkpoint to examine power relationships in that person's framework of values; it suggests the direction the helper should look in order to understand how the individual/family functions. Later in this chapter, examples from different ethnic groups are given to illustrate how the "handholds" relate to the actual descriptions of family life of different ethnic groups.

Variations Within Ethnocultures

It is simpler for the worker to have a word that points to a variety of similar, well-known factors than to remember the exact details of each of the situations. In addition, however, having exact details assumes that agreed-upon descriptions of the cultural behaviour of each ethnic group are available. In fact, it is often hard to get members of a group to agree on descriptions of their culture. This lack of agreement is not surprising for several social and psychological reasons: first, culture is an abstraction and, therefore, what is considered important can vary between people who are doing the abstracting. Many perceptual and psycho-social factors come into play. For example, it can be hypothesized that some members of a group may not wish to focus on some of the characteristics of their culture; they may prefer to downplay those they believe may not be approved of by the host culture; they may wish to put the "best" qualities forward and ignore others. Reitz (1980) has written very fully on this topic.

Second, with more sociological focus, ethnic groups with the same national origin will vary depending on the era in which major migration took place. Since national cultures are always evolving, the people who migrate carry the national culture with them in the form to which it had evolved when they left. People migrating at a later stage carried a somewhat different culture with them.

Again, every national group has many lines of schism within it, along religious, political, racial or other subcultural divisions. Migrations from the country of origin may be drawn more from one set of divisions than another. Thus, in Canada, the religious, political or racial mix for even one ethno-cultural group can vary, from place to place because each setting created a unique set of conditions within which the original culture adapted to become a Canadian ethnicity.

Together, these social and psychological factors lead to great cultural variation within each ethnic group in Canada. When these issues are multiplied by the number of separate and different ethnic groups, the task becomes almost infinite. To have enough rigorous research conducted, where probabilities of the presence of cultural traits could become known, is not practical or possible. There is not the time, the money, or sufficient professional expertise to conduct such studies.

Processual Nature of Reality

Another requirement for a concept to be used in a practice situation is that the processual nature of reality must be taken into account. For this reason, the concepts are presented in a range format. The continua used suggest that a value can be greater or lesser and that some other value may gradually take its place. It is an empirical, but not well-understood, issue how values change within the individual or family. The simple diagram below suggests the change that is possible along one dimension. The left end of the line stands for a high presence of a value or cultural mechanism, which dwindles away to a low level of this value at the right.

High_____Low

An individual or family could be placed on this continuum at one point in time and as the process of acculturation proceeds, could be considered to move towards the other end of the line.

The range format is sometimess used with ideal types. Here a high level of one trait is at one end of the continua and a high level of the opposite trait is at the other end. For example, hierarchical values are seen as opposite to egalitarian values and if formatted in a range could be sketched:

Hierarchical values:

High level_____Low level

Egalitarian values:

Low level_____High level

These could be collapsed into one continuum:

Hierarchical_____Egalitarian

This assumes that these values are mutually exclusive and cannot appear at the same time in the same person. There is some evidence that, sometimes, opposing values can exist at the same time. For instance, some people who are adjusting to a new country see themselves as adding values and not losing any values. It has not been shown how, under normal conditions, this can be accomplished. However, if held in different spheres it is quite possible and in fact probably quite ordinary. In some cases, "compartmentalization" is involved, where the expressions of opposite values are kept separate from each other. For example, a woman may become quite egalitarian in the world of work and expect to be treated in an equal way with men as regards pay scales and opportunities for promotion. However, when she is at home, she may be willing to accept the old hierarchical values in the family, including her husband's authority in family matters. For some people, this "compartmentalization" of values is an acceptable way of living but for others it may seem hypocritical or unintegrated. At the subjective level, therefore, these are very important value issues and may become the subject of counselling or therapy.

Inclusivity

Several other characteristics were outlined as important for multicultural practice work: Inclusivity is one of these dimensions; contexting can be applied to any interaction and everyone, including Native Peoples, can find themselves on the framework of the contexting continua. These continua apply equally to helpers and to those they help, because the question is not whether the values exist in a situation, but rather how much and in what form they exist. Since the scheme is an etic one, it leads to emic questions being asked in each situation. One important question for the helper is how far apart on a continuum is the client/patient from the helper? Thus the issue of mutuality and the provision of a frame of reference is addresseed within the scheme. For example, if the worker has strong egalitarian values and the client has strong hierarchical values, there is a substantial value difference between them, and there may be difficulties in establishing rapport and the worker understanding the client's point of view. Cross-cultural training must ensure both that the practitioner's values not interfere in the helping process and that the practitioner feel comfortable in this situation. In fact, it is exactly in this arena of value difference that cross-cultural training is so essential.

CONTEXTING

A value scheme derived from Edward T. Hall's work on high and low context cultures (Hall, 1976a) is presented here. It has the qualities mentioned previously: it covers variation within and between cultural groups, it reflects the processual nature of reality and applies to anyone in Canada.

Hall's original interest was in contrasting traditional societies with modern ones. In particular, he contrasted Japanese and Middle Eastern societies with the United States (Hall, 1976b). He often used the exemplar of American businessmen doing business in Japan or the Middle East, and with the simple concept of "context," he drew attention to issues that sometimes made the business dealings difficult or impossible. With the use of this conceptual scheme, the businessman could enter another frame of reference. By paying attention to these issues, it was presumed that business improved.

I have adapted Hall's ideas to Canadian multicultural work by assuming that if those problems could occur **cross**-nationally, they could occur **within** a society when those conflicting components came together. In addition to modifying the concept used by Hall, I have divided Hall's original idea into constituent elements and put each into a continuum format to reflect the ever-evolving nature of ethno-culture. And so we proceed on to describe the main concept.

High context cultures are those in which the kin networks are substantially, if not totally, coterminous with the whole society. The most perfect examples of such cultures were the Native cultures present in North America when the Europeans first came. Although much changed and damaged, these cultures are still "very high context." The term "context" refers to the fact that, for those in these high context cultures, kin relationships, established at birth, define completely who one is and their life-long mutual rights and obligations. This description constitutes an ideal-typical case of high context and is at one extreme pole of a continuum of "context." The other pole is "low context," where very little of one's identity, obligations and rights derive from family. Rather, the individual is expected to develop his or her place or context in each new situation and must go through that development activity on a life-long basis. This also is an extreme ideal-typical case. In most instances, the extreme types do not exist but some modified version does. Generally, change is from high to low context values: high context societies are becoming more low context as technological development alters relationships and modern communications permit the fast exportation of ideas from low to high context cultures. Where low context and high context values meet there is often much conflict. Some examples of this will be given later. Also, many ethno-cultural groups and their members in Canada are subject to the pressure of the technological nature of our society and have to shift from a high context to a lower context in their daily lives.

Before turning to the set of continua that are components of contexting, several further observations about contexting need to be made. High context societies or groups are ones in which messages lie largely "in the context," i.e., are implicit in the already established pattern of relationships. When business deals are being made or social or political arrangements being negotiated, very little needs to be said because so much understanding required about trust, reliability, accountability, reciprocal exchanges and so forth, are already largely in place. To have to spell out these basic expectations to the participants would be considered an insult; one's word and reputation are all that are needed to assure the transaction.

Low context people on the other hand, because they do not have a fixed identity into which they are born, have to develop and change their identity and their relationships through their lifetime experiences, have to spell out in every detail and through lengthy negotiations the bases for contracts and trust in their dealings. Where there is insufficient knowledge or awareness by the parties involved of the other's context expectations (Hall, 1969a) conflict can occur.

When contexting is looked at in Canada, much high context life remains in working-class family life, whereas low context life is coterminous with middle-class family life. Rural families are more high context than city families and Canada, on the whole, is more high context than the United States.

This author assumes that, if the practitioner can identify important and basic values in the client's life, then the processes of assessment and service can be speeded up and made more accurate and focussed. If values are identified and understood rapport with the client and the family can be established; methods of intervention can be chosen more wisely; and the outcomes of the helping process will have more predictability. A simple hypothetical example illustrates how knowledge of values might help improve service.

> A family with a high context set of values is referred to a family agency for help with a disturbed child. The family has a very "authoritarian" father and "subservient" mother. Sex roles are clearly segregated and beliefs about what is right and proper behaviour for each member of the family are accepted in an unquestioning way. There is a high degree of interdependence amongst the members of the extended family. The low context expectations by the service worker, (i.e., that individuals in the family will make decisions for themselves and that all parties can speak equally), are not met by the clients and the family breaks off contact with the agency. However, once the worker recognizes this family's values, rapport is established and a method compatible with a family-oriented group is used. The expected outcomes are more congruent with "family-oriented" values; the pace of treatment is slow and careful and the great differences between agency and family values are gradually acknowledged.

CONTEXTING CONTINUA

It is extremely difficult to find dimensions that are **always** true. However, from extended observation, the following value dimensions appear to occur repeatedly in social work practice and other helping relationships where individual and family work occurs. The two lists that are developed group high context values on the left and low context ones on the right. Ten dimensions in all are covered, beginning with the first five in this chapter.

High Context   Low Context

1. Family orientation _____Individual orientation
    (extended family, clan, tribe) ———————— (nuclear family)

The most distinctive trend in post-industrial North America has been the emphasis on the individual. That the individual is expected to live a self-fulfilling life and be able to reach for the greatest personal happiness is a cornerstone of both United States and Canadian societies. This value finds extreme expression with the American emphasis on liberty, an **individual** right, whereas, Canadian society, is more prone to recognize freedom as a group right. Generally, in this respect and others, American society is more low context than Canadian society. Throughout modern, low context societies, however, there are innumerable examples of individualization. Self-help books abound that promote the idea that the individual by him/herself can achieve all manner of personal success in areas from business, money-making, health, family affairs, domestic achievements like cooking and sewing, intellectual pursuits in philosophy, psychology and political science, etc. The individual's achievement of the perfect body has led to a body cult industry. Personal happiness in marriage, friendships and at work is the message emphasized in popular magazines and newspapers. It cannot be over-emphasized here that this value of personal happiness overwhelmingly dominates much of Canadian society.

It is not surprising, therefore, that the individual orientation pervades social work agencies, health care facilities, schools, government offices and commercial establishments. In fact, even "family therapy" practiced in a wide variety of settings is aimed at the health and well-being of the **individuals** in the family; the aim is not mainly to keep the family together, but only to do so if it meets the needs of the individuals who comprise it.

This overwhelming focus about the **individual** strongly contrasts with the concern with the **family** in high context societies or groups. In the traditional high context case, the family is the unit of decision-making and the individual's needs are secondary to what is good for the family as a whole. The family's honour, reputation, prosperity, longevity and sphere of control are the foci for action. Decisions about what will enhance the family are preeminent. For example, the needs of a child, as perceived by outsiders such as social workers or teachers, may be denied if the needs of the family are deemed by the family to be greater. The child will thus be cared for by traditional methods.

In the literature, this family orientation is often described at length. Some examples illustrating the high context family values orientation are taken from a book edited by Monica McGoldrick, et al., 1982. Many of these examples may seem to be extreme levels of high context. Certainly many of them are 'historic' given the date of the citations. To what extent they typify a particular group is not known. However, that they occurred at times, there is no doubt. The authors most certainly have drawn on the best sources that were available. They are given here to operationalize the high context end of the continuum and in that sense they are 'ideal types.' Jewish, Portuguese, Greek, East Asian and Cuban families are described in

McGoldrick's book. References within these citations are found in McGoldrick's book.

JEWISH

(Herz and Rosen, p. 365)

An outstanding study of the Eastern European Culture, *Life is with People* (Zborowski and Herzog, 1952), speaks of the centrality of the family.

> The complete Jew is an adult with a mate and offspring. No man is complete without a wife; no woman is complete without a husband. For each individual the ideal centre of gravity is not in himself, but in the whole of which he is an essential part. (p.124)

While giving priority to the value of the family is hardly unique to Jewish culture, the centrality of the family cannot be underestimated in looking at its dynamics. "Familism" (Bardis, 1961; Zuk, 1978), a belief in the importance of family as a sacred institution, stems from the idea that it is a violation of God's law not to marry. The first commandment in the Torah (Bible) is "You shall be fruitful and multiply." Marriage and raising children — establishing a family — have been the core of Jewish tradition.

PORTUGUESE

(Moitoza, p. 416)

> Indeed, the importance accorded the family appears universal among the Portuguese, with differences tending to occur more at the level of structure. Those Portuguese immigrant families followed by the Egas Moniz Clinic have been found to have both significant nuclear and extended components....

GREEK

(Welts, p. 274)

> Family honour is extremely important to Greeks. Breaking the rules can have terrible implications that dishonour the entire family, and therefore, understandably, would be anticipated with

intense anxiety. For example, men worship their mothers and expect to care for them in old age (Zotos, 1969). If they fail in that responsibility it means not only that they are dishonoured by their own failure to discharge an obligation but that their mothers are retrospectively dishonoured as mothers since they could never have been good if they raised bad sons. Similarly, failure of a son to pay the respect owed his father shames both the father and the son (Peristiany, 1965). The depth of feelings for these matters cannot be overemphasized.

EAST ASIAN

(Shon and Ja, p. 211)

Within the traditional East Asian framework the family is not time limited. The concept of the family extends both backward and forward. The individual is seen as the product of all the generations of his or her family from the beginning of time. This concept is reinforced by rituals and customs such as ancestor worship and family record books, which trace family members back over many centuries. Because of this continuity, the individual's behaviour has a different importance and consequence. Personal actions reflect not only on the individual and the nuclear and extended families, but also on all of the preceding generations of the family since the beginning of time. And individual actions will impact upon all future generations as well. Therefore, there is a burden of responsibility that transcends the individual's personal concerns.

CUBAN

(Bernal, p. 193)

The Cuban family structure is founded on "familism," the cultural attitudes and values toward the family. The family is the most important social unit in the life of Cubans. The Cuban family is characterized by a bond of loyalty and unity, which includes nuclear and extended family members, as well as the network of friends, neighbours, and community.

2. Hierarchy_____Equality
    (levels of power)——————————————————————(equal power)

One of the most dominant traits of high context cultures is an hierarchical structure and the accompanying values that support these hierarchical arrangements. Native cultures exemplify the hierarchical form; there is always a presence of elders and respect shown elders is unequivocal.

High context families are organized usually with the father at the top, the mother and children below. In some societies, such as the Mohawk, women have highest authority. Older people have precedent over younger people. In this situation, the power is used to maintain cultural beliefs in unchanged form, which usually can be seen to benefit those in power or on top of the hierarchy.

An expected concomitant of power is the use of physical force. In the family, in high context groups, it has been accepted practise that men could use physical force on their wives and that parents could use it on children. Today, this issue is now brought forward in practise situations as "battered wives" and "abused children." These problems are found at all levels and in all sectors of society and illustrate that the old values about the use of power still remain even in societies that seem predominantly low context and proclaim egalitarian values. An example of hierarchical remnants in a low context family is a family where both parents are professionally educated but the man does not tell his wife what his income is and her queries are sternly denied.

Certainly, many well-intentioned adults have had difficulty accepting the idea that corporal punishment in schools, group homes, foster homes and institutions for children must be given up. The intensity of feelings about the use of force and the reluctance to break the habit, attests to the deep values and the sense of propriety in which it is held. Excerpts from descriptions of ethnocultural families reflect the pervasive value of hierarchy in the past (McGoldrick et al., 1982). Jewish, Italian, East Asian, Iranian, French Canadian, Portuguese, Greek, Polish, German and West Indian examples are given.

JEWISH

(Herz and Rosen, p. 373)

> She was a perfect Jewish woman, clear, patient, hardworking, and
> silent, submissive to God and to her husband, devoted to her chil-

dren...her own well being was unimportant (Zborowski and Herzog, 1952: 138).

The Eastern European Jewish community was a male-oriented culture where women were regarded as subordinate and where men greeted each day by offering thanks to God "that Thou has not made me a woman" (Hertz, 1960: 21). Woman's role was to serve as a helpmate...

ITALIAN

(Rotunno and McGoldrick, p. 346-347)

The father has traditionally been the undisputed head of household, often authoritarian and rigid in his rule setting and guidelines for behaviour. A kind of benevolent despot, he usually takes his responsibility to provide for his family very seriously. In addition, all male social activities occurred regularly and were considered important. Even work was not to interfere with this.

If the Italian father is the head of the family, the Italian mother is its heart. She is the family's emotional sustenance. While yielding authority to the father, she traditionally assumes total control of the emotional realm of the family. Her life centres around domestic activities, and she is expected to receive her primary pleasure from nurturing and servicing her family. Her personal needs take second place to those of her husband, and in exchange she is offered protection and security from all outside pressures or threats.

EAST ASIAN

(Shon and Ja, p. 211-212)

Within the traditional East Asian framework, marriage does not mark the creation of a new family but rather the continuation of the man's family line. The woman is considered to have left her family of origin and to have become absorbed into the family of the man. Under this patriarchal system the status of the wife is quite low; her position is lower than that of her husband, lower than that of her husband's parents, and lower than that of her husband's older siblings.

Within the nuclear family subsystem, roles and expectations are fairly clearly defined. The father is the leader of the family. He makes the decisions, and his authority is unquestioned. While his authority is great so, too, is his responsibility.

IRANIAN

(Jalali, p. 294)

The traditional Iranian family unit is patriarchal: The father is the undisputed head of the family. Sons and their wives may live in the father's household or compound. An extended family consisting of a couple, their unmarried children, plus their married sons with their wives and children, is common among many segments of the population.

FRENCH CANADIAN

(Langelier, p. 233)

The father is not only the authority figure and economic provider for the family; ideally he is also a moral leader who, in difficult times, provides the family with affection, attention, and support and is responsible for creating a climate of security. According to Garigue (1968), "men regard it as normal for their wives to depend on them and to trust in them" (p. 159).

PORTUGUESE

(Moitoza, p. 416)

The nuclear unit is ostensibly patriarchal, yet, as also described by Smith (1976), much internal and external familial facilitation and negotiation is handled by the female/wife/mother. Authority tends to be organized vertically, flowing from the parental dyad to the oldest son or daughter. All members are expected to make financial contributions so as to make possible the rapid purchase of a house — the repository of family life.

GREEK

(Welts, p. 273)

> Greek men are authoritarian fathers and husbands. They are loving but, particularly to outsiders, appear to be emotionally distant. They are parsimonious with praise and generous with criticism. A Greek proverb, "A man should love his wife with his heart, but never with his lips," illustrates Greek men's feelings.

POLISH

(Mondykowski, p. 398)

> The father and husband is acknowledged head of the household. His authority is to be respected and his wishes obeyed. As one Polish patient told me, "When a Polish husband says, 'Jump!' you ask 'How high?' on the way up."

GERMAN

(Winawer-Steiner and Wetzel, p. 258-259)

> German American family structure and role complementarily reflects the legacy from the fatherland. The husband/father is the head of the household and the leader of the family. The wife takes his name, adopts his family and friends, and gains his social status.

German American women were regarded as hardworking, dutiful, and subservient and were respected for these qualities.

WEST INDIAN

(Brice, p. 128)

> In marriage, the man's primary responsibilities are economic. As the head of the household, he is expected to support his wife and their children. A husband failing to provide for his family is seen as not fulfilling his role, and this is grounds for divorce.

In social life, hierarchical values can be revealed proxemically. For example, in the way people place themselves in a room or round a table. The father's place at the head of the dining table is often an unquestioned fact. The way people walk down a street or approach a desk or counter for service often clearly depicts the order of importance. For example, the husband may walk down the street ahead of the wife or the family will line up, father, mother, older then younger children, as they approach a counter to get help. For the observer, the depiction of these values in social space is not only a visible view of the value, but the behaviour is conterminously the value itself and an expression of respect by those involved for that value. The need to show respect is a built-in behaviour for those lower in the hierarchy. To show respect to elders is one of the most important values in and of itself to be instilled in children. In return for acknowledging higher status, those lower in status expect protection from those above. People who come out of hierarchical family systems may remain sensitive to authority figures all their lives. This tendency can be observed in eye gaze behaviour such as downcast or averted gaze or in social distance behaviour as they keep greater distance from people in authority long after the initial settlement period in Canada. (Chapters 5 and 6 describe behavioural aspects of values).

Men in high context cultures must be seen and understood to be exercising authority and leading the family to protect its honour. In extreme cases, this may mean starting a feud or continuing a confrontation started by a former family head of another family, or a formal organization. Once family honour has been questioned, very little can be done to stop aggressive behaviour until the honour has been restored. Rather than set out on such a long and dire path, usually "back door" negotiations will be attempted, with the help of a third party, for as long as is possible rather than begin something that everyone knows cannot be ended easily. In some cases, there are particular methods laid down to offset the feud possibilty. For example, amongst the Somalis, there is a **dia-paying group**, "which is pledged to collectively support each other, particularly in the payment and receipt of compensation in respect of actions committed by or against their group" (Immigration and Refugee Board Documentation Centre, 1990: 73)

In a similar vein, women in most high context cultures must be seen to be docile and under the authority of men. They must be seen to be chaperoned and exhibit modest and demure behaviour. Always, appearances count a great deal. It is a luxury of the developed, low context societies to be able to say it is what individual people **think** and **feel** that matters.

Not only gender and age fall under hierarchical values, but also race. In the earlier high context eras, one's racial identity could be considered superior or inferior to someone else's without conflict. In anti-racism work, it is very important to understand the history of racist ideas and the milieu in which they could form. In an egalitarian context, it is logically impossible for these ideas to be maintained. That they are still with us to a very great degree, means that we have a long way to go before we can consider ourselves a truly egalitarian people.

3. Unquestioned beliefs_____Beliefs questioned

Within the hierarchical system are strong beliefs that the old values must be retained and must not be questioned. This attitude contrasts strongly with low context situations where values are readily questioned. Children who are encouraged to question and challenge ideas brought forward in schools and children's clubs and organizations, find quite a different view at home if an unquestioning attitude is still prized there.

4. Gender segregation_____Gender integration
    (men/women separate)————————————(men/women together)

Is it possible to distinguish between high and low context cultures in matters pertaining to gender? It is, but with caveats. First, it is not true that the status of women is low in high context cultures and high in low context cultures. There are many instances of women in very high context societies having their own independent sources of power, and of women in low context societies not possessing power, even though great gains have been made about women's rights.

Second, it is hard to ascertain the status of women in high context situations because the **stated** ideal about women's value is frequently very high: the problem lies in the practice of the ideals. According to most religions, women have high value, but the actual expression of that value in national cultures may vary greatly.

Finally, it is hard to get agreement on which practices are considered to be high or low status. For example, for women to be sequestered and have great limits placed on their opportunities to work and have careers would be seen as evidence of low status in low context cultures. However, some high context societies would argue that these limitations on mobility are prescribed not because women are not valued, but precisely because they are valued above all other things. There, women who are free to be mobile and independent are viewed as having low status.

Thus, to talk about women's status as high or low is not a productive basis on which to contrast the values of cultures. However, gender roles can be differentiated on the basis of segregation and integration. This issue also is important to professional helpers.

Gender role segregation is the practice of ascribing different tasks to each gender. Generally this means that women have the domestic arena and children to manage and men have other major decision-making responsibilities in the home and manage the external relations of the family. Out of this separation of tasks emerges a "man's world" and a "woman's world." In every high context society and group, the normative behaviour of women and men is learned in the separate "world" of each. Once again, McGoldrick's (et al., 1982) book provides historical examples; exerpts from the East Asian, French Canadian, German, Greek and Jewish groups are given. (Once again, references within citations can be located in McGoldrick's books.)

EAST ASIAN

(Shon and Ja, p. 212)

> The traditional role of the mother is of the nurturant caretaker of both her husband and children. Until recently, women were not free to engage in the same kinds of work and activities as men, and the care of the family was seen as their central roles. The mother's energy and creativity were to be channelled primarily into raising her children.

FRENCH-CANADIAN

(Langelier, p. 233)

> Amongst pre-WWII and those rural and high-school educated, it is fairly safe to assert that sex-specific roles are well-defined, with almost no sharing of tasks between husband and wife. Marriages are not companionate but oriented toward traditional roles and expectations. The husband's responsibilities are to exercise authority, to punish misbehaviour, and to provide protection and economic support. The wife's responsibilities are to oversee the family's welfare, to manage the daily household activities, to plan leisure time activities and to rear and educate the children. Authority is almost always the man's prerogative, and although in

recent times the father has been losing ground as the sole authority figure in the Franco-American family, he still exercises most of the overt power (Chasses, 1975; Woolfson, 1975).

GERMAN

(Winawer-Steiner and Wetzel, p. 259)

The marital relationship and the division of "labour" between parents tend to solidify the complementarity of a rational, dominant leader and an emotional, submissive nurturer. Yet, the father is not lacking in emotions and might even be quite sentimental. The mother can also effectively lead the family. It is the cultural context, among other influences, that determines who plays what role (Bateson, 1976; Willi, 1978). It is the familial context that maintains the polarity within which each of the partners develops attitudes and behaviour patterns that correspond to their roles.

GREEK

(Welts, p. 273)

Details of the family roles are important because the inability to perform them adequately is frequent cause of distress. The roles themselves are taken for granted; that is, they are not ordinarily discussed. The therapist must know in advance what is expected. Sex roles are highly stereotyped with little overlap between men and women. Men must work and provide. They rarely assist with household or child-rearing tasks. They seek the status of nikokiri or master of their house, and value the companionship and compatibility of their wives (Salamone, 1980). Women, in return, cater to the men's desires, want to build up men's self-esteem, and wish to be considered good wives. As long as there is mutual agreement about these goals, marriages remain stable (Sanders, 1962).

JEWISH

(Herz and Rosen, p. 374)

The sexes were segregated due in large measure to the fear of female sexuality and women's ability (like the Biblical Eve) to lure men into lascivious thoughts or untoward behaviour and away from the study of Torah. Tznius (modesty) as an ideal for women became at least the external and public way of life, defined by demure dress, shaved and bewigged head, averted eyes, and unobtrusive manner (Ganzfried, 1961). It is important to emphasize the extreme limitations put upon women's public deportment and appearance in traditional Jewish life since it was these public restrictions that greatly contributed to their strong, controlling role in the family.

Contrastingly, gender integration is a logical value stance in an individualistic society. It would be very difficult to maintain that the **individual's** happiness and potentialities were central and then circumscribe these potentialities because of gender. Thus, over the last few decades when collective rights and individualization have proceeded apace, the issue of gender integration has gradually enlarged and developed. Unravelling the values and norms about gender segregation has been played out in numerous areas, in particular in the world of work. For example, it is no longer legal in Canada to advertise a job posting as being applicable to only men or only women. The Help Wanted newspaper ads no longer can specify gender.

Much has yet to be done to make gender integration fully operational. For example, research in many western countries shows that where women are working in the labour force, men are not equally helping in the home. In fact, for many women, paid work in industry has simply doubled their labour, because they still have to do the same home tasks. This fact is especially true for most high context women living in Canada. It is probably harder for most high context men to make the changes needed, to help out in the home, than it is for men brought up in a developed, individualistic society.

One concomitant of these separate worlds is that each gender has taboos about interacting in certain situations with the other gender. Generally, it is much more comfortable for women to be interviewed and attended by women, and men by men. This is especially true for health care transactions where women are alone in the home and have to be interviewed there or even in the practitioner's office. Service providers can improve relationships with clients/patients by being sensitive to this issue. It may mean that innovative ways are needed to utilize the service people available. For example, if a man has to be interviewed about a personal family matter, it may be better to have a male interviewer do this task. If there is a shortage of male workers, and if service must be of extended duration over weeks or months, a woman worker could gradually be introduced, first in joint sessions and then alone after a relationship has been established. Attending to this matter in the beginning of service provision can save time later on; valuable time is wasted by unnecessarily irritating or alienating the client.

As pointed out in the previous section on hierarchy, values about gender segregation can be observed in non-verbal behaviour. High context men and women do not engage in direct eye gaze. Averted gaze, respectful gestures and facial expressions communicate these deeply-felt values. There is little to be gained, and perhaps much to be lost, by trying to force a change. The society at large will gradually modify these values; there is usually no need for practitioners to become overly involved with them.

Before leaving this topic, it is worth pointing out that gender segregation in high context societies was nearly always balanced out by very strong ideals that blended the male and female. Joseph Campbell (1949: 149-171), in his world-wide study of mythology, finds the idea of a joined male-female principle existed everywhere. Whether it be Africa, Australia, Native North America, the ancient Greek and Roman worlds, India, China and so forth, all proclaimed in some fashion the unity of humankind. In the highest deities, shamans, legends, sculpture, and even in some puberty rites, the ideas of hermaphroditism, bisexual gods, androgynous ancestors, etc., are proclaimed and worshipped. Thus, the gender integration of low context societies is not new, but merely a new expression of something very old.

5. Interdependence_____Independence
   (prescribed give/take)————————————————————(the self alone)

The final structural variable discussed here under contexting is one relating to the opposing values of interdependence and independence. Where hierarchy and gender segregation tend to divide a social group along status and gender lines, interdependence weaves the group together. In high context societies, there are extremely strong values about mutual rights and obligations. Generally speaking, the emphasis is placed on one's **obligations** to others rather than on rights accruing. In low context society where norms of mutuality also exist, the emphasis is coming more and more to be placed on the **rights** of the individuals. It seems clear that in the long run there must be more of a balance between these forces. In traditional settings where there is an emphasis on giving to others, in many situations reactions have developed over time to put the receiver of help in a lower status position. This is true nearly everywhere and especially true in the highly structured relationship of Hindu society and cultures influenced by it (Wood, 1984).   Understanding these mutual obligations as they are expressed in ethno-cultures in Canada would be important in family and community work.

Interdependence values are ascribed on the basis of status and gender. Men are expected to protect their wives and children. Women are expected to serve their families. Of particular interest to helping professionals is the mother's behaviour and some of the purposiveness that lies behind her devoted, nurturant attachment to her children. Because of her low power position, she must create emotional bonds that will survive throughout her life. Some examples from East Asian, Greek and West Indian families illustrate this (McGoldrick et al., 1982):

EAST ASIAN

(Shon and Ja, p.212)

> This dynamic is quite important in the later life of the mother, after the father has died and the oldest son has inherited the reins of the family. Because of the great emotional attachment the oldest son feels toward his devoted mother, the wishes of the mother are frequently respectfully attended to by the son. Thus, although the oldest son is the ruler of the family, it is frequently the mother who rules this son and, therefore, the rest of the family. This, then, becomes the reward of the woman in the later years of her life. The influence of the wife and mother is more covert, through her ability to influence primary male figures, as contrasted to the overt authority influence of the males.

GREEK

(Welts, p. 276)

> In rural Greek cultures breast-feeding is continued longer for boys than girls (Vassiliou and Vassiliou, 1970). As in other Mediterranean cultures, a woman's cultivation of and identification with her son is both a pathway to power and compensation for her helplessness in a male-dominated society.

WEST INDIAN

(Brice, p. 129)

> There is a strong bond between mothers and sons, and a son is
> doted on regardless of his sibling position. If her husband is
> absent, there is a tendency for the mother to lean on her male
> children. A son's closeness with his mother continues even after
> he marries, and sons are expected to take care of their mothers.

In most low context societies, a great deal of emphasis is placed on
independence rather than on the mutual obligations. This value is congru-
ent with the low context individualistic emphasis: since the State arranges
pensions to the elderly and provides care to those unable to pay for it themselves, there is less need for older people to rely on their children during
their frailer years.

However, the norms about child-rearing remain when high context people come to Canada. Mothers who expect to remain closely attached and
nurturant with their children will continue this pattern. It is here, however,
that conflict with low context professionals may arise.

Child rearing patterns that are stressed in Canadian institutions such as
nursery schools, day care centres and public schools, are based on the belief
that children must become independent and self-reliant as soon as possible.
Thus, children will be encouraged to manage things for themselves. For
example, putting on and taking off winter coats and snowsuits is a personal
activity engaged in daily by millions of children during a Canadian winter.
Teachers expect small children to try to manage this activity on their own.
But, for many high context mothers, this is an activity where she can personally devote herself to the child. Putting on clothing involves closeness
and touching and much nurturing work can go on while this mundane task
is accomplished. Carrying out this task is, for the mother, a great deal more
than a simple instrumental function; rather, it is the communication of
depths of feeling, attachment and security to the child. If such a mother is
admonished to "let the child do it for himself," she may feel anger, confusion, guilt and frustration and yet not fully be aware of why she is feeling so.

Helping professionals can be sensitive to this dilemma. On the one
hand, the mother can be allowed to express her own feelings in the ways
she expects and on the other, the teacher can gradually explain what the
values in the school are. The mother might be used to help other small children who need attention and in other ways turn the potentially conflictual
episode into a positive experience. Generally speaking, high context cultures have their own expectations for children's independence. It should be

just a matter of time before this normative expectation begins to match what the Canadian institution expects regarding independence.

People who have been raised in families that stress interdependence may strive to express these values long after the family members have separated and moved apart. For example, young people who have come to Canada to study in Canadian universities still try to keep in touch with their parents and grandparents at home. One young Hong Kong student I know faced major dental work and phoned home to discuss it with her parents. Her Canadian friends chided her to "be more independent." However, from her point of view, the issue was not independence or the lack of it — after all, she managed by herself in Canada all year — rather it was the joy of interacting with her family over a personal issue and having their attention and advice. She wanted to maintain the interdependence and had very little chance to act out the behaviour that interdependence values called forth; she missed expressing those values.

Many low context people look towards interdependence values with some longing and even envy. The interdependent family has a strong sense of purpose and belonging. In much helping service work, it is these values that are the goals of intervention. Since so many clients feel isolated and lacking in a life purpose, counselling and group work of various sorts aim to help people to feel more connected to society. Although we pull back from extreme hierarchical and gender segregation values, we are much attracted to interdependence values.

In sum, these continua encapsulate several ideas: first, they point at common values found in very disparate ethnic family forms; second, the line denoting a continuum visually suggests variation in the degree to which a value is present; and, third, proposes which value opposites pertain to the two contexting systems. Values can be observed in behaviour and in the way people use social space. Since people do not usually discuss their basic values directly and, in fact, may be quite unaware of them, it is important that the helper be able to "read" the values of the client without the assistance of the client, since identification of values plays a crucial part in delivery of service. At some stage of the relationship, the worker's beginning appreciation of what is important to the client may be shared and corrections made where the "reading" was not accurate. Such sharing accomplishes not only greater specificity for the worker's understanding, but teaches the client about differences in values while acknowledging their validity.

Chapter 4

Five Additional Contexted Values

This Chapter explores five additional continua that are also within the concept of contexting.

CULTURE AND TIME

If it is possible to identify a single important variable in cross-cultural understanding it must be **time** and the seeming passage of time. When the profound world of modern physics is contrasted with that of the Eastern mystics the meanings of time can be explored most deeply (Capra, 1985). However, most of us retain the view of time we absorbed in early childhood.

Conceptualizing time is difficult for many reasons. The behavioural patterns of cultures have rhythms, the timing and pacing of which are unique to each ethnoculture and we learn these rhythms from our earliest years. For example, rural life is usually slower paced than city life. One city may seem faster paced than another. These innate rhythms in cultures are usually invisible to, and unconsciously performed by, members of the ethnoculture; in fact, if cultural values are typically not consciously noted by the owners of those values, even less are the rhythms of those patterns consciously noted. Strangers to a culture can feel uncomfortable and alien when immersed in a new culture, in part discomforted by the unfamiliar underlying rhythms (Birdwhistell, 1952; Condon, 1978; Hall, 1984).

Unless one is a trained linguist or musician, we lack an adequate vocabulary to describe the differences in rhythms. Luckily, most of us do not need to cognitively master this difficult, technical subject; it is enough to know that these processes are going on and that it is normal to experience discomfort — we can identify a universal process and not blame or stereotype those who have the culture with which we are unfamiliar.

6. Polychronic————————————————Monochronic
    (many things at once)————————————(one thing at a time)

There is one set of differences in time usage between high and low context cultures, identified by Edward T. Hall (1976b), which can be described. He called these differences polychronic time and monochronic time. This distinction is very useful to the practical world of practitioners, because it distinguishes the timing patterns of such workers and contrasts them with the subset of clients who have very different timing processes.

Professional people are generally trained to use time in a slotted or monochronic way — one thing at a time — and this manner of working is the basic structure of help-giving. Most workers have their appointment books that lay out each hour of the working day on a page in a linear manner, each hour an identical frame. Time is quantified and people are exhorted to not "waste" time but "save" time and "use" time wisely. The Protestant ethic values underlying industrial-technical jobs of working hard, saving and being thrifty co-exist well with this idea of time. Thus, patients and clients are given help in this time-partitioned, event segregated manner.

If patients must make an appointment with the doctor or other worker, they must manage their medical need so that it can be met in the time frame allotted by the service helper. If a patient's medical need includes hospitalization, another appointment must be made that fits in with the hospital's available time frames. The healing process is also expected to occur within a predictable time and discharge will be planned as much to suit the timetable needs of the hospital as the medical needs of the patient.

Other workers also have appointment books to help them manage their time. Generally, clients must meet the worker's schedule although emergencies are sometimes given priority. Both those helping and those being helped are equally dominated by the clock. However, those who have most power, also have most power over time and the way it is used. The act of "waiting" is more common for those low than high in power. In fact, to keep someone waiting can be viewed as an insult to or a mode of control over that person. The "waiting-rooms" that are found in all agencies and service centres help establish the lower power of those served.

Contrasted to monochronic time is polychronic time. Here time is not considered a commodity and many things are done at once. This way of viewing time is inseparably merged with most other high context patterns. This view is vastly different from a monochronic view of time. There is a more organic flow of activity blending in with the great range of human behaviour possible; it can extend from measured and slow to fast-paced. Indeed, the slow and more-quickened paced activities can often be covered at the same time. Time is not consciously weighed as to its passage, but the focus is on the activity of the people involved with each other and that activity is allowed to "take its own time." Often, monochronic people find it

very difficult to interact with polychronic people because high context timing and pacing is assumed and shared at an unspoken level not available to
clock watchers. On the other hand, it is very disturbing to polychronic people when their activity is compacted and crowded into a mysterious time
frame used in low context society. Moreover, when a polychronic person is
in the low power position, i.e., client/patient role, the rigid timing can cause
anxiety and interfere with developing a relationship with the helping person as the client would want.

It is important for professional helpers to be aware of their own timing
and pacing because this "invisible" dimension of culture has subtle but far-
ranging effects on service delivery. There is no aspect of service that is not
affected and expectations from the unaware helper can create stress and
confusion for the client/patient. Knowledge and awareness of the many
issues involved will improve service.

High Context Cultures and Time

To improve the sensitivity of low context helpers to the high context
use of time it is necessary to briefly enter the frame of reference of high
context societies and recall the conditions under which these societies were
developed.

Cultures are blueprints for adapting to varied environmental conditions.
High context cultures were blue prints developed in a far different world
than the world for which low context cultures are adapted. Generally, the
ancient world (and these conditions lasted with only minor modifications
until quite recently) was one where death rates were high, birth rates were
high and the life span was short. Most countries were agricultural and the
technological level of transportation and communication was low. There
were no political States that could provide the full range of securities needed
to face the many hazards of life. Famine, drought, flood, epidemics, piracy,
wild animals, etc. (Davis, 1951: 33-66) were scourges that had to be fought
directly and family/clan/tribal organizations were the main and best mode
of protection. The family in its high context form was the major protector
and decision-making unit. Native North American cultures already knew a
very high context family form(at) when different versions of the high context
form were later transported to Canada in the minds and hearts of her immigrants. In these conditions, people's lives moved with the ebb and flow of
seasons. The tempo was slow and the circumstances did not require an
awareness of time for itself.

The cultural patterns from pre-industrial times are still with us.

However, the relationship of "people patterns" to time has changed drastically as social forms and technology have evolved. Some of the ancient patterns, including the way time is intricately wound about them, remain. Here some of the cross-cultural issues about time in face-to-face deliberations, such as the professional relationship, will be discussed.

Monochronic Service Delivery and High Context Clients

Often the first connection a client/patient has with a service provider is in a waiting room near their office. This may be the waiting room of an agency and all clients must pass through this room to get to the workers' offices. The first contact for a patient might be in a small room with a receptionist in a doctor's office or a large waiting room in a clinic or outpatient department of a hospital. Waiting room behaviour is understood by monochronic, low context people. Expectations are that there is a "queue" and that clients will be called in order of appointment as the helper becomes free. That one may not get in to see the helper right on time is expected. In the meantime, one sits quietly and looks at a magazine provided by the agency or clinic. It creates tension if people do not follow these implicit normative rules. Asking loudly about the long wait or getting angry about a delay is likely to be considered troublesome behaviour. People unfamiliar with this bureaucratized approach to time may be confused, insulted, or feel rejected. Receptionists can be trained to be alert for signs that a patient/client might not understand the low context approach of slotted time and 'one-patient-at-a-time.' Since the client may not speak good English/French, even simple explanations may take some planning and depend on availability of interpreter resources.

Part of the usual process of inducting a client/patient into the service system is the filling in of forms. This is time-consuming in itself, but even more is it time-related if services are dependent on forms reaching certain destinations in the bureaucracy before services can be delivered. Monetary assistance is given out by government bureaucracies according to calendar time points. To the high context person, unfamiliar with North American bureaucracies, where bureaucrats also have time-slotted appointments, this may seem whimsical and uncaring. Again, simple explanations of what is obvious to a monochronically trained person can reduce anxiety, and also become part of the client's education about the new society.

As the client/patient moves along the intake process of agency or clinic, one of the first things given to the client is an appointment to see the helper. The low context person is aware of this and usually the first move to get service is to ask for "an appointment." This may be accomplished on the phone and often there is a moment of negotiation as the receptionist offers several time slot possibilities and the client/patient chooses the one that suits his/her needs best. If the need is urgent, e.g., a toothache, other previously arranged appointments may be re-scheduled or even cancelled in order to get the closest time available. At other times, if the need is more flexible, then a later time slot is chosen. A weighing of factors often takes place in the client/patient's mind, but always the thing being weighed is the relative merits of time slots. The low context person accepts this kind of decision-making as normal. However, for the uninitiated high-context person, negotiating the appointment-making task is an unfamiliar skill. There may be considerable consternation when the client finds that help cannot be given that day, and that a return trip on another day is needed. Often it is easier for a polychronic person to understand a long wait for an appointment then, than that the help will be given at some future date — a time slot available to the helper, but almost meaningless to the person who feels the need in the present and who does not understand slotted time.

Once the client has reached the office of the practitioner and is ushered inside for the interview or examination, the monochronic person knows that the service is time-bounded. Usually, the length of time is understood and partially predicted by the social worker or health care professional. Since services are classified in various ways, the practitioner has some idea of how long each kind of service will take. A new client/patient usually takes a longer time than a regular one. Certain procedures can be accomplished in a few minutes, whereas others may take an hour. Where a "talking" therapy is part of the service, the time slot may be made a standard length, e.g., the 50-minute hour for psychotherapy is understood well by therapist and patient. In fact, the way the patient uses the time itself may be the subject of some therapy sessions. Whether there will be one appointment or several may be the subject of "contracting." Low context people expect termination of service at the completion of one or more time slotted appointments. For the high context, polychronic person, the course of treatment must be explained and the timing and pacing of it should also feature in the explanatory process.

High Context Cultures and Low Context Knowledge

One other dimension of help-giving that is inextricably time-related is the knowledge base of the physical and social sciences upon which the professional competency of social work, and to some extent the other professions, is built. This is an extremely complex subject and only the general tenor of the concern can be noted here. Knowledge about physical and social development, as it is understood by modern professionals, is rooted in a view of human development along a linear, quantifiable view of time. Even policing and law must acknowledge age and stage of physical development as a factor when evaluating a person's actions, even though it may not be done consciously. Certainly, social work and the health professions have to be cognizant of age and stage of development. For example, a child of three months is half the age of a child of six months and each has an appropriate level of development to that age. Questions, such as when the child cut their first tooth or started to walk, are asked against this basic age-development framework. However, a polychronic person may not have inculcated this basic view of development. Further, questions about life events, such as when was the father born, or when was he hospitalized for mumps, may be data that has been given little thought and may not be remembered according to calendar time.

Polychronic Time in Low Context Society

The person who stays home and does not work for pay in the labour force usually manages a polychronic life style, i.e., does many things at once. In fact, in a low context society such as Canada, the one job that largely remains rooted in high context, polychronic culture is the housewife role (Hall, 1976b). The home is a small system and any system, even if small, needs a manager. The housewife performs management and other functions.

It might be useful to view a mother as a family administrator. Under normal circumstances the administrative functions the mother performs include: assuring nurturance and supervision for the family; disbursing money over a variety of domestic needs; organizing her own and the family's use of time; overseeing contacts between the family and outsiders; setting standards of conduct for family members, each toward the other as well as toward outsiders to the family; and ensuring the safety and security of the family members and home. It need only be mentioned that a mother often administers and provides all these functions simultaneously (Herberg, 1978: 180).

However, the working wife and mother in Canada must manage both monochronic and polychronic time. In the labour force, time is usually very monochronically organized. The work day begins and ends at exact specified times; and any change in the length of the work period is often a subject for union negotiations. The work day proceeds with coffee and lunch breaks established in slotted time format. Work is scheduled in time blocks and deadlines for completed work are determined, based on expectations about how much work can be done in a given time period. The working mother and wife must fit into this mode of operation. However, her role of housewife cannot totally leave her awareness and, even when under monochronic time pressure, the polychronic needs of the home must be considered. In particular, the safety and care of her young children must be managed and assured on a daily basis. This may mean a quick phone call home to confirm that a babysitter has come or that an older child has remembered the smaller child and so forth. There are great strains on anyone managing such disparate chronological systems, especially if one system does not recognize the legitimacy of the other. For example, the employer may forbid phone calls home. Using "company time" to perform home-related duties is usually unacceptable, thus all the home-related jobs must be fitted into the hours not on the job. This leaves very little time for herself or for rest (Forman, 1985).

Women from high context cultures may have an especially hard time if their jobs are in factories and involve shift work. Such women often have families in which the norms about women's roles in the home and gender segregation are very traditional. She may get little or no help from her husband or others at home while coping with poor conditions at work.

The housewife role leads in well to the next contexting continuum. The polychronic style of domestic work is strongly related to "generalist" or holistic role dimensions in that sphere.

7. Holistic_____Fragmentary
    (things seen as a whole)————————(things broken into pieces)

This dimension of culture has to do with a tendency either to see the world in terms of wholes or to experience it in its parts. The former is associated more with analogical thinking and the latter with analytical thinking. Most of professional life is dominated by analytical modes of reasoning. The way to solve a problem is to take it apart and see what is involved. For example, chemical analysis is a method of separating out, in stages, the various components of a substance for its identification. It is assumed that the whole can be named and understood by knowing the parts.

In health care practise, whether it is a public health issue involving many people or the diagnostic process in a medical examination, the process is one of decomposing the subject of concern into its parts in order to deduct what is significant and, through this, arrive at a diagnosis. In social, educational or legal services, the approach is similar.

This kind of thinking contrasts with an holistic approach that starts with the connections of the subject to the whole: Knowledge in this sphere is based on the assumption that everything is connected. For example, in traditional Chinese medicine, the individual's personal bodily system reflects the system of the known universe. The individual's lifestream or energy is part of the Tao or energy in the universe, and bodily problems are understood through a cosmological scheme that links that person's body to familiar parts of the earth, the seasons and eventually to the Tao. Only by seeing the balance in the whole can one deduce what is wrong, i.e., disease or dysfunction is some imbalance in the bodily whole. The aim is to restore the balance — usually through interventions such as herbal medicine, acupuncture, reflexology and other methods that can treat the cause and restore balance (Wallnofer and Rottanscher, 1975).

The holistic approach is found throughout the world where high context people still remain. Even in what low context people would call "psychological matters," the holistic way of thinking still pertains. A high context person who is psychologically troubled may be seen as one who has not carried out some action required for interdependence in family roles. Perhaps some ritual needed to show respect for ancestors has not been attended to or in some way he/she has let down the family or clan group. The low context professional who tries to explain a problem as being understood by individual personality or motivation only, may not be trusted by the person steeped in holistic thinking.

One of the most obvious results of analytical thinking is the production of specialties. In the process of breaking down a problem into parts, it appears that each part requires more and more knowledge for its comprehension; no one can learn all the information that is available and so specializations emerge. In health care, this is most obvious. Each part of the body has a specialization attached to it; for example, orthopaedics, nose and throat, internal medicine, oncology, dermatology, psychiatry, etc. The patient's experience tends to be a fragmented one; no doctor fully sees the whole person or the connection between the different problems and treatments seen by others.

In the social sphere, similar dissection and categorization goes on; monetary assistance is given through one agency; child welfare services somewhere else; deviant behaviour is managed through a third and medical needs through a clinic or hospital. In this, many professionals from different bureaucratic structures serve the same family.

8. Religious_____Secular
    (the spiritual connects all)——————— (the spiritual separated out)

Clearly connected to the holistic dimension is the religious one. Students in multicultural courses could well spend time on the various religions that have been brought to Canada. Buddhist temples from several Asian countries are established here; Islamic centres are springing up in most major cities; Hindhu temples devoted to the worship of Brahma in his various aspects are also laying down roots in Canadian places. These different religious world views need on-going study for most Canadians rooted in the Judeo-Christian faiths. One writer who has plunged into the psychological depths of some of the existential questions raised by these different religious views is Richard A. Shweder (1991). His work starts from the standpoint of research done in the countries of origin. These are advanced conceptions and not usually suitable for beginning classes; he challenges any simple ideas of how multicultural societies can meld different world views when some are so very different from each other.

The term "religious" is used here in the way anthropologists first referred to preindustrial societies. They discovered that in such societies, there is always a religious or spiritual aspect to any behaviour or idea. There is no division between matters pertaining to the spiritual realm and matters pertaining to the material one. Everything is joined. In these high context societies, the spiritual expression of an ordinary momentary event may be verbal as in a prayer or expression like "God be with you"; it may be gestural such as a "warding-off" sign with the fingers, for some cultures, (the tip of the thumb protrudes between first and second fingers) (Morris, 1979: 147) or sometimes crossed fingers (Morris, 1979: 15). The expression of the supernatural presence is apparent as an aspect in most ceremonies whether it be to cement a political alliance or marriage, celebrate the birth of a child, or perform a death rite. It is also highly visible in the sculptured artifacts displayed in museums specializing in ancient cultures (Coe, 1976).

This preoccupation with the spiritual or supernatural flows from the belief that gods or spirits controlled everything and that because the gods were often viewed as "human," they were considered to be approachable, and open to influence. It was important to be aware of the supernatural level; disregard of it could lead to bad luck, unhappiness, and other poor outcomes. In Canada today, many of these beliefs and practises have become separated from their original high context setting and are now deprecated as "superstitions." This is demeaning for those who have these practises and they may be reluctant to share their concerns with low context practitioners in case they are viewed as uneducated or "simple." Actually, many people still carry residual concerns, of varying intensity, about the supernatural, in the form of "superstitions," e.g., knocking on wood, throwing spilled salt over the shoulder, reacting to black cats, and not walking under ladders, to name only a few.

Practitioners should become aware of the great variety of beliefs carried in from high context cultures, beliefs that are often so strong that a course of treatment seen as useful by low context professionals may be quite useless to the religiously-minded person. The religious context has everything connected to some central core of "power," "force" or omnipotent "will"; it thus is possible to see any of life's difficulties in terms of that supernatural connection.

Since high context people have long-term and deeply involved relationships with each other, it is very likely that these relationships themselves can become a focus of religious activity. For relationships that are deeply caring and devoted, actions will be taken to protect these people. In contrast, if feelings involved in the relationship are ones of suspicion or hostility, defensive action will be taken. Moreover, power may be perceived in people or things; intuition and imagination combine powerfully to produce an interpretation of events that differ quite markedly from a low context view of them. Some examples from my communicants in service work follow.

1. A young man left his high context home in Toronto to find work. His searchings took him across the country to another province. This young man leaving home without a job prospect left his mother distraught. Her reaction was to seek help from a healer; within three months the son returned home. She believed the healer's prayers returned her son to her. The helping professional might have explained his return as an inability to adjust to a new environment, an assessment that might well be totally discounted by the mother.

2. Another man had difficulty finding work. The low context helper perceived a cycle of difficulty in obtaining work combined with feelings of discouragement and a deepening fear of rejection each time he was unsuccessful. His mother-in-law, however, perceived the situation quite differently. It was clear to her that someone was interfering with him. It was not clear who, but soon jealousy was raised as the causative reason. Later, an ongoing curse placed on his mother, was seen as the reason. The curse was perceived as harmful to anyone associated with her, and in this case it was harming her son. A healer was sought to exorcise the curse on the

man's mother. The healer identified the source of the problem as the house; according to him it was possessed or haunted. At first incense was burned, but later, incantations and healing rituals similar to ones used by T.V. evangelists were used. None of these remedies worked and the woman continued to search for more powerful healers.

3. Other examples include rituals for removing the evil eye for stomachache and other bodily ailments. In another case a child's prolonged fear of going to bed at night was related to the house being possessed.

All of these examples involve issues with which social service, health care and other practitioners might often deal — unemployment, maladjustment and bodily ailments are very common problems. In each case the high context solution involved a client perception of supernatural power and some countervailing supernatural power was then wielded. Problems were not seen as being "in" an individual, but instead, somehow lodged in the links between one individual and another or with one individual and some object such as a house. If one goes back to the family\clan organization as the basic unit and remembers the intense, ongoing involvements within and between extended families and long-term acquaintances, as well as the holistic view of life, then these interpretations about life's difficulties become easier to understand. Nowhere in that view of life had there been a place for the "rational/scientific," secular, individualized and specialized way of the low context professional.

Practitioners are usually unaware of their clients' beliefs, and if told about them they may be sceptical or bewildered. First of all, the high context client has learned not to discuss these ideas with low context people because the usual disbelief or contempt is often quickly communicated, and when one is in a low power situation they quickly learn to cover up disapproved behaviour. Second, even if a person does feel free to discuss these beliefs, they probably are inexperienced in articulating their total view of life and the way a particular problem is caught up in their different cultural elements. Finally, for most low context people, these beliefs are difficult to grasp because they are so alien to the urban, post-industrial views based in physical and social sciences. However if a particular course of recommended treatment is not being followed or if people do not return for follow-up appointments, it may be that the low context practitioner should step back and try to uncover the client/patient view of the problem. This may take considerable time because a solid trust must be built up before the client's real concerns come out. Obviously, when the practitioner cuts or demolishes deeply held cultural beliefs, little helpful work can result.

9. Oral_____Written

One of the most striking characteristics of professional and technical schools is the emphasis on written work. Usually, great importance is attached to students being able to write well. Most evaluations of students are based on their written material; reports, exams and essays are all inextricably tied up with writing skill. The other side of this is reading proficiency; the ability and willingness to read a great deal, and be able to comprehend easily what is read. As students in professional training move through years and years of intensive reading and writing in their field of study, they become more and more adept at using and understanding the language of their occupation. These languages are rooted in academic disciplines that also rely heavily on reading and writing. The conceptualizations in these writings are usually a long distance from the language and culture of the unschooled person and when reports or information brochures have to be translated for various client populations, it is very difficult to capture the multiple layers of conceptual meaning that underlie any phrase or sentence.

For example, a simple information sheet that tells about a programme for children in a recreation agency will at least refer to age ranges and gender of the children who are expected to attend. The introduction of "age of child" is rooted in the cognitive-developmental model that says there is a gradual development of the physical, social and mental abilities of children, and that any planned activity should be appropriate to the age of the child. To any person educated in this industrial-urban liberal arts manner, that idea will be so deeply rooted it will be almost unconscious. But to someone outside of that life experience, this idea may not be understood.

In fact, to the high context parent reading the brochure translated into their ethnic language, the "age of child" contingency may either seem whimsical or else not be noted at all. If the programme was for young children, an older child may be sent along to keep an eye on the child. To the parent, the older child's role is to babysit the younger one. To the recreation director, the presence of an older child may be unacceptable, because bureaucratic rules must be followed or she/he may feel the parent is "palming off another child on them" and is insensitive to the programme needing to be geared to the younger age group. Sometimes the programme director may even feel insulted by the parent's behaviour. In each case the cultural assumptions of the other have not been explicated.

In contrast, high context cultures rely to a very great degree on oral culture and knowledge passed traditionally from one generation to another by the spoken word. Of course, those high context people in Canada who are well educated, adapt easily to this aspect of Canadian life. However many high context clients who have had slight education, especially in their countries of origin, will have great difficulty with the over-riding reliance by service providers on the written word and their client files. Access to the service, as well as participating in the service, requires people to read brochures, forms, articles, signs and so forth. For example in the waiting rooms of most clinics and agencies there are brochures giving information about a wide range of subjects, including the functions of that service. Not only are many people not accustomed to learning that way, but if they read the brochure the professional language may not be understandable. More research is needed about how best to inform people who are not accustomed to acquiring information by reading. Traditional societies use street plays, puppet theatres, slogans, outreach visits, storytellers etc. and, of course, daily conversations to get across the message, sometimes via the electronic media. It is quite possible for low context agencies to reduce their reliance on the written word and turn to some other medium more familiar to those from an oral culture.

10. Sense of place_____Mobile
    (a specific place is home)————————————(any place is home)

Generally speaking, high context cultures are founded and rooted in "a place." Even nomadic groups did/do not wander aimlessly, but went from one particular place to another, usually familiar to the group from many past visits. Originally "the place" might have been beside a stream, in a certain valley, or on a mountain plateau. Later some of these places developed into farming hamlets, communities, villages, or towns. Historically, the life of the people was intimately interwoven with the physical features and climatic conditions of the "place." Music, poetry, stories and legends became associated with "the place" and the life that they led there.

Native Peoples have the deepest connections with the land and "places" in Canada. The connections were/are spiritual rather than the legal and economic ones of ownership. Tribal groups across North America ranged from the nomadic to the highly settled depending on the resources of the land that derived from climate and terrain and the stage of tribal social development. Every rock, stream, and plant could potentially become a spiritual landmark. Often particularistic relationships were felt; one rock could not stand in for another; one piece of land could not substitute for another.

In contrast, low context cultures have people who are very mobile, and the mark of a successful low context person is in being able to move from house to house, city to city, without maladjustment. The search for work is the driving force that moves people from place to place. The unemployed move to locations where jobs are expected to be. Those who are employed move to other sites where promotions and better opportunities exist. Families become separated by greater and greater distances as people move across the country or across the world.

For high context people who migrate, the same kind of mobility means that the web of obligations between people becomes distended or disintegrates. The network of bonded relationships that is strained may be eventually modified (Litwak, 1965). Although many strive to retain the bonds and go through great deprivations to give high priority to expression of relationships, these high context needs often have to be put aside. In the place of origin, however, the "fiction" of that person being in the network is still maintained. For the high context migrant it is a painful and often slow process to put down roots in the new country, away from the place of origin in which they and their ancestors resided, sometimes for millennia.

SUMMARY

Each of the ten values in this Section has been presented in the contrasting form of a continuum. Each of the ends of a continuum has expressed a vast contrast to the other end. Each end encapsulates a value, that is, a deep sense of an idea of what is right and proper for that culture, even though these ideas may not be explicitly articulated. Neither side of a continuum is absolutely "right": both high and low context ends make sense given the conditions under which each has emerged. However, when both high and low values are placed together as they are in contemporary Canadian society there is always the possibility of misunderstanding and conflict. Awareness of the issues and an ability to empathize with one who has differing values from oneself, can make it possible to improve the delivery of service.

Values in Behaviour: The Non-verbal Modes

THE NON-VERBAL MODES

These two chapters, 5 and 6, are about identifying values in behaviour. Since most of social life is more non-verbal than verbal, it is necessary to be able to start "reading" what is important to people as one interacts with them or as one is able to observe their behaviour.

Without being aware of it, we are all giving out messages about what is important to us as we walk and talk and move around. Our behaviour has been conditioned since we were born and is not easy to change. We communicate how we feel about authority, and about cross-gender interactions; our weaknesses, our strengths, our anger, fear, and joy are all deeply embedded in the way we conduct ourselves.

As we communicate, our deeply contexted values are reinforced through our behaviour and these values are acted out without conscious thought, in a culturally approved way in concert with our verbal behaviour. We can even value behaviour itself as "proper" behaviour. Through the use of our eyes and other parts of our face and body, we let others know about what is important to us. We also have rules about what is proper or mannerly behaviour.

Since each culture has variations about how to convey what is important and what it values as mannerly and proper, we can make mistakes as we interpret what is being communicated. It is important to have a simple vocabulary to talk about our behaviour and to examine those behaviours that might be misunderstood. Chapters 5 and 6 cover six non-verbal modes thatare important behavioural arenas for communication.

The reader should be aware that it is difficult to talk/write and even think about the non-verbal arena. Logically, the result can only be partially satisfying — the reader needs to put together some actual non-verbal work with these written words to get to the heart of what is written about. In addition, since there are no hard data on what different people might mean by any particular behavioural trait, this part of the work is only suggestive of what may be present in any one situation.

Chapter
5

Non-Verbal Modes: Gaze, Sound of The Voice, and Social Distance

INTRODUCTION

Another major conceptual sector for the multicultural method is that of Non-Verbal Behaviour. The great bulk of the collective life in society is the patterned, normative behaviour of individuals interacting as pairs and in small and large groups.

This patterning derives from basic societal values, expressed in the normative behaviour of gestures, gaze, tonicity, social distance timing and pacing and tactility, each of which is discussed in this Section. Norms attached to these aspects of behaviour are deeply rooted and, along with other aspects of culture, are largely below the level of conscious control. These two ideas, that non-verbal behaviour is governed by norms, and that there is generally low awareness of these norms are central to the kind of understanding human service workers need to gain. The latter idea of low awareness has particular importance for how training is carried out.

Those who share a culture, interpret and experience social life in much the same way. There are minor variations but if the cultural assumptions are similar, there will be agreement and common understandings. Conversely, it is expected that if people come from very different backgrounds there will be misunderstandings. In the Canadian situation, with many cultures, the question arises as to how good we are at communicating with each other, given that a range of norms exists.

One would expect that when Canadian-born people have been together during childhood, and gone through the same school system, they should have large areas of common understanding. Where there is an open attitude to issues or to improving communication, there should be less misunderstanding, more sorting out of differences, and attention paid to variations in understanding.

In some cases, the culture surrounding a subject can itself carry messages about how open or closed that subject is for discussion and investigation. For example, in the case of "race" and "race relations" a variety of attitudes exist, but it is becoming more clear that in Canada, "race" is not a subject that is generally open for candid discussion. Some of the consequences of this are discussed in Chapter 10. The message that a subject matter is taboo, can be conveyed non-verbally through eyes, voice, movements and/or body tension.

The sense organs are therefore of great interest to professional helpers; as stimuli are processed by sense receptors, and "understood" by the brain, the culture of that person (also "in the brain") effects how the stimuli are perceived. The perception of the stimuli is translated into behaviour. Cultural patterning can delete, add, or reinterpret what is perceived and effect behaviour. Pierre Casse has explicated this idea well in his book, *Training For The Cross-Cultural Mind*, 1979.

For purposes of the cultural investigations of this book, the six particular behaviours to be studied are called "non-verbal modes." Knowledge about these "modes" can be traced back to investigation carried out by numerous non-verbal communication researchers (Wolfgang, 1984). Although six non-verbal modes are developed here, these, of course, do not cover all of non-verbal behaviour. They do represent major aspects that have been subjected to intensive research and thereby have been well categorized and conceptualized. It is difficult for non-specialists, as are most professional helpers, to talk about some non-verbal behaviour such as facial expressions or general bodily movements that cannot be easily described. However, there is some ability to discuss the six that have been chosen.

These six dimensions of behaviour are easier to identify and compartmentalize in an objective way. For example, it is easier to identify and describe gaze and gaze aversion than the numerous movements that the whole head can make. Head movements and eye movements are both part of non-verbal communication but the latter have been more studied and are easier to discuss, and thereby noticed, by one who is learning anew about these phenomena. Thus, **eye gaze** is one of the six modes presented here, but this does not imply that the concomitant head movements are not important.

In this chapter, the six modes are discussed first of all in relation to the sense receptors in which they originate. Applications of findings about each mode can lead to self-awareness and greater understanding of the range of meanings in behaviour. With a spirit of openness and a willingness to take risks as well as an awareness of the range of meanings in non-verbal behaviour, service workers can research the "ordinary" life in the agency/clinic/office and discover for themselves what misunderstandings exist and the inappropriate power relations that can be maintained.

THE NON-VERBAL MODES

A great deal has been written about perception, starting with the basic level of the physical organs of perception all the way to the psychological and social level of perception, under different conditions and in various situations. Service providers should be steeped in this knowledge because the processes of assessment and intervention are rooted in seeing and hearing; the eyes, ears, nose and kinaesthetic sense are sources of the information on which helping services are built. Much is said about "selective" perception (Sikkema and Niyekawa-Howard, 1977: 22-27) but from a cultural point of view all perception is selective. The aim of cross-cultural training is to widen and increase the capacity of the senses to take in and to process information as well as increase awareness of perception in the process of assessment.

THE SENSES

The senses are physical organs of the body as well as processors of physical stimuli from the environment. *The Hidden Dimension* by Edward T. Hall is a basic, practise text for the consideration of these subjects from a cultural view point. He divided human sensory apparatus into two categories (Hall, 1969: 41):

1. **The distance receptors**, the eyes, ears and the nose;
2. **The immediate receptors**, the skin, membranes and muscles.

He pointed out that:

> There is a general relationship between the age of the receptor system and the amount and quality of information it conveys to the central nervous system. The tactile or touch systems are as old as life itself; indeed the ability to respond to stimuli is one of the basic criteria of life. Sight was the last and most specialized sense to be developed in man, vision became more important and olfaction less essential when our ancestors left the ground and took to the trees.... Stereoscopic vision is essential in arboreal life. Without it, jumping from branch to branch becomes very precarious (Hall, 1969: 42).

Hall's view of the senses includes what he calls the **infraculture** (Hall, 1969: 101), which is behavioural and much rooted in the biological past, and **preculture**, which is physiological and very much in the present. There is also the **microculture** that is the proxemic level of culture most of us are aware of and mean when we talk about culture. Another way of understanding these ideas is that cultural expression in social space is determined by the physical capabilities and limitations of the senses. We can understand the senses more fully if their evolutionary development is recognized.

Training for Increasing the Non-verbal Repertoire

The neurological basis of behaviour in each person starts from the moment the embryonic layers related to the nervous system are laid down **in utero.** The cultural training will start immediately at birth. These primordial activities are highly specialized areas and beyond the scope of this book. It is enough to be aware of the depth and complexity of this functioning and realize that any tinkering with the programming laid down so early must be most carefully approached and the intricate processes at work handled with care and respect. Any intervention considered in this book is viewed with caution and awareness of the dangers that may be present if the basic behavioural life of the person is deliberately pushed off track. My experience from conducting simulations suggests that there is a severe disorienting effect when culturally programmed behaviour is deliberately changed. Since simulation experiences are introduced in training with safeguards, the dangers are limited. However, to take the simple role plays of the simulation and transfer them without reflection and care to the real world could be dangerous because of the disorienting effect.

For this reason it is **awareness** that is stressed and not **directly changing** behaviour. In simulations, the activity of changing behaviour is undergone for a short period, perhaps no longer than five minutes. In this very brief time, participants can become aware of their behaviours and feelings. In the debriefing session I employ after each simulation, participants are asked to fully describe their feelings, images and thoughts during the experience. They are instructed that the aim is to know what is there, but not to change it. There should be a long process for the learner of exploring, noticing and paying attention to those feelings. Knowledge can embrace feelings on the deepest level and connect to words, concepts, ideas that have personal meaning. From this open-ended activity comes a clearer view of the "behaving self." Meanings below the level of conscious knowledge gradually come to the surface and become "known." Eventually, behaviour change can come about, but in a way that is integrated at the level of consciousness and thus is of little danger to the person. The length of time before change will occur varies greatly between individuals and between the sensory systems being changed. The ability to modify some behaviour will be more difficult for some individuals than others, whereas, different issues will be more easily addressed. We actually know very little about how these changes occur or the range of differences between people.

GAZE AND GAZE AVERSION

The Eyes as Sense Organs

The eyes come from the latest developing embryonic layer and have a highly complex interplay with the brain. It is very difficult to compare one sense receptor with another in terms of the amount of information conveyed by each to the brain, but on the basis of quantity of neurons alone, the optic nerve contains roughly eighteen times as many neurons as the cochlear nerve of the ear (Hall, 1969: 42). Not only do the eyes sweep up an enormous amount of information; they also convey a great deal of what we want to communicate. How the eyes are used in practise settings is extremely important; there is the stare that subdues or humiliates or there are the beaming eyes of welcome or acceptance; the communications are subtle but clear. If a great many demands are placed on the eyes, practitioners comment that sometimes after intensive interviews their eyes are very tired. Thus suggestions are made here for the care of eyes.

Exercises

First, there is need to acknowledge the part that the eyes play in communication. As well, the eyes can be under stress and fatigued from the glare of artificial lighting, from very strong sunlight, chemical fumes, dust and from the heavy load of work from reading and writing.

Second, the eyes should be prepared for eye exercises. To begin, bring awareness to the eyes; allow the work of the eyes to be let go; allow the relaxation of tiny muscles around the eyes to occur; pay attention systematically to the area all around the eyes. Eyes also reflect feelings: interest, a "sense of responsibility," concern, friendliness and the like. Such feelings can then be noticed and released. This expression of feelings through the eyes relates to personal goals in the practise situation, and an awareness of this phenomenon helps identify important values in the person. This example is only one illustration of how values are expressed and appear to be "embedded" in the body.

Next, the eyes can be exercised in a physical way. An example is an exercise practiced in yoga; relax the whole body and sit straight, then gently and carefully look to the right of the visual field and then to the left. Returning to the centre, look up and then look down. Look diagonally from the bottom left to the top right of the visual field. Allow the eyes to come down from that position and move to bottom right and then the top left of the field. During the exercise, the neck muscles are kept relaxed and the head should not be moved. The eyes are never forced in any direction. These kinds of exercises acknowledge the presence of muscles adjacent to the eye sockets and that the same care given to other muscles in the body should be extended to them.

Finally there is a meditation exercise for the eyes useful in cultural training; to begin, sit comfortably and relaxed. Focus concentration on the eyes by not allowing any words to pass through the mind. For as long as possible, just look and look around. As soon as a thought involving words comes into the mind, acknowledge this has happened and allow the words to float away. This can be a very difficult exercise because the mind is constantly involved with ideas and words and these can flood in even when one desires to stop them. Two things come with this exercise. First the energy is focussed on seeing and not diffused on conceptualizing. This process alone can be relaxing. Second, the power of the cultural filter, i.e., the words and concepts (which are always culturally based), is reduced. For brief moments, it may be possible to "really see" without the cultural filter: to become aware of what has been there but has not been seen, and see what has been seen but is not there (Casse, 1979: 64).

These issues pertaining to the care of the eyes and the eyes as organs that sweep up information are crucial to practitioners who are involved in demanding jobs and are also, through their eyes, evaluating people and situations as part of their work. From a cultural view it is crucial that what is **seen** becomes consciously available for reflection, and consideration. We generally put too much store on visual information or use visual information incorrectly, as for example, when we always notice a visible minority person's race and perceive race as a major part of that person's identity. This section emphasizes that practitioners need experiential knowledge equally as much as cognitive knowledge.

Meanings in Gaze and Gaze Aversion

There has been much research in the field of gaze aversion, on both animals and humans. The power of the eyes is of great interest. For example, in some fish, there are "eye spots" that accentuate the eyes and, it is hypothesized, thereby, ward off predators (Argyle and Cook, 1976: 1). Here, no particular work by the fish is necessary but a message of power is communicated, nevertheless. At a higher evolutionary stage, some birds and mammals developed eye rings. Among many preliterate groups the eyes were accentuated by masks, paint or other paraphernalia during rites of passage and other rituals. The eyes thus treated would carry magnified power and would communicate the seriousness of the ritual activity and that danger might follow any trivialization of the event or of unfulfilled commands.

Even today, the eyes carry great power. The fear of the "evil eye" originated in preliterate times when it was believed that evil or danger could come simply from someone looking at you. Throughout the world, in modern times, variations abound on this theme in expressive and pictorial ways.

Psychologists have long studied the bonding of infants to the caregiver and the locking of eyes with the care-giver has often been noted (Argyle and Cook, 1976: 9-16). Quite early, a child learns about the importance of respect to elders; one kind of behaviour that shows respect is the dropping of eye contact as a gesture of respect: gaze aversion. As the child gets older, eye behaviour again comes into focus with sexual development. There are strong taboos in high context societies on eye contact between the sexes. Many and varied prohibitions on interaction between the sexes will prohibit eye contact because the "dance of eyes" in sexual contact is almost instinctive. In addition, the hierarchical relation of men and women will be normatively portrayed in gaze; women may not be allowed to gaze directly at men because this would communicate equal power, a value contrary to the established order. The combination of sexual attraction and power in gaze behaviour is enormously complex and controlled at a very deep level. Socialization about these values starts at birth, and while it is modified by age level, is never suspended.

In low context societies, strong emphasis is placed on individuation and egalitarian values; therefore, direct eye contact is highly valued. The person who does not have a direct gaze often is sanctioned, even if indirectly; speculations abound about what the person is hiding; is the person guilty of something; is something suspicious going on.

It is not uncommon for parents to discipline children with a "look"; such "looks" carry enormous power. Part of the difficulty with an averted gaze is that the one who expects constant eye contact does not know if attention is being paid to what is being said. When a child or even a subordinate is being talked to or chastised and does not look at the parent or teacher, the adult may say, "look at me when I am talking to you." This will be threatening to a child or underling but is part of the parent's or teacher's need to be attended to. To not look is a way of avoiding the frightening power of the eyes.

When people are angry with each other or if there is dislike, gaze aversion is a way out of the situation. If people are particularly disliked or seen as very inferior, the gaze may be such as to "look right through" someone. Thus, where racism is very pronounced, people may treat each other as if the other does not exist and gaze aversion expresses that those involved do not acknowledge each other. Sometimes, in relationships where these feelings have gone on a very long time, this gaze behaviour may be almost unconsciously performed. I believe that this can happen in both high and low context situations.

Thus the eyes carry many meanings and these meanings vary with culture. Where there is great emphasis placed on eye contact, gaze aversion tends to be viewed negatively. In other cases, direct gaze may be considered rude, and politeness between older and younger people or between men and women demands some gaze aversion. Gaze aversion may also imply guilt or shyness, and direct gaze may be seen as threatening. In some cultures, direct gaze is needed to assure that proper attention is being paid (Erickson, 1978: 99-126).

Thus, it is very necessary in cross-cultural situations to make allowance for different meanings in gaze behaviour. The method suggested here involves awareness of one's own normative gaze behaviour and a willingness to put off final judgement about the meaning of another's gaze behaviour. A "hypothesis-forming" attitude would be desirable; that is, a tentative meaning to the behaviour should be defined and further observations would be engaged in to test that hypothesis. It is not possible to give prescriptive instructions about the meanings of gaze for peoples of different backgrounds. Rather, the skill that should be developed in multicultural and multiracial situations is the ability to hold off judgement about the meanings inherent in specific gaze behaviours, while at the same time being aware of the effect on oneself from that client behaviour. For example, professional people who have strong eye contact norms need to become deeply aware of the meanings they possess in cases where gaze aversion is taking place. Extra care in evaluation will need to be given because the meanings to the low context helper are often negative and to gain practice with these situations, simple role playing exercises can be employed: in varying situations, the gaze behaviour can be modified to give practice interviewing someone with different norms about gaze.

THE SOUND OF THE VOICE: TONICITY
OR NON-VERBAL VOCALIZATIONS

The Ears as Sense Organs

While the eyes can sweep up information quite efficiently to a mile distance, the unaided ear is markedly different in capacity. Up to twenty feet the ear is very efficient.

> At about one hundred feet, one-way vocal communication is possible at somewhat slower rate than at conversational distances, while two-way conversation is considerably altered (Hall, 1969: 42).

It becomes immediately apparent that the social space of offices/clinics/classrooms must take into consideration the physical capability of the ear. In fact, the ear is the limiting factor for communication since the eyes have such greater capacity. The placement of desks and chairs must take into account where sound will be coming from and unwanted noise such as voices from other desks/offices. Sound-absorbing panels have been used with some effect but it is still an indicator of low context prestige if you have a 'quiet office' space.

The telephone is the predominant aid to the ear and virtually all offices/clinics in Canada have them. The telephone however creates culturally-based problems for those who cannot communicate comfortably without visual contact. But being able to use a telephone is so basic to Canadian culture it is difficult to imagine anyone who has not used one.

Having your own phone in the office or clinic is a signal that you have achieved an established position: a desk of one's own with a phone is a mark of being personally identified in an office. Modern phone technology is expanding the functions of the phone; 'camping' on someone's line; having conference calls; automatic ringing of a busy number and so forth make the ear even more available — sometimes too available — for communication.

In another way the telephone can be a trap: sometimes new immigrants, devastated by their distance from the family group, use the telephone to keep contact but accumulate extremely high phone bills which cannot be immediately paid; they then may experience the resulting humiliation of having the phone "cut off" by the phone company, an insult, of a kind, to honour.

Another hearing-related aspect is "tonicity" or non-verbal vocalization (Scherer, 1984: 4) which refers to all the sound in voices that is not specifically the **words** of the voices — pitch, timbre, loudness and tempo. Thus, there is a non-verbal aspect to speaking. As the eyes both give and receive information, the voice of others is perceived and one's own voice, communicates. Thus, awareness of what one "hears" and what others "hear" is important in cross-cultural work.

Before considering the ears in service communication, as awareness preparation can be done for the eyes, the same can be done for the ears.

First the ear can be consciously acknowledged as a physical mechanism for transferring sound waves to the brain. The ear deserves care and protection from overly loud and irritating noises. Many potentially destructive sounds cannot be avoided but achieving an increased awareness of the ear as an organ with needs, capacities and limitations should be a goal.

Exercises

The preparation of the ear for the demands of cross-cultural work are similar to that for the eyes. It is difficult to think of relaxing the ears but when attention is paid solely to the centre of hearing, the feelings perceived in hearing can be noticed. As in other exercises, the effort is towards noticing and paying attention to the feelings, not to changing them. When concentration is focussed in this way, it may also happen that other parts of the body relax as well.

A meditation exercise for hearing is similar to that for sight. To begin, sit comfortably relaxed. Determine to focus on the ears by not allowing any words to pass through the mind. For as long as possible, just listen and hear sounds. It might be easiest when first focussing on hearing to be in a place where sounds are varied and pleasing, such as a garden. As soon as a thought involving words comes into the mind, acknowledge this has happened and allow the words to float away and return to just listening and hearing sounds. Do not berate the self for being unable to hold concentration on this task. A patient attitude directed towards the self is no more than is expected with a client. Becoming aware of sounds in their fullness and with the cultural filters dropped is the objective.

Meanings in The Sound of the Voice

The sound of a voice may bring great joy or fear or sadness. The voice of a loved person, whether child or parent or lover, can elicit great emotion. The words may not matter nearly as much as the cadence of the voice. Just as easily, the voice of someone who is feared or hated can call forth great negative emotion. A child can be disciplined by the sound of a stern parent's voice, as much as by the words of that parent. (This parallels what is possible with a "look" from that parent, mentioned in the last section).

For high context people, especially for Native Peoples, the sound of the voice is extremely important. When an elder or healer is telling a story or reciting some ritual, the voice is an instrument for communicating many nuances of meaning and emotion that the actual words themselves may not carry. Hence, to write down what someone says may be experienced as a violation of the holistic value that is being communicated. The verbal and non-verbal, fused together, carry the identity of the culture.

In healing circles, the tone and inflection of the voices of those interacting is easily as important as the verbally expressed ideas. Often what is heard in the voice tells more about the inner life and meanings of the person who has come for healing than what they actually may say. It is up to the listeners to truly "hear" what is being communicated, even if it is not consciously understood by the person receiving a healing. Well trained therapists in low context society also heal in this way, by hearing what lies beyond the words, although the therapeutic setting may be quite different from that of a healing circle.

A great many factors can affect the sound of speech. Brain damage can affect speech production as can abnormalities in mouth or pharynx. The physical condition of voice-producing organs should be understood because mental competency may be inferred unconsciously by the sound of the voice. No one **means** to negatively judge someone with an impairment but the evaluation can occur below awareness. The issue of particular interest in cross-cultural work is the sound of the voice that is influenced by culture; the **accent** of the voice. The variables involved in accent include syllabic emphasis, pitch, tempo and others.

A very influential investigator, John C. Gumperz, a socio-linguist, did pioneering work in England on non-verbal communications in the workplace. The film, *Crosstalk* (1981), produced vivid insights into communication problems that can occur when people of different background and race each speak a different kind of English to each other. It was shown how different attitudes and different expectations about the manner of speaking, deriving from culture, emerged in vocal production.

Misunderstandings and misinterpretations can come from different emphases on syllables of English words. People can be perceived as angry, arrogant or rude for example, just from the sound of the voice, and/or from different use of words. Some of the findings about what can be troublesome between Asian and non-Asian English-speaking people are summarized from the video role play in the film.

What Can Confuse Non-Asians and Lead to Irritation

a. Certain uses of high or low pitched voice and loudness (e.g., raising voice in "No" to contradict).

b. Lack of stress (e.g., not marking clearly the difference between "last week and this week").

c. Use of Yes/No (e.g., saying "yes," meaning you have heard what is said, but not meaning that you agree).

d. Lack of cohesive features in discourse so that the Asian speaker appears boring or confused (e.g., misleading intonation patterns, unclear pronoun references).

e. Wrong use of turn-taking (e.g., persistently interrupting in the middle of the speaker's utterance).

What Can Confuse Asian People and Lead to Irritation

a. Tone of voice: high pitch or stress on particular words. This can be interpreted as emotional and impolite (e.g., when someone wants to explain or emphasize a certain point).

b. Apparent not listening, when in longer chunks of discourse the Non-Asian may switch off, or change subject.

c. Many forms of unexplicit or indirect statements and questions.

d. Apologetic or polite and repetitive uses of words (e.g., much use of "please" and "thank you").

These may appear quite technical, but are very apparent when presented in a video role play, where the participants are **seen** and **heard**. Adding to the understanding, a sociolinguistic analysis of the speech sounds and patterns coterminous with the sounds is presented in this important film. (This is a place where an actual simulation or video would greatly add to the verbal analysis presented here).

It is clear that professional people usually do not have the expertise to analyse, in a technically correct way, the sounds of speech in their work. It is also not practical to try to understand the very great variety of speech sounds and patterns that are possible. However, the practitioner can quite quickly become aware, through training, about the effect of the voice on the listener, and from there start to develop awareness of this non-verbal aspect of communication.

Awareness would start with noticing the feelings you experience that are generated by the sounds in voices. Then you need to consciously partial out the effect of these on judging the person. With regular practise, as happens with cues from other non-verbal sources, it becomes part of the helping process to note these mental cues and make adjustments. Once again, experiential and cognitive knowledge work together.

The work of Gumperz throws special light on this non-verbal mode, the sound of the voice. It can be noted that Gumperz also draws attention in his work to broader issues: he points out there are cultural assumptions about what is and is not appropriate behaviour in various parts of the work situation and there are culturally different ways of structuring conversational information or a logical vocal argument. These sorts of examples deeply connect culture with vocal production and with language itself, and show how important these connections are in the whole communication process. In Ontario, there is available a Canadian video entitled *Crosstalk in the Workplace*, a teaching tool based on Gumperz' work.

SOCIAL DISTANCE

A very important non-verbal mode, which is treated in a separate and distinct way in the research literature, is "social distance." This is the micro, face-to-face environment one experiences and, literally, in terms of physical space. The social distance concept referred to here is distinct from the scale of social distance used in ethnicity and race relations research. That scale refers to differently distanced relationships or feelings of acceptance of other group members as neighbours, fellow worker, in-laws or other relationships.

In practise it is difficult to keep the social distance mode separate from the other modes because the other modes — gaze, vocalizations, touching and gestures and smell and taste — are occurring simultaneously and influencing the spatial arrangements people keep in their face-to-face deliberations. As with the other modes, people have norms about the physical distance they like to be apart from others. Also, as for the other modes, the purpose of the communication and exactly who the people are makes a difference to how close or far the spatial arrangement will be.

At one extreme is the close physical intimacy of lovers and of mother and baby; at the other, far distance, are public figures or complete strangers. Edward T. Hall has written extensively about social distance (Hall, 1969: 113-129 and plates 10,11, 12 following p.106). He conceptualized four categories of distances:

THE FOUR DISTANCES

Intimate Distance

1a. Close phase involves touching and an increase in the play of olfaction and the sensation of radiant heat. The high possibility of physical involvement is uppermost in the awareness of both persons. In the maximum contact phase, pelvis, thighs and head can be brought into play; arms can encircle. When close vision is possible within the intimate range — as with children — the image is greatly enlarged and stimulates much, perhaps all, of the retina. The eyes' high potential for influence, is maximized at close range and conversely can perceive the detail of face and body.

1b. Far phase is 15-46 cm 6"-18" distance. In this distance, appropriate in some cultures for ordinary interaction, many North Americans will feel intruded upon. For such people, the eyes are too close, and there is a feeling of strain as the focal length shortens. There is social discomfort from the physical proximity and a sense of a taboo being broken; as a result there often is an instantaneous reaction of moving away from the other person.

In Canadian cities, however, there are many occasions when one must be in extremely crowded buses or subways. People who habitually are in these "inappropriate-distance" situations, develop many defenses against experiencing the discomfort. Averted gaze, motionless body stance and a withdrawn consciousness protect the person from the repeated symbolic trauma of having to be overly close (Hall, 1959: 117-118). An exercise concerning social distance is to observe oneself and others in conditions of different distances, and note both one's physical and psychological reactions and how the defences work.

Personal Distance

2a. Close phase is a distance 1/2 to 3/4 meter (1-1/2 to 2-1/2 feet) apart. This is the distance that is sometimes called the 'personal bubble.' Hall's work was, in part, rooted in studies of animal behaviour, in which it was found that these distances vary for different species. This clearly relates the idea of a personal bubble back to our animal ancestry. With animal studies as background, it is an easy step to understand the emotions elicited when another person inappropriately moves inside one's personal distance bubble.

2b. Far phase is between 3/4 to 1-1/4 meters (2-1/2 to 4 feet). Keeping someone at "arms length" or, a distance away that one cannot easily "get his hands on" someone else are expressions that capture this distance (Hall ,1969: 120).

Social Distance

3a. Close phase is 1-1/4 to 2 meters (4 to 7 feet). Impersonal business usually occurs at this distance and people who work closely together tend to be within this space. Offices are usually organized around this parameter.

3b. Far phase is 2 to 3-2/3 meters (7 to 12 feet). This is the distance to which people move when they are asked to "stand away so I can look at you." As these distances increase, less and less detail of the face is retained. Odour and body heat are rarely noticed and the eyes must work harder to retain attention in any prolonged conversation.

Public Distance

4a. Close phase is 3-2/3 to 7-1/2 meters (12 to 25 feet). There are important sensory shifts in the transition from personal to social to public distance. This last distance is outside the usual circle of involvement. One's voice must become louder and the choice of words alters slightly to accommodate the louder volume; a more "formal style" seems to emerge at this distance. Details of the face are blurred; eye colour begins to be imperceivable. The head size is perceived as considerably under life-size.

4b. Far phase is 7-1/2 meters (25 feet or more). Hall stated that "thirty feet is the distance that is automatically set around important public figures" (Hall, 1969: 124). His example is from a description of the behaviour of men, also powerful, as they approached John F. Kennedy when his nomination for President became a certainty. "The others in the room surged forward on impulse to join him. Then they halted. A distance of perhaps thirty feet separated them from him, but it was impassable." (ibid.: 124).

It is from careful observation of real life situations that the most useful hypotheses are derived. Practitioners can develop their own hypotheses about social distance norms from careful observation during their daily activities at work.

MEANINGS IN SOCIAL DISTANCE

I have summarized Hall's analysis of social distance here for several reasons. The first has to do with the reporting on the nature of the detail of social distance for classification purposes. It is helpful to see a classification and consider its value for our work. In this case the analysis combines the physical capacities and limitations of the senses with the behaviour that follow from those capacities and limitations. Thus, when in cross-cultural situations one can be aware of the degree to which behaviour must take account of the "universal" human body and the degree to which, in different cultures, behaviour varies.

Second, we can use Hall's detailed descriptions to practice our own observations of ourselves and others. As we practice noticing very ordinary behaviours and sensations in new ways, we can become aware of our own norms and expectations about social distance, and as with the other nonverbal modes, become able to hold off making judgements about others.

Hall has commented about the social meanings he derived from social distance research, including:

> The use of intimate distance in public is not considered proper by adult middle-class Americans even though their young may be observed intimately involved with each other in automobiles and beaches (p. 118).

> A wife can stay inside the circle of her husband's close personal zone with impunity. For another woman to do so is an entirely different story (p. 120).

To stand and look down at a person (from close social distance) has a domineering effect, as when a man talks to his secretary or receptionist (p. 121).

A feature of social distance (far phase) is that it can be used to insulate or screen people from each other. This distance makes it possible for them to continue to work in the presence of another person without appearing to be rude. Receptionists in offices are particularly vulnerable as most employers expect double duty: answering questions, being polite to callers, as well as typing. If the receptionist is less than ten feet from another person, even a stranger, she will be sufficiently involved to be virtually compelled to converse (p. 123).

Hall also discussed the many differences he noticed between North Americans and Middle Eastern peoples and many other groups. His observations are worth reading.

In learning simulations, where people are forced to interact at very close distance, I have found that the experience of the personal bubble can be introduced very easily. Some participants have reported that the failure of others to observe social distance norms is more upsetting than the experience of varying any other non-verbal mode. Once again, the objectives of such simulations is to become aware of one's feelings; in this case to identify the feeling of possessing a personal bubble and notice our own instant assessment when someone invades that perimeter.

Three Additional Non-Verbal Modes: Gestures, Touch and Timing and Pacing

GESTURES

The Sense of Movement: The Kinaesthetic Sense

In the simplest way, the kinaesthetic sense is our awareness of our muscles or our "muscle sense." As the muscles are worked, nerves called proprioceptors feed information back to the brain. These nerves help the body to work smoothly in its environment; they therefore occupy a key position in what Hall calls "kinaesthetic space" (Hall, 1969: 55). This concept connects the moving, active person with their social environment. Thus, the people involved together in a work environment can examine their separate kinaesthetic spaces and those that are shared. Hall discusses "hidden zones in American offices" (Hall, 1969: 52, 53). He suggested three zones:

1. The immediate work area of the desktop and chair;

2. A series of points within arm's reach outside the area mentioned above;

3. Spaces marked as the limit reached when one pushes away from the desk to achieve a little distance from the work without actually getting up.

   An enclosure that permits only movement within the first area is experienced as cramped. An office the size of the second is considered "small." An office with Zone three space is considered adequate and in some cases ample.

Given these criteria, much of the work environment falls into the "cramped" and small categories; these could be quite unpleasant working conditions for those who culturally feel the need for more space.   Offices, lecture halls, interviewing rooms, hospital wards, clinics etc., can all be examined from the viewpoint of physical comfort and efficiency of movement. These spaces can also be viewed more subjectively because different cultures define what is restrictive and what is adequate spatial provisions. In addition, the degree of involvement with others can be culturally regulated.

These issues about kinaesthetic space interlock closely with issues taken up later in "tactile space," (p.91 of this chapter), "touching" being another non-verbal mode subject to cultural influences. Hall calls his study of the way space is used to express cultural ideas and values, "proxemics." He spends some time studying proxemics in literature and art (Hall, 1969: 77-100) and these artistic fields give further insights into the proxemics of a national culture.

Body Awareness

Becoming aware of one's kinaesthetic sense overlaps with an area of study called body awareness. From the perspective of service to people, the cultural values of low context society give somewhat conflicting messages. On the one hand, the individualistic emphasis provides legitimation for fulfilment of the person, and possessing an integrated mind and body is part of this fulfilment. On the other hand, a strong mind-body dualism persists in western culture and makes feelings, and the body itself, suspect, with the implication that the body and feelings are of dubious relevance in the work sphere.

Contrastingly, in the Orient, especially in Japan and China, considerable attention is paid to the body and movement in the work setting. For instance, workers do exercises at prescribed times near their work stations. That Westerners have difficulty getting "in touch with the feelings" engendered by body and movement, is attested to by the great number of courses, workshops, retreats and books on this subject. The values mentioned earlier in Chapter 4 on Contexting, which also contribute to a mind-body compartmentalization in Canadian society, are the loss of holism and a fragmented approach to problems. Monochronic time values that emerge into the monotonous lock-step of slotted time and that prescribe that activities **must** be engaged in whether one feels like doing so also leads to a body-mind separation. In both the concepts of fragmentation and monochronic time, feelings are submerged, in favour of the unrelenting machine of work, whether it be professional work to help people or to develop "widgets" on a factory line. Finally, the intense materialism of modern society forces our perspective to be on externalities, on appearances, on what is **seen**, and can be counted, not on what is felt. Research on most service spheres emphasizes what can be explicitly quantified and measured, another aspect of materialism.

In contrast, body awareness needs periods of protected time when attention can be paid to the non-uniform flow of feelings; it is in this kind of time-space that the body, as a moving, acting, communicating entity, can be reflected upon and understood. All of the non-verbal modes, of course, need this kind of quietness and slowed-down time for reflection. It is through awareness of bodily movements, especially with the guidance of trained professsionals, that many of one's deeply held values can be identified. Attitudes toward work and play, relationships that are loving or hating can be discovered in attending to the details of the body's behaviour.

As with the other non-verbal modes, a meditative process can lead to increased bodily awareness. In one exercise, the mind first is emptied of words and of efforts to think. Any simple activity like opening a door, tying one's shoes, washing the face or simply walking can become the focus. While the activity is carried out very, very slowly, the mind is free to observe the activity as it is done in "slow time." Through this, awareness develops of the preprogramming that directs even the simplest motions and of the difficulty of changing them. Buddhist monks use this sort of exercise to increase "mindfulness" (Sayadaw, 1977: 58-65)

Meanings of Gestures (Emblems) and Other Bodily Movements

That gestural movements are involved in communication is well known. However this behavioural material can be difficult to conceptualize because there are so many parts of the body that can be moved. The face, arms and hands, however, play a very significant part in both receiving and giving information. For example, the expressions of surprise, disgust, pleasure on the face, register receipt of information and the facial expressions or other behaviour that follow the initial recognition will broadcast messages, often paralleling verbal communications.

How varied and complex this can be is exemplified by a set of hand-arm gestures, called "emblems," which carry particular meanings depending on the culture of the people using them. Desmond Morris' research on twenty emblems reveals that each emblem may have several meanings and that the frequency of predominant meanings can be found through survey techniques. For example, an emblem, the "Fingertips Kiss," has the following description:

The tips of the fingers and thumb of the right hand are pressed together and pointed towards the gesturer's own lips. At the same time the hand is raised towards the lips and the fingertips are lightly kissed. As soon as the kissing movement of the mouth has been made, the hand is tossed lightly forward into the air, the fingers opening out away from one another as this second movement is executed.

The true fingertips kiss is usually a rather gentle performance, having little vigour, but when it is imitated by foreigners who do not normally employ it, it is nearly always heavily overemphasized. When used frequently it often lacks the actual hand-to-lips contact, the fingertips stopping just short of the mouth. Some individuals reduce it even further bringing together only the thumb and forefinger and brushing them gently against the lips. (Morris et al., 1979: 2)

Research from 1200 informants on gestures was drawn from 40 locations in 25 countries in 15 languages, with a range from northern Europe to North Africa and from Spain to Turkey.

The percentage distribution of meanings of the Fingertips Kiss was found to be as follows:

1. Praise   50%
2. Salutations   31%
3. Others   4%
4. Not used   15%
                    ─────
                    100%

Another emblem, referred to in Chapter 5, was "the Figa" (Morris: 147). Here "the hand is closed so that the tip of the thumb protrudes from between the first and second finger." This ancient gesture has contrasting connotations: one as an insult and the other as a protective device. In Morris' study, the distribution of meanings was as follows:

1. Sexual comment   19%
2. Sexual insult   17%
3. Protection   7%
4. Nose Joke   6%

5. Nothing	3%
6. Others	3%
7. Not used	45%
	100%

Once again, the variety of meanings in behaviour can only be under-stood in cultural terms. As seen, the use of the "figa" as supranatural pro-tective device was the meaning referred to in Chapter 4. In reports from a few social work students, this protection device is used frequently, often covertly and like other gestural movements, is very quickly synchronized with verbal communication. Thus, under normal circumstances, one can be considered fluently non-verbal. Fernando Poyatos has done extensive work at the University of New Brunswick on verbal-non-verbal cultural fluency (Poyatos, 1984: 431-459). This Canadian resource should be better known by service providers.

Emblematic gestures are relatively easy to study because these hand-arm forms lend themselves to clear conceptualizations and labels. However, other bodily movements, which are usually more important than emblems in daily service-delivery, are much harder to partial out as clear identifiable movements. Therefore, observational skills are exceptionally important here, as is the need to hold off final judgements about the meaning of behaviour until corroborating evidence comes to support/contradict the ini-tial assessment.

TOUCHING

The tactile or touch system is as old as life itself. Unlike the eyes, which are the most recent evolutionary development (Hall, 1969: 42), the ability to respond to stimuli that "touch" (contact the entity) is a basic criterion of life. Response-to-touching functions for the organism are protection, infor-mation-gathering, security and pleasure. Touch can be connected to active aggressiveness and assault but it generally is viewed positively as a means of communication and associated with comfort and warmth, as when people seek to touch and to be touched (Henley and LaFrance, 1984: 359).

Human babies need touch more than any other stimulation to develop in normal, healthy ways. In many, if not most high context cultures, mater-nal involvement with infants provides unambiguous touching opportunities for mother and child. In preliterate and peasant societies, it is common for babies to be carried during much of the daytime hours, via some form of carrying-shawl, sling or carrier that keeps mother and child together in an intimate, shared environment. Under such conditions, breast feeding when the child indicates hunger is easy and natural. The suckling reflex and mother touching functions occur according to the child's own inner timetable, and stroking and fondling occurs during this supremely satisfying activity. This whole behavioural sequence occurs "naturally" in high-context societies/groups.

In sharp contrast to these practices are ones which exist in low context societies. In modern urban settings, many of the opportunities for parental contact with children have been structured out. Use of bottle feeding, perambulators, separate sleeping arrangements that place children away from mother, even separate bedrooms for parents and children lead to less contact, whether people intend or not to be less touching. Urban houses contrast sharply with simple dwellings such as tents, cabins, or huts; permanent walls, heavy furniture keep people physically separated. Offices, clinics and schools are also organized for isolating, non-contact effects.

It was the scientific (very low context) approach to babies and children that led some doctors in the early part of this century to advise against both breast feeding and picking up crying children, and who advised the abolition of the cradle, and promoted by-the-clock feeding. In this same time period, it was discovered that children in isolative residential centres for foundlings suffered from "marasmus" or the wasting away of body and life; death rates for these children were extremely high but not from physical disease or trauma. It was established during the period when tender loving care was viewed as unscientific that when abandoned children in orphanages were picked up and fondled, even by strangers, they survived and flourished. From there, the invention of foster care for children became part of a growing child welfare movement. This "invention" in modern societies was, of course, used in all high context societies, the only difference being that it was less formalized.

As with other non-verbal modes, the aim for the service-provider is to become aware of their own and clients' personal norms about touching them as they arise in a variety of professional encounters. If negative feelings about being touched are observed in oneself no attempt should be made to deliberately change these feelings. Likewise, if the client shows distaste for touching, there should be a careful respect for these feelings. If possible, the worker should reflect on their own feelings over a period of time. Eventually, there may come, at least in a superficial way, a more flexible and relaxed feeling about clients touching them. The decision to actually reach out and touch is also a behaviour that can be examined. However, deeper changes for the student learning in this fashion about the meaning of touch, may be much longer in coming, if they do at all.

Much attention of late has been paid to the need for touch stimulation as a healthy part of life. For example, the professional masseuse is increasingly being sought out because of the stress-reduction properties of the massage. For many, their hairdresser is the only non-family person who touches them. For people confined to residential facilities or deprived of contact with others because of age, or handicap, hairdressing services are provided on a regular basis. There is thus a legitimate opportunity for contact and self-esteem is enhanced. As with any individual case, however, there is not always the expected reaction. In one case reported to me, an elderly woman in a nursing home, who had a previous liking for such services, suddenly reversed her response and any touching was viewed as invasive and unpleasant.

The Skin as a Sense Organ

A great many aspects of the skin as a sense organ could be discussed here. Probably nothing is as important as the skin as a **thermal receptor** (Hall, 1969: 54-59). The sensation of "being cold" is a complex one and has varying effects starting from the birth experience, when a temperature change is first perceived (Montagu, 1986: 102-107).

For many of the immigrants to Canada who come from warm climates, the experience of our dark, cold winter months is a severe trauma. The sense of "being cold" can trigger various deep emotional feelings, and when these are joined to the difficulties encountered during the settlement phase of acculturation to Canada, lifelong unpleasant memories sometimes accompanied by lifelong discomfort can remain. For some immigrants, the cold weather can inhibit their adaptation; some may not venture out of their apartments, while others may dress their children in an overly-warm way, restricting movement and making them uncomfortably hot. In conversation, discussion of the cold weather can bring memories of the misery of those lonely, problematic early years in Canada. And for some of these people, feeling physically cold (as in air-conditioned or otherwise cool offices) can bring back to them the same feelings of problem, worry and the like.

Meanings in Contact and Non-Contact Behaviour

In role playing situations where people are directed, while conversing, to touch the person in a prolonged way, there are various outcomes. The simulation directs the role player to hold the hand of the other person while some simple conversation is going on. For some, the act of holding hands was very difficult, either for the person who reached out to hold hands or for the person being held. For some of the participants, handholding was acceptable because in their own culture that was a common practice. For others, the handholding was embarrassing and distracted them from the conversation. Some people saw the action of reaching out as a sign of dependence, not a positive trait. Others felt that in a cross-gender situation the person was soliciting sexual interest. Many people felt vague feelings of discomfort that they could not easily describe. As with other non-verbal modes, one's character was often instantly imputed on the basis of this behaviour. The important outcome of the simulation is to become aware of one's own norms about touching thereby continuing the process of cultural self-awareness. This individual objective exists in addition to the information-sharing.

The meanings that can derive from touch in non-verbal communication are as broad as is life. They can stretch back in history or connect to any number of present issues. For example, the **smile** is believed to be connected to the early sucking action of infant at mother's breast (Montagu, 1986: 93-94). Two centuries ago, Darwin hypothesized that after the mouth completed its sucking, and the relaxing of the sphincter muscle, the "smile" of pleasure and contentment was produced. The origin of the smile is thus associated with infants' oral-tactile pleasure at the maternal breast. Darwin also emphasized that the degree to which people smile is culturally conditioned.

Another important behaviour is that of **shaking hands** as a method of introduction between people. It is important to know cultural norms about handshaking. For some people, to not shake hands is an insult, and even children shake hands. In other cultures, women take the lead in shaking hands. In still other cultures, at introduction there is no contact, but bowing and/or displaying one's own hand-to-hand form to the other, like the East Indian namaste. With patients and clients, it is useful to observe how often touching occurs and how the people involved regard their own touching behaviour. Some may wish for more contact and others may feel abused by it.

One line of research connects dominance and touching. Henley and LaFrance have shown that men touch women more than the reverse; they related this behaviour to the socialized dominance of men over women (Henley and LaFrance, 1984: 359-60). In other words, the higher status person has more power to touch the lower status one. Child physical abuse and child sexual abuse stem directly from this expression of power of adults over children and of males over females.

It is also through cultural means that this power can be mitigated; most cultures have practises that give some protection to the weaker party. For example, the abuse of women may be tempered by the power of her male relatives who may step in to modify excesses. For children who are abused there may be other relatives to whom the child can turn. However, the breakup of the extended family when migration to Canada occurred may reduce even further the few protections that existed. Service providers are, on the one hand, now in the difficult position of knowing that many clients/patients need to be touched because there is a severe deficit of this stimulation in their lives. On the other hand, because of the abuse of the touching response there is great reluctance by workers to risk being misunderstood. Court cases of abuse and harassment of clients have great visibility in the media and serve as a warning to service providers to think through their touching behaviour very carefully.

Interestingly, it is in the area of touch that social service workers and health care workers can be differentiated. In my experience, few social service providers see it appropriate for them to touch their clients. The delivery of health care in the home, clinic or hospital, though, usually requires that the patient be manipulated directly either for diagnosis or treatment.

Smell (Olfaction) and Taste, and Their Meanings

Whereas the other senses had non-verbal modes attached, the senses of smell and taste do not have behaviours attached that can be partialled out in the same way as sight and hearing, gesture and touch. Behaviours result from smelling and tasting, but people do not actively control or exhibit taste and smell the way some animals do.

The brain's limbic system, involved with emotions and memories, is intimately connected to the sense of smell. This system activates the hypothalamus that regulates the pituitary gland. In turn, smell messages are tied to internal body chemistry involving the endocrine and autonomic nervous systems (Gibbons, 1986: 337). The neurological research on smell is very complex but it is enough for practitioners to be aware of the depth of the effect of smell on themselves and on their clients, and to realize that these effects are not easily turned aside.

Each of our reactions to smell is connected to our own background — patterns of behaviour, relationships and events. Each person brings these deeply programmed responses to the workplace — they cannot be checked into a closet with our coat and boots when we slip behind our desks. These responses are conditioned by culture. Positive and negative feelings attached to these smells are evoked without conscious effort and can therefore affect our perception of colleagues and clients. Once again, a developed awareness is the most effective protection against unwarranted assumptions about other people.

The closely connected sense of **taste** is much better understood than that of smell. In fact, one of the most accepted areas of cultural difference is that of ethnic food. In any Canadian city the range of ethnic foods available is great. Part of the reason for this is that for immigrants without saleable skills, there is always the possibility of opening a restaurant or at least working in one. Since there is a large market for new and interesting food, and although competition is keen, it is possible to make a living this way. Almost all Canadians, even though they may know very little about other cultures than their own, enjoy the food of another cultural group.

It is important to notice that it is one thing to actively choose to eat a particular ethnic food, it is another to smell foods inadvertently. At some times and in some places, the odours connected to foods in storage or being cooked can evoke disgust and even fear. This also, of course, holds for eating certain prepared foods of another cultural group that, according to your own culture, is unusual, prohibited or unpleasant.

The reasons for such strong reactions are many, but it is well understood that we absorb strong reactions to the food given to us in childhood. Not only are we being fed food in those early developmental years, but, we might say, also being fed cultural values. The values have to do with very many things, including what is "good" food and, by implication at least, what is "bad" food. "Good" people are ones who eat "good" (our) food and bad, untrustworthy, inferior people eat other things. The person interested in overcoming these ingrained dislikes should reflect on their early training and experiences with beloved parents, caregivers etc., to ascertain the bases for their current values about tastes and smells.

These attitudinal correlates of food are usually acquired by children without much thought by them or their parents of their meaning and consequences. The values we have about our own cultural foods are very important and often connected to very meaningful traditions. These need not be changed. What needs to change are beliefs and behaviours that hurt or demean others. We may denigrate people because they eat certain foods that to us are strange, bad or disgusting. Such attitudes should be self-identified and discharged.

Raymond Sokolov is a regular columnist in the journal of *Natural History* on the subject of taste. These are engaging and erudite articles and also useful to acquire a cross-cultural view of food. In the November issue

(Sokolov, 1987: 107) Sokolov pointed out that we can learn to put labels on various aspects of what we taste and thereby increase our memory of different tastes. This concept reflects the theme here of the need to develop self-awareness as a tool to gain mastery over our senses and to information they convey about clients.

Related to self-training about food are attitudes about odours people have that are caused by foods they eat. When people are perceived as having odours, it may be because they consume certain spices or foods. The odour attached to people is a very personal and emotional subject in our sanitized, hygienic low-context culture, in which "odour" usually means an unusual odour, defined as disagreeable or unclean: generally discussion about person-odours are taboo, even though they are noticed. It takes a special effort to discuss these openly, and in-service development time can be spent profitably helping staff to discuss their feelings about client smells they encounter in their work. Such staff development time might also help the professional learn how to discuss with the client what is offensive in this culture. It is not fair to staff or to clients that this important subject be left for each person to handle alone. The pressures, both from having to endure odours offensive to oneself or to be the one who feels isolated because of odours, are a serious source of stress and undermining to self-esteem, as well as the ability to render service.

Finally, there is much positive work that can be done with food. For example, being aware of one's own foods (ethnic food to someone else) should be each's fundamental knowledge and a cultural source of strength and nurture. For the client to have to eat strange food while also adjusting to new places, new people and new customs is an extreme stress situation and any help given with obtaining familiar foods would be concrete evidence of caring.

During training periods, staff can be sensitized to the traumas of adjustment if in a reverse role simulation they undergo a period of eating only unfamiliar food. Such an intense learning experience can only be done with the agreement of the participants, and support during and debriefing after the experience are essential.

In discussion, peoples' feelings about having been in situations where they were unable to get their own food can be elicited. Food can be the *entre* point to revealing about almost any topic — childhood memories of relationships, present economic problems, adjustment of family members to work, school and community; it is the most universal tool there is.

TIMING AND PACING (CHRONEMICS)

Timing and pacing is the last non-verbal mode discussed. Whereas time could be contexted according to polychronic or monochronic differences, timing and pacing is a universal dimension for any culture. In fact, timing and pacing might be considered the most basic dimension. It is the different rhythms, pacings, and beats inherent in behaviour that makes one culture very different from another, make the newcomer feel ill-at-ease, not at home.

Thomas Bruneau spent his professional lifetime on this subject. He defined chronemics as "the nature and meaning of human tempo and temporality" (Bruneau, 1983: 1). He stressed that the "daily rhythmic" activities in biological, perceptual, psychological, social and cultural contexts are of paramount importance in human conduct and communicative interaction." In fact, the mind itself is integrated by time. He sees proxemics, kinesics, paralinguistics, touching behaviour, silences etc., as not yet having been fully integrated in their temporal dimensions.

The study of chronemics could be expanded to overlap nearly all knowledge. Hall gave particular credit to early investigators of this topic like Birdwhistell and Condon (Hall, 1976: 72-76): He describes Condon's work on "synching" — how people in interaction move together in whole or in part.

Condon analysed, frame-by-frame, 16mm film of people talking to each other. Each movement, no matter how minor, was recorded along a time line. In this way the smallest movement of each person could be aligned in parallel at the instant of time that they occurred. From these analyses he demonstrated that everything a person does is under the control of "body synchronizers"; that all interactional movements are synchronized. Such movements include the blink of an eye, and barely perceptible movements of hand and finger. These movements, in turn, are in synch with specific parts of the verbal code — words, pitch and stresses.

Condon spent years studying the behaviour of infants, finding that newborns initially synchronized the movement of their bodies to speech regardless of the language, e.g., American babies synched with Chinese language as well as with English (Hall, 1976: 73).

Later work by Condon showed that people's movements were "in synch" with words, even if nonsense syllables were introduced. When a third party entered the conversation, however, the synchrony stopped. Subsequently, Condon showed that the underlying factor in synchrony was that the brain waves of the interacting people were moving synchronously. When a third party entered in the interaction, EEG recording pens no longer moved together.

Further analyses showed that these patterns of communication are "culture specific" learnings. After years of viewing microanalyses of film, Condon commented:

> that it no longer makes sense to view human beings as...isolated entities sending discrete messages to each other. Rather it would be more profitable to view the "bond" between humans as the result of participation within shared organizational forms. This means that humans are tied to each other by hierarchies of rhythms that are culture specific and expressed through language and body-movements. (Hall, 1976: 74)

Others have studied large numbers of people and found that even quite large groups such as "all the children playing together in a school yard" (Hall, 1976: 76,77) are involved in a synchrony and sometimes this can be traced to one individual who, usually unconsciously, is leading the rhythm through their behaviour. It is quite likely that future research will show how informal leadership also is associated with synchrony between leader and group followers, and between members of a family.

For service providers, these studies provide an underpinning to the experience that non-verbal behaviour is patterned: all are characterized by tempos, and that the behavioural norms vary between and according to culture.

Meanings of Timing and Pacing

In spite of the pervasiveness of timing and pacing norms, they are not well understood at the level of being a constituent of ordinary daily activities. The first task of training involved here is to demonstrate this at a vivid level. In a learning simulation this is accomplished in a very simple way:

One person is instructed without the other knowing to carry on a conversation but hesitate for a ten-count before responding to any comments by the other person. This change in tempo from the normal Canadian rhythm of conversing becomes distressing to both parties. The person in the slowed-down role finds it difficult to concentrate on the topic and is subject to many accompanying feelings of being rude, incompetent and/or difficult. The other person typically does not wait for the response, but interjects with more comments and questions because the silences feel strange, even unbearable to them. The slowed speaker is sometimes assessed in these simulations as deaf, or developmentally handicapped, or not able to speak English. Acknowledging the instantaneous evaluations one makes is helpful in learning how our minds work, even in simulated situations.

A slow tempo is part of the culture of many Native Peoples. In these groups, what is considered desirable is quite different from normal urban-technological (low culture) speech. Here, what is spoken may be considered at length before response is made; the silences created are shared silences and full of meaning as opposed to being considered empty or wasted time. The very slow and deliberate pace joins group members and permits a humane and spiritual connection. Outsiders who participate may feel great discomfort.

However, it is possible for someone to become able to feel comfortable with different tempos. First, one can practice becoming aware of their own tempo. For example, when driving a car, to many people a red light means slowing down a fast tempo and waiting for the green light go-ahead. Observing oneself at the red light to see if impatience and increased tension are present is a first step in awareness.

Many opportunities are present to observe time-pace and waiting behaviour; waiting for elevators, appointments, meals, children and so on. As for the previous non-verbal modes, a meditative approach can help. The central activity is reflection on your feelings and whether those feelings are what you really want. Any tendency to become impatient with yourself should be noticed and allowed to drift away. After reflection — the duration will vary for different people — it becomes easier to relax and sink into the tempo of the situation one is in. This should feel "natural"; there should not be a feeling of wanting to force a tempo change. If there is, one should return to reflection and self-analysis.

There are many situations in which a slowed-down tempo is important. Very young children and teenagers (for different reasons) are often very slow in their reactions, yet are behaving within normal limits. Certainly the tempo of young children is very different from that of adults and often a source of difficulty for people learning to be caregivers. For foster parents, a new child in the home is difficult until the child adapts to the synchrony of the home. If fragile elderly are the concern, caretakers need to slow down their behaviour to match the tempo of those whose physical and/or mental state does not permit a faster speed. People who are under sedation for some mental illnesses are slowed down considerably in all their functioning. In all of these examples the helper is required to adapt to the ability or functioning of the client/patient.

These examples of tempo change have been from fast to slow. Occasionally the direction is changed and people have to react faster. This direction of change may make it more difficult to keep a relaxed frame of mind and keep from becoming too tired. However, it should be noted that people whose tempo is normally very fast, usually enjoy the fast tempo. Driving, fast-paced professionals are often quite happy maintaining this pace; they feel productive, energized and alert at this pace. Closer examination of one's internal experience of pacing may reveal that it is possible for you to be quite fast-paced and yet be internally calm and serene.

Whatever the tempo or rhythm change, awareness of one's own norms and appreciation of the validity of those norms is the foundation for competence in serving clients/patients. The next stage in competence is to be able to make an assessment of the situation and then consciously decide whether to alter one's own norms in the interest of the client/patient, and/or whether to bring the matter forward as a point of discussion between staff and an advisory group for those being served.

TRAINING FOR AWARENESS

The training side of non-verbal awareness may be unsatisfactory to those who want neatly packaged activity and targeted goals. The subjective internal work that is required is not readily monitored from the outside and it would be damaging for someone to be too intrusive into this subjective process. Reflection and the increase of awareness is personal and therefore individually variable.

Teachers need to be sensitive to the pace of learning that learners exhibit. In a positive, proactive way, teachers can aid the process by maintaining an open atmosphere, by keeping up an encouraging ambience, by allowing discussion to emerge, and explicitly supporting an ongoing effort to improve and increase self-awareness by the learner and awareness of others. There should be no competitiveness, however. Each person's work should be respected. We do not have the baseline criteria on these behaviours and thus do not know what constitutes "enough" movement or "significant" movement in awareness. We are dealing with **consciousness**, the most mysterious idea in the universe.

SUMMARY

Six non-verbal modes have been analysed separately for awareness and contemplation as behaviours with norms in the service provider's behavioural repertoire. The idea of directing attention separately at each one is a pedagogical tool and once each mode has become vividly revealed and known they become entwined with each other and intermingled with verbal communication. Special emphasis here has been placed on not forcing behaviour to change.

These behaviours — a glance, a gesture, a touch — can be viewed as being very ordinary, even trivial. However, it is through them that we can appreciate, not only our own cultural values, but those of others, and begin to gain control of forces that deeply affect our work.

Tracing Back to Value Origins
With the Acculturative Framework

THE ACCULTURATIVE FRAMEWORK

In the three chapters ahead, 7, 8 and 9, a scheme is presented for understanding from where the cultural values that exist in the present, originate.

A framework is developed that can be used by anyone in Canada to trace their cultural heritage. This "etic" model (see page 23), links the major variables related to any culture change. The culture change that is developed here is that which comes from immigration or migration.

The variables that are considered basic to understanding culture change are placed on a "time line," a simple line with an arrow pointing along to the right of the page. They are named in a very abstract, simple way and can thus be applied in a variety of contexts, settings and time frames. The variables or Benchmarks are placed on the time line, which can be any length of time — for the individual, the family, or the whole cultural group — that is relevant to the situation under analysis.

Chapter 7 covers the first three of the Benchmarks; this early stage of the culture change process has been the subject of research for many decades and in many countries and thus more is known about it. It is also a period to which professional activity is specially directed because of the psychological difficulties associated with culture change.

Chapter 8 discusses the next two Benchmarks, the last one of which is called Ethnocultural Identity, the product of the other variables in the framework. Chapter 9 covers the identities of people in Canada of the second and remaining generations as well as the host community.

The chapters cover topics, along the way, associated with the Benchmarks that are being discussed. The reader should be cautioned that they may find the whole framework somewhat attenuated for this reason — it takes all the chapters to get to the end of the framework.

Fig. 7.1 — The Acculturative Framework

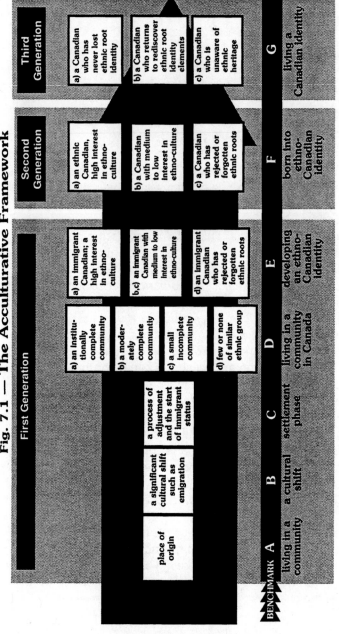

Chapter
7

The Acculturative Framework: Part 1 — The First Generation

INTRODUCTION TO THE MODEL

Thus far in the book, a contexting scheme has been presented that highlights many of the major differences between traditional and modern cultures. In addition, six non-verbal modes were described, showing how basic values can be expressed in behaviour. That helpers and clients each have their own norms of behaviour was emphasized. These were the object of awareness exercises in order that practitioners could more consciously know and employ them.

The Acculturative Framework is a third major model and it provides a systematic way of organizing cultural information about individuals, families or even Native or ethnic communities. The next three chapters are about this Framework and how to use it.

In the beginning section of the book, characteristics of a multicultural method were outlined. The Framework is a conceptual tool that expresses these characteristics. First, the method is inclusive; everyone can analyse their own life or the history of their family with this framework. Thus, a person of any ancestry, whether a renderer or receiver of service, can conduct the same process of analysing their own acculturation in and to Canada.

Second, by specifying the information in the framework, a service provider can start entering someone else's frame of reference and, when desired, compare a client's and their own frames of reference.

Third, the Framework is an "etic," or a culturally generalizable, concept. It permits important information to be outlined without stereotyping individuals or groups. However, within the framework, any individual or family experience can be explicated and the complexity of any one situation be collected, acknowledged and analysed.

The Death-Rebirth Paradigm

This Acculturative Framework paradigm draws on one of the most basic themes of human life — that of "death and rebirth" (Campbell, 1949: 30). In Campbell's work, these points of the mythological path are placed in a circle. However, the Acculturative Framework lays these points out, in modified form, in a straight line.

This archetypal form allows consideration of culture change on many levels. At one level, it can illuminate how our country has been and is constantly transformed by the infusion of immigrants. At other levels, in close-up, we see many "death-rebirth" phenomena as people go through the archetypal steps: separation from homeland; settlement in a new country and, eventually, a rebirth or return to life in a new community.

The pain of the "death-rebirth" cycle in immigration is not overstated by this analogy to archetypal form. Many theorists have documented the trauma of emigration and drawn on metaphors that capture the deep psychological changes that immigration sets in motion. That immigration trauma is likened to other rites of passage trauma only intensifies our understanding. For example, Parkes (1971) has reported illustrations of what he calls, "psycho-social transitions." He uses widely differing examples of "disasters, bereavements, childbirth, changes of occupation, retirement, migration, major physical illness and disablement" (Parkes, 1971: 101) to illustrate events that involve a loss and a necessary readjustment to that loss.

Not all "changes of state" result in happy outcomes, however. In some cases, the end result will be worse than the one promoting the change. A component affecting the outcome is the type of change and the source of motivation for change. In the case of normal immigration, immigrants voluntarily go through the trauma of expatriation in order to gain a better life for self and family. For the refugees, on the other hand, the expatriation is forced and unwanted. Yet, for either immigrants or refugees, the outcome may be that acceptance of the loss of homeland is never fully accomplished. The many ways in which the transition takes place and the transitions' varied outcomes is the subject of the Framework.

Because this archetypal trauma is a repeated pattern in social life, it is one understood and experienced by all helping professionals. Health care professionals see this transcendent form in the grieving process when patients are dying and when family and friends of the dying patients also come into professional focus. Teachers see rites of passage as young people move through puberty into adolescence and from adolescence to young adulthood. Social workers see young adults becoming parents, and, sometimes families breaking down through separation and divorce. All of these processes have in common an aspect of the "death and rebirth" phenomenon. Each one has, like migration, a wrenching change, a period of readjustment and then "return" to life. This, then, is a recurring process for helping different peoples and is common to different helping situations.

Where there is a recurrent process among the helping professions, this can become a basis for interdisciplinary understanding of clients/patients/students. The Jungian death-rebirth phenomenon and the psycho-social transitions of Parkes refer to the same "changes of state" as the Acculturative Framework.

The Acculturative Framework is as abstract and simple as the archetypal process described by Joseph Campbell (1949: 30). Thus, the scheme can be used for individual clients or patients or it can, on another level, be used to understand waves of immigration of people from the same country of origin. It can be used to understand the cultural identity of any Canadian person or ethnocultural group because the framework is elaborated to include people of different generations. In every case, the "rebirth" or end phase results in a new identity that combines the historical process of the change as well as the new life/community to which one is adapting.

A Practice Tool

As a conceptual tool for practice situations, the Acculturative Framework, as depicted in Fig 7.1 can be considered as a model or representation of (Samuels and Samuels, 1975: 79-99) the acculturation process by allowing discrete pieces of information to be put together and ordered in a meaningful whole. It is at this point that it is necessary to comment on the metaphors used to depict this change process. The Acculturative Framework is a simple processual flow-chart consisting of a "Timeline" and Benchmark points or stages of acculturation, each of which needs exposition. In this visual format, even imperfect or partial information can be put into place and used to "solve" or understand the client's identity state. Also information that is missing can be quickly identified. Earlier in this book in Chapter 2, the image of a river with many tributaries was used to capture the situation of a whole country undergoing change from immigration. Later another metaphor, that of growth rings of a tree, is used to visualize the way the effects of change are laid down especially for the individual engaged in that change. Readers will have their own images or metaphors and are urged to develop them.

THE FRAMEWORK FOUNDATION: THE "TIME LINE"

The simplest way to portray the river, mentioned above, and symbolize the passage of time in a monochronic way is a straight line or wavy line going in one direction: This, the straight line,

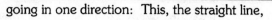

or the wavy line,

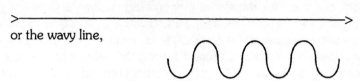

stands for the passage of time under consideration. (A wavy line or a curved line may be more comfortable for people who see time in a more curvilinear way).

The line can represent one individual's life to the present time, with the pointed end representing a particular time point. The line may also stand for a family's history in Canada and can include time prior to coming to Canada. Previously (Herberg, 1988), the time line was applied, in very broad terms, to an ethnic group's experience in Canada. But for now, in the case of a very new family in Canada, where acculturation has just begun, the time line could be used to project possible future outcomes for the family. If individuals or families have moved several times, several time lines can be used to project a profile of change:

```
                                                      time 1
>─────────────────────────────────────>

   time 1                                  time 2
   ───────────────────────────────────>

   time 2                                  time 3
   ───────────────────────────────────>
```

If the individual leaves Canada, the time line can indicate that activity:

```
                                                    ^
>──────────────────────────────────────── ¡──>
```

BENCHMARKS OR STAGES IN ACCULTURATION: FIRST GENERATION

Because this framework has been developed for human service practitioners who as helpers often cause change by their actions, a practical outline is needed where concrete events can be organized to "explain" what is happening.

Practitioners, as well as clients, are acculturating to Canada. Events in this process need to be picked out quickly; the framework can depict critical junctures of the adaptation career in Canada. Thus, the chart can be envisioned as a longitudinal slice of experience that depicts multiple "time layers" all at once; the lines above are examples of the time layers. To keep the chart consistent, each time layer starts afresh when a new cultural shift occurs. Another metaphor is used to talk about these cross-sections, that of the growth rings of a tree.

The time layers can be thought of in much the same way as the concentric circles visible in a cross section of a tree trunk. A forestry expert, looking at these concentric rings, can deduce environmental conditions for each year of the tree's life. Conditions of draught, fire, excessive moisture or cold temperatures can be imputed by the particular pattern of the rings. Wide rings suggest more optimal growing conditions whereas narrow rings suggest deprived growth conditions. The tree, at any one point of time, is the product of all these past conditions.

**Cross-section
of a tree trunk**

There are many practice implications deriving from the profile of changes: for example, an individual who has moved many times may have a more tenuous personal identity because of the frequent uprootings or, in some cases, the situation of many moves may be associated with more knowledge or skills. The age and stage of personal development at which the moves are made will have a crucial bearing on the meaning these moves have.

The analogy between tree and human being or family (or group) has vivid similarities, but the analogy cannot be taken too far. The human being has a mind and a mobile body and these alone make analysis of the human condition infinitely more complex. However, an uncomplicated chart, depicting important points in cultural change, can assist analysis of this extremely complex and variable phenomenon.

Since people have different ways of using their imagination to grasp concepts, other ways of depicting these changes should be experimented with.

Several basic variables must be found in the "time layers"; they are needed to capsule approximately where acculturation of worker and client are. These variables are called Benchmarks and are located on the time line. They are similar to the ones used in collecting oral histories from ethnic respondents (Harney, 1979). What is added are the time perspective and chronology of events in the respondent's life.

For the sake of convention and systematization, each Benchmark has a letter and meaning. The five basic Benchmarks are:

1. **Benchmark A is the Country of origin**, the origin of the ethnoculture;

2. **Benchmark B is a Culture Shift** such as migration, immigration, illegal entry, or culture contact;

3. **Benchmark C is the Settlement Phase** where the individual or family makes the initial, large adaptive changes as they settle into their Canadian locale;

4. **Benchmark D is the Ethnocultural Community** in which the person is settling and its ethnocultural characteristics, relative to the person studied; alternative possibilities of community structure are included; and

5. **Benchmark E is the Ethnocultural Identity** or the identity deriving from the country of origin (A) blending with "Canadian" identity elements. Possible alternative identites are specified.

The Framework also includes other Benchmarks, Benchmark F and Benchmark G, that make it possible for acculturated people in the second, third and beyond generations to find their place on the Framework, making the Framework inclusive of everyone. These later Benchmarks are discussed in Chapter 9.

In the simplest way, the Framework, using time line and Benchmarks for immigrants, can be expressed thus:

A	B	C	D	E
Country of Origin	Culture Shift	Settlement Phase	Ethnocultural Community	Ethnocultural Identity

The Benchmarks that are covered in this chapter are the first three on the time line from Fig.7.1:

living in a community	a change such as emigration or migration	a process of adjustment and the start of immigrant status

$$\longrightarrow$$

Benchmark A place of origin	**Benchmark B** a cultural shift	**Benchmark C** settlement phase

BENCHMARK A: THE PLACE OF ORIGIN

The present identity of oneself, one's colleagues and clients started in the past. In a multicultural society, except for Native Peoples, it means going back to some society beyond Canadian borders. It is necessary to be clear what we are looking for in the past. Ashley Montagu's definition of culture is particularly appropriate to understand the Acculturative Framework:

> Culture is the man-made part of the environment, man's symbols, ideas, values, traditions, institutions, it is what remains of man's past, working on his present, to shape his future. (Montagu, 1961).

The Acculturative Framework operationalizes this definition of culture. In Benchmark A, the cultural remains from the past are acknowledged because they affect the present and shape the future. This past "layer" must be taken into account to understand what happened along the way and to help "explain" what is happening in the present.

The concept of culture is applied to a wide variety of social structure levels: nations, sub-groups within a nation, families, and communities. The culture of a nation is an extraordinarily complex phenomenon and is difficult to specify. However, the people who live in a country appear to understand the values that are present even though values gradually change and even if not all members of the society subscribe to all the values. With Benchmark A, the service worker's task is to identify relevant values from the country of origin, of the individual or family being studied, because these values were brought along when the family emigrated. Later on in the Framework, at Benchmark D, the Ethnocultural Community, the concept of culture is again applicable to consider how the values imported into Canada become transformed by contact with Canadian community life. In the

Chapter 9 section on Discovering Ethnocultural Root Behaviour Patterns, residual forms of these original cultural values are shown to still affect people's lives many generations later.

Hence, the Framework starts with the place from which the person or family originally emigrated. It also includes the places prior to immigration in which the person or family made significant adjustments in their way of living. Thus, for example, if individual 1 immigrated directly to Canada from Guyana, that one-phase experience is noted by one time line:

Individual 1

A
Guyana   Canada

and information about Guyana should be collected at Benchmark A on the line. If individual 2 emigrated from Guyana to England, and ten years later immigrated to Canada, this experience is collected with two time lines:

Individual 2

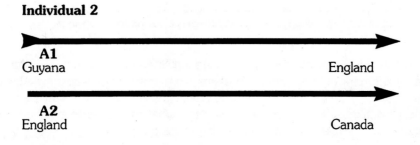

A1
Guyana   England

A2
England   Canada

For individual 2, important cultural information will have been picked up in England prior to coming to Canada. Both Guyanese and English information will have been integrated in that person in some partially predictable and partially unique way. For example, England is generally a more low context society than Guyana, and Individual 2 will have gained some knowledge about this form of societal organization that Individual 1 will not have. How he/she reacted to the economic opportunities in England, on the one hand, or the racial climate, on the other, will have a personal, unique impact on them. All of these experiences will have been brought to Canada and affected their adjustment here. The term "Country of Origin" covers effects from both Guyana and England because each country is considered a "country of origin" in its respective time line. Of course, the ethnic label that will follow either Individual 1 or 2 could be either West Indian- or Guyanese-Canadian. How each may feel about the label cannot be predicted and, as pointed out previously, the best strategy is not to rely on ethnic labels to guide one's understanding, but to allow Individuals 1 and 2 to develop labels that fit themselves.

Given that the past effects the present and shapes the future, there are many aspects of "Country of Origin" that can assist the helping professional enter the client's frame of reference. A comprehensive listing of these factors follows under the headings of "Demographic," "Language, Literacy and Educational Systems," "Government-Judicial Systems," "Socio-Economic, including welfare, System." At any one time, only a very small subset of this information is needed by the practitioner. Posing questions that focus on the type of problem under view, would narrow the field of past information that is required. The following listing suggests the kinds of information that might be needed.

Demographic Characteristics of Country of Origin

Geography and Climate

The terrain and weather provide an important backdrop to the culture of any society. Canada's climate and the enormous distances between regions of the country will contrast greatly with the past experience of most newcomers.

Place

Related to geography is the importance of "Place." People from high context societies have very close ties to the actual place or the specific site from which they come. Low context people are not as attached to any one place but are mobile and expected to adapt to urban places wherever they are.

Racial Composition of the Society

Is the society of origin predominantly of one race or a mixture? Is it a predominantly white society or is the ethno-racial diversity of Canada a new experience? With what race does the person identify? Is race for this client an issue that is ignored, forgotten, denied or strongly affirmed? Is the person linked to any organizations on the basis of race?

For example, in the Caribbean Islands there is a mixture of many races, because in the earliest colonial period the invaders were white and these intermarried with the aboriginal peoples. Later, Blacks, Chinese and people from the Indian sub-continent were brought in at various times as labourers. Thus the society became a very mixed one. What many West Indians have not experienced is a predominantly white society. Individual 2 in the previous example would have had that experience. This issue is discussed more in Chapter 10.

Social Class

Every society has at least two socio-economic strata and in many societies a middle class also is developing. The class level from which a person comes will have a very great deal to do with the kind of adjustment that is made in Canada. In fact, social class is the one variable which, in my experience, human service providers mention most often as affecting the helping relationship and the way Canadian services are understood and used. It also should be emphasized that social class effects often are mixed up or confounded with urban-rural residence. Of course, as education is introduced universally, these differences level out. In Canadian cities, working-class neighbourhoods tend to operate in a more traditional (high context) way and it is, thus, tragic when urban renewal pushes through such neighbourhoods and destroys the web of involvements that have developed. In any case, to the extent that working class or peasant class is associated with low levels of education and high context culture, then they will be more unfamiliar to service providers in Canada.

Religion

Is the country dominated by one religion or are there multiple religions? To what extent is there a religious/secular split in the society? Is there a monotheistic emphasis or is the religious life heavily constituted by animistic and magical elements? To what extent do the clergy influence sectors of the society that in Canada are considered "non-religious"? How has their culture brought the client to appreciate that most services are extended non-denominationally, but that many child welfare services in Ontario, and especially in Toronto, for example, are provided under religious categories? At the other extreme, how well does a client understand that in Canada, Church and State are separated?

Family Structure

If the family comes out of a high context culture, there will be a strong extended family emphasis, with a tendency to hierarchical form, usually with the father/grandfather as head of the household and the women and children subservient in authority to the head. Boys are often given freedom to move about the new country, whereas girls are expected to work in the home and help to maintain the traditional family culture. Also, the "Family" extends well beyond the nuclear unit; close relatives are necessary to the family's functioning and all will be done to sponsor relatives to Canada as quickly as possible.

Language, Literacy and Educational Factors

Language spoken

Many people immigrating to Canada do not speak English/French. This is especially true of sponsored relatives of the original immigrant in the family to come into Canada. If a newcomer comes from a country where English or French is one of the main languages of business and government, then there is greater likelihood that they are fluent in one of our official languages. Adjustment to Canadian life revolves greatly about the ability to converse with employers, shopkeepers, school teachers, police and other public officials. The sense of belonging to this country and understanding its social life through friendly conversations, listening to television and reading English/French newspapers, is critically mediated by English/French language competence. For high context people there is a need to be able to "build up contexts" in new situations in order that others can understand who they are and what is needed.

Literacy

Literacy is a prime requisite for moving into Canadian community economic and social life. It is likely that immigrants who have entered Canada under the point system of the Immigration Act in effect since 1968 will be literate, but sponsored relatives may not be. If they are not able to read

English/French, is the person literate in his/her own language? Moreover, participation and progress in English as a second language programmes usually are affected by literacy in their own language.

The Educational System

Each country has at least a developing educational system whose organization is arranged to meet that country's needs, given the resources available. Some systems are advanced while others are just beginning universal education. The attitude in the country of origin to school's and teachers' authority, as well as beliefs about the way education should be carried out and what should be taught, will be important factors in the adjustment of children and parents alike to Canadian schools.

Government — Judicial Factors

Type of Government

Is the nation of origin in the Western bloc of countries, within the (former) Soviet orbit, or from the so-called non-aligned group of nations? What type of government has the family been used to? For example, are they used to government involvement in many aspects of life as is the case in Canada? Do they expect the government to find them housing and a job as is done in some socialist countries? Are they used to bureaucratic government operation? Do they understand the use of forms, schedules, manuals, licences, public notices, memoranda, minutes of meetings, agendas, etc.? Do they understand the debate about public and private sectors; about "more" or "less" government? What is their experience with government officials; do they expect officials to require extra remuneration to do things for them; do they understand what a civil service is and how it works?

The Legal and Justice System

The definition of what is legal, the nature of a country's system of according justice, and how the family relates to both of these vary widely around the world. Do immigrants expect that basic legal problems will be solved by the kin group? Is restitution for wrongs handled by one's relatives? Do they assume police will be corrupt and rule by fear and violence? What is their attitude to law and order issues? Are they used to the policing of non-violent crimes such as traffic and parking infractions, petty theft, fraud, etc.? What is the attitude towards human rights and the role of the government?

Socio-Economic Factors

The Economy and Business

Is the economy in the country of origin a "free-enterprise" type or is it centrally controlled? How is business carried out on a day-to-day basis? Is it strongly entrepreneurial, corporation-dominated or communally organized? Business and jobs for newcomers in Canada have to be explained from the point of view, first, as a consumer, and second, occupationally, where a person holds a job as a livelihood. Expectations of government aid or assurance for obtaining employment may need to be addressed.

Health

How is sickness managed in the country of origin? Is the family the mainstay and healer in times of illness? Are supernatural forces believed to be closely involved in illness? What are their indigenous pharmacopoeia and folk remedies? What is their experience with modern medicine? Have they experienced the bureaucratization of medicine into hospitals, health insurance and other extensive residential services such as nursing homes, rehabilitation clinics and so forth? Do they understand "doctor's appointments," "regularly scheduled treatments," and time-slotted care of all sorts? Do they understand the concept of illness in the analytical way of modern medicine, i.e., the patient is viewed in terms of diagnostic and treatment categories? How do they understand the role of the sick person? Do they understand the "achievement orientation" of medical personnel, (i.e., the patient's job is to get well as quickly as possible and co-operate with the prescribed treatment regimes), or is their orientation to expect the same outpouring of sympathy and caring from medical staff as they expect from family and friends?

Welfare

Will the family be the main source of help if times are hard? If there is a shortage of food, or if their house is destroyed, will they seek help first from relatives? When they are old, do they expect to stay with their family, and/or have their children support and look after them? If they are female and unmarried, will they expect to stay in their parents' home? What is their expectation of government assistance in times of trouble? What experience, if any, has been had with professional counsellors?

SUMMARY

These separate topics cover the main categories of information relevant in professional helping. Not all are needed in any one interaction, of course. Details about each person's situation can be elicited from the client. However, helpers need to increase their knowledge about their clients' "Countries of Origin." The information can come partly from the media, but much that is valuable will be learned from the arts and translated writings and poetry of national artists and from writings in Canada by members of the group. Important traditional and current ambitions and the yearnings of the people are vividly communicated. Gaining familiarity with some of this background will greatly enhance a helping relationship, and trust in it will be furthered.

Particular professional helpers will have specific areas of interest. For example, the police may wish to know about attitudes to law and order and the general view about police personnel. Employment counsellors and immigrant settlement officials may find it helpful to know the expected level of government involvement in peoples' lives, the degree of their experience with bureaucracies and whether they expect the government to provide jobs and housing. Health care professionals will be interested in beliefs and attitudes toward disease and the processes of healing. All workers will find information about "contexting" (Chapters 3 and 4) useful in understanding the newcomer's frame of reference.

BENCHMARK B: A SIGNIFICANT CULTURE SHIFT

A
                                                    B
                                          Culture Shift

This process starts with the decision to migrate, and occurs when the break with the original culture is initiated. The circumstances of this decision have great portent for later adjustment. What precipitated the decision to migrate? Who was involved in the decision: women and men; children and parents; the elderly and the middle-aged? Was there agreement about the decision? Were some fearful or reluctant to go? Was the decision made in a hurry? In secrecy? Is there fear for those left behind? Is the decision a commitment to the new country or is it a decision for only a temporary stay in order to make some money for an eventual return home or as a place of refuge until their own country returns to a state of normalcy?

This emigration period, here called a "cultural shift" is a legal process; there are also psychosocial aspects and there is a physical uprooting and shift of lives. In terms of the archetype, "death-rebirth," this shift begins this process.

For most immigrants, the cultural shift has beginnings in some kind of personal or family upheaval that resolves in a decision to leave the home territory. For some the choice of Canada is a response to the local immigration recruitment literature such as posters about Canada. For others, the choice to go to Canada is part of family reunification. (For the phenomenological development of this process see Disman, 1981.) The cultural shift may occur over a relatively brief period, or it may consume many years. The actual physical shift, often taking a few hours by plane, but in some cases the end point of months or years of wandering and displacement, will be only the outward manifestation of a very complex, drawn out experience.

Reasons for Emigrating

Economic reasons

Economic resons for emigrating, in the past, included poor opportunities for self and children in one's home country. There were often few job opportunities, or agricultural land had been depleted, either due to the spread of urbanization or because it had been subdivided between relatives beyond a reasonable return. Often, land reforms were slow in coming and people saw little hope for economic survival. Poor economic conditions stemmed from past colonialization of the country and economic production had been skewed in favour of serving developed nations, not organized in the best interests of the indigenous people. Now, migration is as refugees, frequently due to impoverishment due to extended civil war or drought.

Political Reasons

Political reasons for emigrating often stem from economic reasons. For example, where people's reform movements are oppressed by regimes in

power, those involved in reform often have to flee persecution or risk tor-
ture and imprisonment. In a growing number of cases, people are expelled
by a political regime and they become political refugees. The Ugandan
people who fled Idi Amin's regime in the early 70s, were only the first of
many groups to experience displacement. The "boat people" from Vietnam
fled because of their unwillingness to accept a Communist way of life and
felt threatened by the new regime. Recently, many peoples in Latin
America, Africa, Asia and Europe have had to escape from hostile powers.
The future of Canadian immigration will be dominated by these movements
of refugee peoples. In each case the service provider should be familiar with
the political conditions from where people have come. Often this information will help explain what people have been through and what their outlook is for the future.

Other Reasons

Other reasons for emigrating may be lodged in the opportunity structure of jobs. Sometimes the main source of jobs in the country of origin
was the civil service and if literacy and educational levels increased rapidly,
there may not have been sufficient outlets for well-educated people.
Sometimes where foreign corporations dominate, the only non-agricultural
jobs available are in these foreign-dominated industries. Such employers
may be more concerned with profits than in the people of the country and
jobs available to people are limited to the less skilled, lower paid positions.
   The Classes of Immigrants admissible under the Immigration Act
are defined in detail in the *Immigration Handbook* (Canada: Employment
and Immigration, 1981 and updated). The main preoccupations in the later
years of the 1980s and the 1990s are the refugee movements around the
globe that have had and will continue to have a large impact on who tries to
enter Canada.
   Refugees are often processed as "landed immigrants," sometimes by
emergency-teams of officials prior to admission to Canada, but the psychosocial processes may be considerably different. Refugees are fleeing,
often in disorganized panic, from conditions of natural disaster, political persecution or terror in their own country. Their aim is to find haven in a
country that will provide refuge. The eventual choice of country may not be
the first choice, but what is immediately available.
   Once in Canada, they may enter the refugee determination process.
This process may take months or years to complete. In many cases people
become "illegal," either because they do not enter the refugee determina-

tion process for fear that once in the adjudication process they will be refused — for example, economic refugees will not be granted status — and will be sent back, or, they did apply and their application was refused and they are afraid to or cannot return to their country. Other illegal immigrants are those who came in on a visitor's visa and have stayed beyond the time limit of their visa. A few offshore students are illegal also because they have stayed on beyond their student visa limit.

In both immigrant and refugee situations, the connection to the original culture is broken and a significant culture change starts. Those refugees who arrive in Canada without a landed status will have a particularly difficult time until their status is determined by the Refugee Determination Board because they are not eligible for most services.

In the case of illegal immigrants, a culture shift also occurs, but it occurs under conditions that make later adjustment very precarious because of the insecurity of their tenure in Canada. The circumstance of illegal entry puts the helping person in a very difficult position. A helping person may be tempted to "look the other way" and not draw attention to the illegal status of the client, especially if the client is or has a child. Whatever is done, there will be stress imposed on the helping person.

For most people coming to Canada, the actual physical shift that must be undergone is accomplished, nowadays, in a few hours by aircraft to Canada. Some decades ago, a boat trip usually preceded the immigration process. In earlier days still, this took months in sailing ships and often was a hazardous process. In tales related down through the generations, some of the perils undergone by immigrant ancestors are retold, thereby becoming part of one's ethnic identity. For Canadian Blacks, there are stories to tell of the Underground Railway (Winks, 1971). For Jews, there are stories of refugee ships searching for a haven and sometimes being turned away (Abella and Troper, 1982). For Chinese and Sikhs, there are stories of sea journeys to Vancouver and refusal of entry (Krauter and Davis, 1978: 66-87). For each ethno-racial-religious group that immigrated to Canada before the modern era, there exists a series of historical and mythical reports of travail, but also, usually, eventual success.

Finally, how do we consider Native Peoples in terms of this framework and "significant culture change"? Obviously, Native People did not leave one country to move to another, but that they underwent significant culture change is not in doubt. In fact, the main reason for phrasing this part of the acculturation process, "significant culture change," is to include Native Peoples in the Acculturative Framework and bring forward their needs and plight as part of our knowledge base. In terms of this Framework, their significant culture change took place over scores of decades following the invasion of their lands by Europeans and continues today. Their way of life has been under attack for four centuries. The processes of colonialism drastically changed the original native culture. What is left is only an analogue of an ethnoculture; the original culture has been vastly altered to meet new conditions of colonization in what was their own land. In Chapter 10, analysis is made of the many cultural shifts that First Nations Peoples endured.

Of course, First Nations People are not the only people to have significant culture shifts within Canada. Up until about 1931, most of Canada was rural. Following this most groups experienced the move from a rural to urban location. These moves brought with them large cultural changes most of which can be understood as a shift from high context to lower context values.

All these statuses—landed immigrant, illegal immigrant, refugee, pioneer/invader, colonized people—relate to the way the separation from the original culture came about. In each case, the fortunes of the people are affected by the manner in which the original culture was disjoined. And, in each case the knowledge has significant and practical importance for the practitioner. With the exception of First Nations People, and other internal migrants, the period of Significant Cultural Shift ended with arrival in Canada.

BENCHMARK C: SETTLEMENT PERIOD

A   B   C
                                              Settlement
                                                 Phase

The Settlement Phase (Benchmark C) starts once the immigrant has passed through the immigration process that is carried out at airports, seaports or border crossing-points. This phase includes the first few years in Canada and the initial period of psychosocial adjustment, the beginning of the "rebirth" period, the beginning of acculturation to Canada. Individual people and families vary in the length of time before they begin movement into the mainstream of Canadian life. For some, Benchmark C is largely completed within one year, but it can be much more extended. Experienced movers and people with optimum situations — money, jobs, prestige — can settle into a new country quite quickly.

For most people who are not highly experienced in moving and with only ordinary resources, it can take 5–7 years. This time lapse is necessary for them to experience the seasonal variations in the culture several times and for these to become familiar environmental factors. Finally, a small proportion of people do not feel adjusted even after 20 years, and indeed may not ever feel adjusted, no matter what their objective situation is. The caseloads of helping professionals may have an over-representation of these kinds of immigrants because their lack of adjustment can result in a high incidence of health and social problems for themselves and their families (Herberg and Herberg, 1987).

Culture Shock

Culture shock is the term given to a variety of reactions to the experience following a cultural shift, that is, during the Settlement Phase. Often, there is very loose application of the term "culture shock"; people can use the term to apply merely to experiences of discomfort. "Culture shock" as used here means the conflict and experience of the contrast in beliefs, expectations and values between the culture of the place of origin and the new environment. Culture shock can produce a range of problems, varying from mild discomfort and disorientation to severe dysfunctions of thought and behaviour.

The process of adjustment and the experiences during this period follow a somewhat predictable sequence. This is the case for the well-endowed, experienced mover, mentioned before, as well as the less experienced person. In a 1981 article, Dr. Alistair Munro, who perceived himself as an experienced mover and in a favoured category, discussed his own personal experiences prior to and following the immigration to Canada of himself, his spouse and teenage daughters. He described nine stages that occurred for him within a two-year period.

Stages

1. The disengagement process began prior to leaving for Canada. This included reactions by friends and associates who also were disengaging from him. By the time he left, he had so successfully disengaged that he was pleased to leave because he no longer felt he had a place to work.

2. He called this stage "Jet-Lag et al." Symptoms here included sleep disturbances and mild stomach upset in the days immediately following arrival in Canada.

3. "The pseudo-holiday spirit," in the early post-landing weeks was a

defence against anxiety and included doing a great number of things that could have waited, but which, in retrospect, were done to substitute for having to think about the new situation.

4. The "honeymoon" period lasted about two months and was related to a beginning low job pressure. There was mild euphoria, yet some anxiety. There was some difficulty in remembering things, as new work routines were encountered. There was also a pronounced sense of weariness.

5. The recurrent infection phase. About four months long, for him it involved many upper respiratory infections and influenza-like illnesses. There was lassitude, inertia and irritability.

6. Eidetic images or flashbacks of British scenes occurred while awake. Strong emotional association with these "places" was noted, but the experience of the flashback did not produce any specific emotion, though it was attention-consuming.

7. Reality: pleasant and unpleasant. Around the fifth month, feelings of dissociation largely disappeared and the learning and memory problems resolved. These improvements coincided for him with the finalization of house-purchase and the arrival of his belongings from England. However, periods of profound tiredness and irritability remained. Any hint that coming to Canada was a mistake produced self-justifying responses.

8. Adaptation was felt in strong ways as friends were made and activities extended. The periods of the "blues" were briefer and less frequent. There was a greater feeling of energy and sense of well-being. Occasionally "flashbacks" returned, but actual visitors from Britain were not interesting as sources of information about Britain but as listeners to his talk about Canada. Any patronizing remark about Canada caused Dr. Munro and his wife to bridle.

9. Going "Home" on vacation reinforced feelings of belonging in Canada and the return to Canada was filled with keen anticipation. Much of the tiredness had by then disappeared and his irritability reduced. Munro reflected on his vacation as the "$1,000 cure" to his homesickness.

Obviously, one person's experience of homesickness is not identical to everyone's experience. However, these stages, remarkably contracted into 1–2 years for this person, can lengthen for those with fewer resources and less experience. Sluzki (1979) described an adaptation experience that resolves into 4 stages and expressed them along a time line in terms of a "curve of performance." These are listed below.

The Preparatory stage

As the family prepares to migrate, the curve of performance varies slightly up and down while the person prepares for the move. The tendency is for the family to pull together the energy anticipated for the uprooting and, depending on the circumstances, perform first "up" with euphoria and then "down" in a short period of overload. These ups and downs are normal, preparatory to emigration. This preparatory stage parallels Munro's disengagement phase, Stage 1.

The Period of Over-compensation

This period referred to the first few months after emigration and fits with Munro's "pseudo-holiday spirit" and "honeymoon" periods. (These less technical terms are valuable to remember when dealing with clients who might find the technical language a barrier to communication).   Sluzki, like Munro, found that the heaviest stress does not occur in the weeks or even months immediately following emigration.   Often immigrants are unaware of the stress they are under and the cumulative nature of it. There is a task-oriented efficiency as energy must be focussed on what in the past was routine activity.   These activities are no longer routine, however, and require minute attention because of the mismatch between personal expectation and what the new cultural environment actually requires.

A sense of being alien in the new environment in every movement and gesture is the core of the culture shock experience. Over-compensation by a narrow focus of consciousness is the normal way to react to overwhelming stress.   Psychosocial conflicts and physical symptoms tend to remain dormant as the body gears up to survive in the new environment. These coping strategies can last only for so long, and for some there can be a final collapse triggered by even some minute thing in the new reality, six months or more later — a crisis from cumulation of stress.

The Period of Undercompensation

The period of undercompensation follows and the curve of performance, previously well above normal, now slips down below normal. In Munro's case there was physical illness, eidetic images, feelings of dissociation, irritability and profound tiredness.

Sluzki also discussed the way that family roles are played out in this period. For example, a split between instrumental and affective roles may deepen in the adaptation to the new environment. Some people cling to the past or cling to another family member. Others will move out and make new connections that may threaten other family members. In a few cases, deep family pathology may occur. Such families, however, are just the ones whom helping professionals may find over-represented in their caseloads; people who adjust well often do not need their help (Sluzki, 1979).

Normalization

Gradually, in the final stage of normalization, the family begins to feel less alien and more as though they belong to Canada. Many factors effect a return to normal functioning: the presence of an adequate job and sufficient money to meet new needs will help adjustment greatly. Much, though, can work against adjustment: one's race and accent can be readily perceived cues to being different. If racism is experienced, adaptation may be slowed down because the need to belong to Canada is thwarted (Herberg and Herberg, 1987). Also, a feeling of being alien can persist beyond a normal time and the sense of solitude can be deepened by discriminatory experiences.

Many immigrants, even those with positive commitments to Canada in the first place, can experience the "myth of returning" to the homeland. If this final stage goes well, as in the case of Munro, the actual returning experience helps solidify the acculturation already accomplished. Life in Canada afterwards is less afflicted with homesickness.

Another work that depicts culture shock is the monograph referred to previously by Sikkema and Niyekawa-Howard (1977). Here some journal entries from students placed in a deliberate culture shock experience are presented.

Working With People in the Settlement Phase

The most basic cultural adjustment for a newcomer may be related to how those personal characteristics which have highest visibility — race, gender and age — are related to by people they meet in Canada. There is an expectation gap when the way a person is treated in Canada differs considerably from the way they were treated in the place of origin. For example, at point of entry to Canada a white middle-aged couple is met by an Immigration Officer who expects that the man is the wage-earner, and takes the leadership in family matters. The woman is cast as the wife, a homemaker and mother who supports her husband's leadership. However, if the woman is a professional who has her own identity, it is a shock for her when she is passed over and only her husband is included in questioning or discussion. The gap in expectation is felt as culture shock by her. Although this example is a Canadian one, the Immigration Officer in this case is more high context in orientation than the incoming people. This Immigration official will manifest an unconscious expectation gap and can feel and act rather negatively toward the couple.

Likewise, the experience of being treated as a racial minority person can be a culture shock for the non-white person accustomed to a predominantly non-white society. To see white people everywhere and even throngs of white people in the streets can be an overwhelming experience. However, this first impression is not immutable, because a person can adjust to a society that is different visually than their original one: it is the feeling of being different and of not belonging and not being wanted that can be lastingly painful. It is in later housing and job searches that the person can experience these devastating attitudes.

Evidence that there is a toll experienced by non-whites was provided by Breton's recent research in Toronto, and in many more ad hoc Committee Reports. In some situations the non-white groups studied were only half as likely as the white respondents to report feeling accepted by the majority of Canadians (Breton, 1981: 4-6). In a later study by the Social Planning Council of Metropolitan Toronto, (Henry and Ginzberg, 1985), actors in the experiment, who applied over the phone, reported that over one third of the sample of non-white-sounding job applicants experienced discrimination.

Different expectations for age groups can also be a shock. The elderly may suddenly find themselves without a purpose and respected place in the community. The young may find a kaleidoscope of expectations in school and neighbourhood that differ from those of the home country.

USING THE FRAMEWORK TO ENTER
A FRAME OF REFERENCE

If we return to Individual 1 and Individual 2 mentioned earlier, we can start to sketch out a hypothetical profile of each, building in individual characteristics, to demonstrate the application of the Framework.

Individual 1

Benchmark A	Benchmark B	Benchmark C
born in Guyana	immigrated to Canada	settled in Toronto
1930	1970	

Individual 2

Benchmark A	Benchmark B	Benchmark C
born in Guyana	immigrated to London	in London for 10
1940	England, age 20	years, 1960-1970

Benchmark A	Benchmark B	Benchmark C
in London at	immigrated to Canada,	settled in Toronto,
age 30	age 30	1970

Individual 1 and 2 differ in the range of experience each had before arriving in Canada. Individual 2 experienced a white, industrialized country for a significant portion of their life. Both people originally had a Guyanese cultural background.

To operationalize culture a definition of culture given by Ashley Montagu (1961), specified that:

> culture is...the human made part of the environment, human symbols, ideas, values, traditions, institutions. As the late Sir John Meyres put it, culture is what remains of man's past, working on his present to shape his future...

Thus, the effect of each Benchmark goes on through time, and the next Benchmark effects are superimposed on the previous one. If one could use a series of transparencies, one for each Benchmark, this would capture the cumulative effects in a vivid manner. Without the means to introduce transparencies in this book, the following chart attempts to portray some of the cumulative effect of each previous Benchmark.

A general picture can be drawn and, with some imagination, the effects can be seen going on through time:

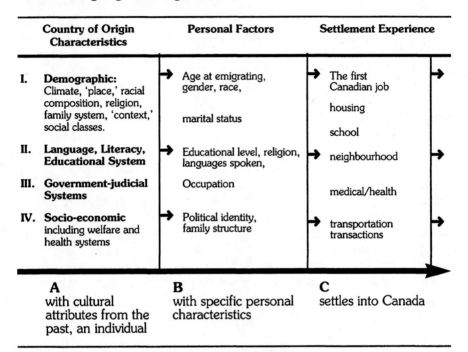

Country of Origin Characteristics	Personal Factors	Settlement Experience
I. Demographic: Climate, 'place,' racial composition, religion, family system, 'context,' social classes.	Age at emigrating, gender, race, marital status	The first Canadian job housing school
II. Language, Literacy, Educational System	Educational level, religion, languages spoken,	neighbourhood
III. Government-judicial Systems	Occupation	medical/health
IV. Socio-economic including welfare and health systems	Political identity, family structure	transportation transactions

A with cultural attributes from the past, an individual	**B** with specific personal characteristics	**C** settles into Canada

The individual at Benchmark C has been through a specific cultural shift and brought with him/her a complex set of beliefs, values and attitudes from the Country (or Countries) of Origin. The professional person, working with the individual at time C may need to look back along the time line to Benchmarks B and A to get that person's frame of reference. The arrows across the chart show that the effects from Benchmarks A and B are conveyed along at C and colour every transaction, whether it be job or housing search, school beginnings, neighbourhood exploration or medical help. And these effects continue on in the life of the immigrant and into the lives of the follwing generations.

The person at place C is in a particularly vulnerable position. They have suffered the loss of familiar physical and cultural surroundings, but because of overcompensation may not be aware of how the psycho-social pressures could be building up. It is not unusual to find people behaving very busily, in some cases working at several jobs.

An additional vulnerability comes from lack of preparation for the realities of Canadian life. Jobs can be very hard to find and/or the jobs to which a person is accustomed may be closed to them because of "lack of Canadian experience." They also may be unused to finding their own housing, using mass transit or be confused by the system of medical care, etc.

The actual home base they acquire after initial immigration processing, may affect much that happens later. On the one hand, well-meaning sponsors may keep them from directly learning themselves about available opportunities. On the other hand, being alone in a rooming house may lead to many months of loneliness before friendly contacts are established. Finally, to the extent people are snubbed or slurred because of their racial identity, the feeling of cultural alienation and shock can persist long after a sense of belonging would normally have begun.

Practitioners who become involved with immigrants at this stage should be aware that an apparently good adjustment in this phase does not automatically assure good adjustment later on, although it makes it more likely. It should also be noted that both clients and professionals who are themselves in this phase may be very uninterested in the topic of ethnicity and at times even impatient with a topic that seems either obvious or irrelevant to them. People are generally unaware that they are viewed as "ethnic" or that their cultural patterns, which are simply "a way of life to them," are regarded by other Canadians as "ethnicity." In addition, people at this stage of acculturation often have not yet learned "to objectify" and analyse their own cultural experiences (see Chapter 2). Any language difficulties, marked accents or different cultural practices identify them to others as newcomers.

There are specific therapeutic measures that can be taken with newcomers. The most powerful help is simply to listen to what the person is concerned about and the emotions they are experiencing. Considering some of the problems the person undergoing transition has — somatic problems, anxiety, "seeing things," (eidetic images or flashbacks), irritability, extreme tiredness, loss of memory and so forth—it is normal at this stage to be concerned about oneself. Providing reassurance about present symptoms and preparing them for other symptoms can legitimize their culture shock experience and reduce both their negative reactions and the duration of culture shock dysfunction.

When there are feelings of depression, normalizing activities should be recommended. For instance, the person should be helped to find compatriots from his/her Country of Origin or friendly people from the mainstream. Meaningful objects from home should be kept with them.

Importantly, the practitioner's legitimation that these reactions to transition are normal will in itself communicate reassurance and benefit. Of course, if severe symptoms are found, the appropriate professional help should be sought.

The description of the settlement phase here is ended by noting that later-born Canadians have all "had" these settlement experiences in the past history of their ancestors. The earliest settlement phase of whole communities was, of course, that of early French and English pioneers in the 16th through 19th centuries. It is because of this pioneer relationship to the country that many members of these charter groups do not see themselves as immigrants. Rather, they see themselves as founding peoples with special rights. The hardships endured by the pioneers in settling the country are regarded with pride. Even so, this re-definition does not change the immigrant status of these groups. Black people who also were pioneers are often not recognized in the history books. This omission is slowly being corrected.

Finally, taking the "first people" last, the analogous phase in Native People's history can be considered to stretch from the early years of involvement with the British and French — fighting in their wars, developing the fur trade for them, assisting in their exploration and survey of rivers, mountains and plains (which they already knew so well as holders of the land) and numerous other involvements. It was a mixed period. Natives then still believed that it was possible for white and Indian to live side by side, despite the broken promises and bloodshed. Before long, though, the realities of vastly different cultures, imported from Western Europe, began to be felt. This "Settlement Phase" for the charter groups, ended for the Native Peoples with their increasing isolation and loss of their indigenous culture. As noted earlier, these changes are analysed, by means of the Acculturative Framework in Chapter 10.

SUMMARY

The first three Benchmarks have been outlined. It is emphasized that everyone in Canada has some connection to them. Thus, the acculturation process can be seen "close up" in the lives of present day immigrants but also in deeper perspective in the experience of pioneer groups and Native Peoples. The process of shift from place of origin through migration to the new place, to the place of settlement is a complex and potentially problematic sequence, not the least of which is cultural shock.

Chapter
8

The Acculturative Framework:
Part 2 — The First Generation

The next two Benchmarks, D and E, are placed on the time line, though their sequential place is not nearly as clear cut as the previous three benchmarks. Benchmark D is the relevant Ethnocultural Community for the immigrant individual or family under consideration (Fig. 8.1). Benchmark E is his/her Ethnocultural Identity (Figure 8.3). Obviously, identity is not confined to a point in time like the process of settling into a country (Benchmark C), which can be roughly bracketed in a specific period. It is placed on the time line, however, because it is an important outcome of the processes considered thus far and relevant to the work of service providers. After Benchmark E no other Benchmarks for the immigrant generation exist in the scheme.

BENCHMARK D: THE COMMUNITY; THE ETHNOCULTURAL ASPECT

The ethnocultural elements, described in the last chapter under Benchmark A, come to be felt in the community within which a person lives and works. These are a logical focus for multicultural work. However, at the onset it is well to remember the other communities within which the ethnocultural community exists. Breton, in his early work, talked of three communities for the immigrant: the community of his ethnicity, the receiving or host community and the other ethnic communities" (Breton, 1964: 193). There are services related to all of these communities and all of them can have an effect on the immigrant. The Framework, however, spells out only the ethnocultural aspects. In addition ethnocultural communities or enclaves vary in type, size, and complexity from one Canadian locale to another, and the particular ethnocultural origin mix is unique in each place.

How do the different kinds of ethnic communities depicted at Benchmark D emerge? They may be considered to be laid down over time in the course of the flow of people over the Canadian landscape. As people move in and out of locales, looking for jobs or searching out kin, they stay and set down roots, eventually developing their group institutions—businesses, places of worship, recreation, educational and cultural centres, newspapers, and professional establishments. As numbers increase, the entrepreneurial motive is sharpened by the demand for ethnocultural goods and services and the range and number of ethnocultural organizations and businesses increase. The size and complexity of enclaves can wax and wane as circumstances change, especially the flow of subsequent immigrants. Thus, the study of ethnic communities is complex and requires special expertise. Fortunately, such a special field of study has emerged: Canadian Ethnic Studies.

Canadian Ethnic Studies

Canadian ethnic studies, with at least three decades of research to its credit, is an important resource for those in multicultural work. Very often the reports from this field are somewhat remote from the professional person's field of action — intervention with an individual or family — but nearly always the material provides important background understanding of the multicultural dimensions involved.

One of the factors causing remoteness from the action framework is that, in the past, academic researchers have been largely interested in what contributes to or prevents high ethnic group cohesion and have, therefore, chosen to study groups with which professionals have relatively little contact. Groups such as the Native People, Doukhobours, Mennonites, Amish and Hutterites have strong religious ties and tend to live in isolated enclavic settlements. They are highly cohesive and seldom use outside professional helpers. Of course, at the nexus of contact, through schools or hospitals, or social agencies, some ethnic studies would be valuable. However, the outcomes of sociological studies are given in summary probabilistic and aggregate terms and cannot be applied directly to individual situations (Rosen, 1982).

As pointed out in Chapter 2, however, sociological research is useful to the practitioner by raising questions that might otherwise not have been considered relevant to direct practice work. In addition, if the research includes the instruments for data collection, then the practitioner can become more informed about a concept and how to inquire about it in their own service activity. The professional outlook is, therefore, enriched by this examination.

Institutional Completeness

When possible, one should consider community variables that not only affect the adaptation of people to Canada but also are useful to professional work. Many issues could be built into the Framework: Some of these are the nature and constituent elements of the community; its geographically concentrated versus dispersed character; the range of political ideologies extant; the level of education of its members and the range of occupational achievement; the (racial) visibility of its members and so forth. However, because the Framework ends in a Benchmark that is about ethnocultural identity (Benchmark E), the Benchmark previous to it must be related to this kind of outcome. For this reason, a concept about the nature and constituent elements of ethnic communities is employed. This concept is called "institutional completeness" (Breton, 1964; Herberg, 1988).

If an ethnic community becomes entirely self-sufficient — individuals living their lives entirely within this community without going outside it for any purpose — it is called institutionally complete. This concept was developed by Breton and an examination of his report can help in determining how the issue can be examined and what correlates can be expected.

In the Framework at Benchmark D, it is the community of the individual's or family's ethnicity that is being charted. As pointed out earlier, the receiving or host community and other ethnic communities surround and are implied in the chart, but not included explicitly in order to keep the Framework as uncluttered as possible. But they must be kept in mind. In Chapter 9, the host community and the work of professional helpers is commented on.

The community of the person's own ethnicity provides an alternate route to integration within the wider society. It has an important function in shaping the life of the immigrant; the size and nature of that community will have a sharp effect on that shaping. There are obverse or complementary effects from the receiving or host community, either directly on those functions where the ethnic community is not effective, or indirectly, in the attitudes and feelings that are present towards the ethnic community. (The host community is considered more fully in the next chapter, Chapter 9.)

When people from a newly-immigrant or refugee group settle into a neighbourhood, it will be particularly hard for them to adjust if the group is racially visible and also the subject of media attention. If political activities in their homeland are controversial and routinely publicized in newspapers and T.V., the group may encounter gossip and hostility from members of the host community. As the ethnic enclave enlarges, it can become a source of comfort wherein newcomers can be with like people, especially people of the same race.

Breton's findings about the concept of institutional completeness suggest what the nature of the community itself is and what is especially important (Breton, 1964). In addition to the informal networks of friendships and cliques are the more formal organizations — religious, educational, economic, arts-cultural, media, political, social-recreational, governmental, social and health services. Some have organized welfare and mutual aid societies (Herberg, 1988: 268-271). It should be noted that the term "completeness" in the concept suggests process and variation, and such terms have good potential use in a practice or action context because the variation and change of the "real" world can be taken into account.

In addition to just naming sectors in which ethnic institutions could be found, Breton discovered that first, some institutions are more important than others; and second, having a range of sectors developed is more important than simply the total quantity of organizations. For example, "one church" has far greater impact than "no church," but "more than one church" does not make a great deal more difference (Breton, 1964: 200). Newspapers and other publications are extremely important to in-group cohesion, but, again, reading two newspapers or more does not have much more impact than one. But not reading an ethnic newspaper at all reduced cohesion markedly (Breton 1964, p. 197).

In the D Benchmark, with Breton's observations in mind, four shadings of institutional completeness can be developed — from an institutionally complete enclave to the condition of all institutions being absent. The two intermediate ones are classified into relatively high completeness and relatively low completeness. Ethnic settings can then be classed in one of four ways:

Da - institutionally complete, i.e., a complete range of institutions
Db - organizations in many or most but not all sectors
Dc - organizations in some, but not a majority of institutions
Dd - organizations in no, or only a few institutions

The Acculturative Framework can be extended to show Benchmark D.

Fig. 8.1 — Ethnocultural Communities

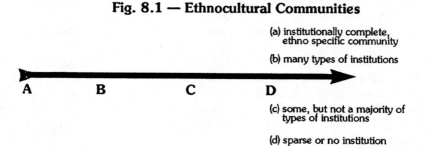

(a) institutionally complete, ethno specific community

(b) many types of institutions

A   B   C   D

(c) some, but not a majority of types of institutions

(d) sparse or no institution

For example, in Toronto, the Italian community would be characterized as D_a, (institutionally complete) but in Winnipeg, the Italian community might be D_c, much smaller and less varied (moderate to low range of types)

As will be shown for Benchmark E, these alternate ethnic routes are hypothesized to have an important affect on identity and integration into the society. Breton's work suggested four ways the communities can effect this integration.

First, he suggests that an ethnic organization can be used as a substitute for one from the receiving or mainstream community. For example, Grace Anderson's work, on immigrated Portuguese men, showed how networks based on kin and acquaintances from the place of origin formed the basis for contacts about possible jobs (Anderson, 1974) instead of a federal employment agency.

Second, Breton points out that immigrants who belong to ethnic organizations can extend the network of participants in such organizations and thereby nourish and sustain a sense of attachment to the country of origin among themselves and, perhaps also among non-participants and those with weak attachments to the ethnicity.

Third, organizations and associations can raise new issues or reactivate old ones and thereby bring the ethnic group's presence forward in the public mind. For example, Armenian activists who sought out and killed Turkish diplomats in 1982-83, reactivated in Canada the old issue of the Armenian holocaust in Turkey nearly 70 years ago. Or, following the 1980 catastrophic earthquakes in Italy, the Canadian Italian community founded special organizations and brought the issue of Italian relief work to the general public. Many, many examples of these kinds of community institutional activities could be listed.

Finally, leaders of ethnic organizations can actively attempt to maintain or enlarge the participating group, especially if immigration is declining. This kind of activity occurs because leaders generally do not like to lose their spheres of influence, and also, of course, have real attachment to their group (Breton, 1964: 197-8).

Before going on to make connections between Benchmark D and E, some further comments about the ethnic community and practitioners should be made. The perspective of the Framework is always a relative one and, therefore, we can look at the ethnic community from the "outside," mainstream position or we can look out at the mainstream from the ethnic perspective. This is the case because service providers may well have an identity within an ethnic community. They may work either in an ethnic health or social service organization such as an "immigrant aid," "mutual benefit society," ethnic association or clinic, or, such a person could work in a mainstream agency and in that agency exhibit either an assimilated perspective or feel part of an ethnic community. Both of these perspectives are frames of reference as discussed earlier and are important to differentiate.

Service Delivery and Institutional Completeness

Regardless of the frame of reference one has established, service delivery would include services both ethnically originated and from the mainstream. One's repertoire of service information should include all service systems. After that range of possibilities is established, it becomes a matter of assessing how and by whom a client is best served. People who are new to Canada are often served best by those who have a similar background, but, as will be shown later, this is not always the case. If it is the function of an organization to assess gaps in service, it should be the whole service network that is examined. For example, in a recent Toronto study, the National Congress of Italians showed that a serious gap in services for Italian-speaking people existed. They looked both at mainstream agencies and Italian community social services, and surmised that the demand for social services from Italian-speaking professionals far outstripped the supply. This is a difficult problem to remedy quickly, but service providers can begin a course of action for the long term to encourage Italian-speaking people to earn social service qualifications.

Research Questions

There are many ways that ethnic community variables can be used to analyse extent and adequacy of services in any one time period. For example, correlations can be made between the presence and nature of services with community characteristics. For example, in a specific locale institutional completeness and presence of services of a particular type could be correlated in a four-celled table for different ethnic communities. In Figure 8.2, the institutional completeness variable is posed against the degree of diversity in the community of each group noted in the table. For example, Jews have very diverse backgrounds — the Sephardic group come from the Middle East and the Ashkanazi come from Europe. Within each of those major subdivisions there are many other political, racial, and national origins. This group also has a wealth of services given in Yiddish or Hebrew as well as English/French languages. They thus occupy a place in the table characterized as high diversity/high completeness. At the other extreme are Jamaicans who have a fairly homogeneous community and have a small number of services provided by fellow Jamaicans. They are thus low diversity/low completeness.

Fig. 8.2 — Diversity of Social Services in 1980s

		High Diversity	Low Diversity
		Jewish	Italian
	High		
Institutional		Chinese	Portuguese
Completeness of			
Ethnic Communities			
in Toronto in 1980s		Native	Greek
	Low	People	
		Latin	Jamaican
		Americans	

SERVICE DIVERSITY AND INSTITUTIONAL COMPLETENESS OF COMMUNITIES

The information on both these variables in Toronto is from impressionistic perceptions, rather than from any detailed statistical data. If a more rigorous picture is desired, it is not too difficult to get information using such resources as the phone book, community services handbooks, and ethnic informants. If a low degree of formal services are discovered, the more informal ones, such as are given through ethnic community associations, could be investigated. In the process of surveying these variables, a dynamic picture of an ethnic community can be realized and impressionistic views can be revised by later, more precise information. In fact, the very act of surveying the services in an ethnic community can induce that group to become more organized about information and notice gaps in service. For example, as one group sees another group developing for itself social service directories and handbooks, that idea can instigate similar activity. Other variables can be correlated with services, and might raise questions such as, are communities, characterized by low levels of education, served by appropriate social services? If the organizations are mainly under religious auspices, are services diverse enough to cope with the exigencies of modern city life? In a highly dispersed community, are services also dispersed so as to be readily available? If political organizations, representing rival ideologies, are dominant in community life, are parallel social services also provided? If they are not available, should they be provided? These questions represent only the most obvious few of those that can be posited for any ethnic community. As these questions get answered, policy questions could be raised, such as, should more resources be spent on ethnospecific services or should mainstream agencies be modified to accommodate the identified needs?

Benchmark D and the Family

The Framework implies an ongoing process in order to express an individual's experience. From that point of view, there may be no distinctive line between Benchmarks C, the Settlement period, and D. For many people, the community at D is the same one as at C. For such people, Benchmark D draws attention to the person's growing sense of belonging to that community and a growing ability to pay more attention to issues other than strictly survival ones. A family may have chosen the community for its ethnic component or it is certainly possible that there is little awareness by a family of what is available in the community or which ethnic groups are represented.

The process of the family coming into Canada and settling down might include sequential migration of family members. Thus, before all the members are settled at Benchmark D, many years can elapse, and each new family immigrant will go through the process of settling in at different times, and under different family and community conditions. This type of immigration is extremely stressful to a family and many social and health problems can result. Occasionally members of a large family have the resources to buy housing stock in an area so that kin and acquaintances can settle down in proximity to each other. Here, the family becomes centred in a location that highly supports ethnic identity.

Of immigrants who are sponsored, especially under refugee conditions, many end up a long way from the location at Benchmark C. For example, a few Vietnamese refugees were sponsored by groups in northern Canada. When sponsorship ended, they drifted closer to other Vietnamese people in Southern communities, a cultural shift that could be almost as severe as the original one from a refugee camp.

Benchmark D and Native Peoples

Finally, again putting the "First People" last, for Natives the "community phase" or Benchmark D would be the movement to treaty lands and reserves, away from their ancestral homes. The story of these moves has been written about in many ways: there have been government versions of what happened; historians and anthropologists also have documented many aspects of this era of Canadian history. Now, Native People themselves, as they become professionally trained, are writing about it from their perspective. Obviously, practitioners of whatever background, need to know much about this phase of Native history and the different perspectives about it. The most recent shift is the movement of Natives from the reserves to the cities. The city as a "community" for many people of Native ancestry has yet to be thoroughly documented. Perhaps this time the documenters will be of Native ancestry.

BENCHMARK E: ETHNOCULTURAL IDENTITY

Ethnic Identity and Professional Work

Any discussion of ethnic identity leads back to the ethnic group with whom one is associated. Once again, as in Chapter 7, the image should be drawn of layers of transparencies, one for each Benchmark, depicting the ongoing effect of the forces set in motion at Benchmark A, the place of origin.

For the practitioner, there are a number of immediate issues. First, because a person's appearance has so much to do with our expectation about identity, the problem of stereotyping a person's identity is very pronounced. This issue has very high salience for our interaction with colleagues, clients or patients. Age, race and sex are the first visual signs of identity and are the three important dimensions along which stereotyping occurs; much societal attention is now being paid to these dimensions. All three are related to culture and in Chapter 10 the difficulty of identifying people by their racial appearance is examined. Suffice it to say here that racial appearance is a poor predictor of cultural identity, and race, age and sex tell little about interests or competence.

Another aspect of identity is non-verbal behaviour. In Chapters 5 and 6, various dimensions of non-verbal behaviour were explored: the sounds of voices, accents, eye contact, the social distance maintained while interacting and so on, carry meanings that are rooted in cultural expectations. Very often people are not aware of their non-verbal behaviour and the meanings they may unconsciously communicate. This arena has been little studied in Canada, but for practitioners it has far-reaching consequences. Once again the outward, behavioural signs of ethnicity may not convey what is meant and felt by a person, and those interpreting the signs may collect inaccurate information about the person's identity. For example, a person who speaks softly and does not make eye contact may erroneously be assessed as having low self-esteem. In actual fact, it may be that person is expressing what they deem is the proper respect for a professional helper, and has high self-esteem. A value from one cultural framework often cannot be accurately used to evaluate the behaviour derived from another.

A very large aspect of identity has to do with cultural values. In Chapters 3 and 4, through a method called "contexting," cultural values important to identity were organized in a way that is both universalistic and yet permits individuation. However, the practical application of these ideas is very complex and some examples are given. Following this, ethnic identity research in Canada is briefly described.

Applications of Ethnic Identity Phenomena

Ethnocultural identity is a complex phenomenon. Superficially, it seems easy to identify someone as "ethnic" if they speak English (French) with an accent, live in an ethnic enclave and eat ethnic food. However, those who have been studying ethnic identity for decades in Canada, as well as in other countries, find the issue quite complex and a very varied phenomenon indeed. Whatever this ethnic identity represents for an individual or family, it is an important topic for helping professionals.

The term "identity" in some sense summarizes all that has been said so far and can be considered a resultant of all past experiences by the individual. Understanding it is an essential route to entering a person's frame of reference and understanding how the relation between one particular individual and a professional helper will proceed.

For example, if a woman is from a traditional setting that proscribes any familiarity with men not in the family, then a male doctor at her bedside can deeply offend her and her family. Likewise, if a person is from a cultural milieu in which the "balancing of forces" is a crucial part of healthful living, then modern medical help provided in such a way that it cannot be placed into this traditional framework can be very upsetting, more a problem than a cure. And again, if a person is from a setting in which "respectability" has high value, then he/she may react very strongly if a police officer confronts them publicly and thereby threatens his/her "respectability."

The professional helping work that must be done will be more effective when it is based on understanding how the person's identity can be used in a positive way or, at least, be taken into account. It is a "rule of thumb" that working **with** identity elements will be more successful than working **against** them, or even working as if there are no differences between people when workers apply their usual methods as if unassailably generic.

Ethnocultural identity is focussed on as Benchmark E (Figure 8.3), although, of course, this identity exists from early in the person's life. It is placed at this point here to show in a systematic way the many contributing influences on it. In particular, the ethnocultural community of Benchmark D is an important source of ethnic identity. However, there is not always a good "fit" between these community variables and any particular individual or family identity.

For the remainder of the chapter, various ethnic identity research is touched on in order to show what kind of research has been done and how it might be useful to practitioners. However, full justice to the magnititude of the work that has been accomplished is not possible here.

Canadian Ethnic Identity Research

Scholars of Canadian ethnic studies have spent much time trying to account for the varying nature of ethnic identity. Researching this topic has proven quite difficult and the research outcomes often only moderately satisfactory. A short examination of the kinds of studies that have been completed will reveal why it is difficult to predict or even fully describe cultural identity.

A major problem in studying identity is that some aspects are observable and hence relatively easy to conceptualize and measure while other aspects are purely internal and subjective, measurable only by asking attitudinal-type questions. Since identity is a life-long process, it matters as well when the measurements are taken or questions asked. Moreover, researchers have to make decisions about issues such as what weight to place on internal versus external indicators of identity, because we do not have well worked out ideas about what we exactly mean by ethnic identity. It is a concept that is at best vague and shadowy in the minds of most Canadians, and this is reflected in the inexactitude of research on ethnic identity.

Of course, part of the social researchers' job is to operationalize the concepts which are to be studied, and different scholars have focussed on different facets. In one way or another, all the measures focus on ways people may interact with like-ethnic people.

Objective Components of Ethnic Identity

Raymond Breton has looked at the extent to which the ethnic community is viewed as a resource to people. People need several kinds of resources and he looked at two major areas: one, the broad area of becoming fully incorporated in the society, and the other, problems of cultural loss. The former includes problems of social acceptance and discrimination, and the latter was concerned with the maintenance of traditions, customs and the use of the group's language. Breton (1981) compared nine ethnic groups in their propensity to use ethnic organizations to solve a variety of problems. He found great variation amongst the nine groups he studied as regards their willingness to use and optimism about their ethnic leadership and organizations as sources of help.

Occupational Segregation and Identity

Another researcher, Jeffrey Reitz, looked at "work role segregation," i.e., the degree to which a person worked in a setting in which employers, supervisors, co-workers, etc., tended to be from the majority group, his own group, or some other group (Reitz, 1981: 2). Also the issue of occupation itself, the nature of daily work, is a topic of importance to service helpers. In terms of ethnic identity, it certainly will enhance and develop ethnic identity if co-workers are of the same group; conversely, if there are very few majority group or mainstream people with whom to interact on a daily basis, there is less opportunity to learn about the wider Canadian culture.

Reitz studied the same nine groups as Breton and found wide variations in work role segregation. He developed an index that measured the concentration of an ethnic group in a particular occupation (Reitz, 1981: 35) in 1978. Some examples of high job concentration by ethnicity were:

Italian Men:	brick and stone masons and tile setters, barbers and hairdressers;
Italian Women:	various fabricating, assembling and repairing occupations; textiles, leather and fur;

Jewish Men:	medicine and health occupations;
Jewish Women:	supervisors, sales occupations, commodities;
British Men:	firefighting occupation;
British Women:	supervisors, reception, information, mail and message distribution;
West Indian Men:	medicine and health occupations, welding and flame cutting;
West Indian Women:	nursing aids and orderlies;
Chinese Men:	chefs and cooks; waiters, barbers and various other service occupations;
Chinese Women:	sewing machine operators, textiles.

The occupational indices of concentration varied greatly: e.g., of those men who were brick and stone masons it was 16.8 times more likely than average that such a wage earner was Italian. This high figure compares with sewing machine operators where of women so employed, it was only 3.5 times more likely that Chinese women were there. As is the case for any statistical information, care must be taken to understand what the particular statistic actually means.

Residential Segregation and Identity

Warren Kalbach has looked at yet another aspect of ethnic identity. In addition to interacting with each other on the job, it is obvious that how much people interact in their neighbourhoods will affect the nature of their ethnic identity. He developed an index of ethnic residential segregation, and studied eighteen major ethnic populations in Toronto, using as a reference, one population of English origin in 1971 census tracts. He found that people were aware of the ethnic character of their own neighbourhoods and that the residential proximity was consistent with their perceptions. He emphasized that one's attitude about the importance of their ethnic origin, as well as the levels of ethnic-related activities were linked to residential patterns. Finally, he said that the ethnic character of a neighbourhood appears to serve as a facilitator or inhibitor of participation in ethnic-related activities. Put in another way, those who lived in areas of low ethnic segregation appeared more assimilated into the mainstream culture.

Subjective Components of Ethnic Identity

Although sociological studies will always lead from the social/group level of analysis, some studies focus more deeply on the subjective/internal consequences of membership in a group. Of the many scholars interested in this aspect, two, Reitz and Isajiw, are briefly considered here.

In a 1980 study, Reitz examined the nature of identity more broadly. He developed concepts of membership in ethnic groups. There is the person with **"full"** membership who interacts and identifies with his/her ethnic group. Another kind of membership is called **"nominal"** where a person does not interact with like-ethnics but does identify as a member of the group. The reverse of this last is called **"latent"** membership where a person interacts with people of the same group but does not identify as one of that group (Reitz, 1980: 93).

Although full ethnic membership seems readily appreciated, there are pitfalls even in this for the service provider. For example, if a community has major cleavages along religious or political lines, a professional helper needs to know on which sides of these cleavages the client or colleague is. A worker who identifies with one political or religious faction may not be accepted by fellow ethnic colleagues or clients on the other side. This issue has important implications for hiring personnel and for the way clients are served.

The underlying dynamics of the nominal members are suggested by Reitz and important to understand in a helping relationship. Sometimes a nominal member is cut off by distance from interacting with fellow ethnic group members. Others, however, may disdain the local ethnic community. Sometimes this attitude comes about because the community is "old-fashioned," i.e., was formed many years prior to this person's entry into Canada and the ideas maintained in the community have long ago been overturned in the home country. Ideas as basic as morality and as superficial as fashion may be involved. Sometimes, the disdain may come as a reaction to perceptions from other Canadians who seem to see this community and its ways as quaint or unimportant. In the rush to belong and integrate, there may be a wanting to get away from old country patterns and contacts. These sorts of dynamics are important for helpers to understand in order to maintain positive relationships. Blindly assuming that all newcomers want to retain ethnic patterns or are like older-resident members of the ethnic community is poor professional work.

Latent members, those who interact with fellow ethnics but deny ethnic identity may be a puzzling and difficult syndrome for helpers. Reitz suggests that such "de facto membership" may be due to a belief that ethnic communities do not or should not exist in Canada. These people may have patterns of behaviour that are externally identified as ethnic, but do not admit or are not aware of them as "ethnic" (Reitz, 1980: 93). As mentioned earlier in this book, workers should not label people by their ethnicity and, therefore, people should be worked with on the basis they project, and from where they begin — possibly identifying simply as "Canadian," but at times exhibiting behaviour patterns that seem "ethnic."

In different work, Isajiw (1981) added to an understanding of ethnic identity by researching factors relating mainly to the "felt" identity or internal, subjective one. The first dimension is "**cognitive**" and includes self-images and images of one's group. These images may be stereotypes. It also includes historical knowledge of the group and the selections made here may have important symbolic connotations and play an important part in identity.

The second aspect is "**moral**," the feeling of obligations to the group. For Isajiw, this is a central aspect of subjective identity and obviously of importance to helping professionals who are assisting in a network of helping relations or where the absence of a network is felt by the client (or ethnic professional).

The third aspect is the "**affective**" one referring to the feeling of attachment to the group. These feelings include feelings of security with group members as well as with the cultural patterns of the group. The fourth dimension is "**fiducial**" or trust in the group. This aspect is the obverse of the feeling of obligation—if one fulfils obligations to others then one should be able to count on support from them when needed.

Isajiw sees these four dimensions being differentially retained or lost in different areas of social life and, therefore, needing separate analysis. He compares the retention of feelings of obligation, language retention and so forth between ethnic groups and between generations (Isajiw, 1981: 44-62). The values in probabilistic terms or percentages are not very useful for the professional, but the idea of variation between groups and between generations along identity lines is an important backdrop for multicultural work. It prepares the mind for variability and gives the conceptual labels to follow some of the variability as it emerges.

Benchmark E: Its Place in the Framework

Though these studies were about ethnic groups, for practitioners it presents interesting ideas about how clients and patients might vary in the way they relate to these issues and identify with their group. For social workers and others frequently involved in helping clients find assistance of various types, the clients' ethnic community is seldom considered, although many ethnic agencies are developing various programmes. As these workers become more aware of those resources, they will also have to be sensitive to the range of ways any one client may view the resources: some may feel such resources are ineffective whereas others may perceive some positive and encouraging help available. Also, some may feel closely identified with agencies within their ethnic community, but others will seek out mainstream services. In addition, since any one researcher's findings apply to a particular locale in a particular time period, the exact findings may not be equally applicable to all who read them. Thus, as pointed out in Chapter 2, p. 8–10, academic work often should be used more for the raising of questions than for specific answers.

Now the Benchmark for identity can be sketched in. As can be seen from the dimensions laid down so far, like the Ethnocultural Community at Benchmark D, this one is also very complex and not easily reduced to simple terms for a chart. However, given the many variations on ethnic identity, a simple typology from high ethnic identity to low or no ethnic identity can be used. These categories should raise questions at least about which identity dimensions and for what purpose identity is "high." Reitz's and Isajiw's categories mentioned earlier form the backbone of the typologies.

> Ea - high in ethnic identity and in interaction with like-ethnic members
> Eb - moderate sense of obligation or closeness to other ethnic members
> Ec - low sense of obligation or closeness to other ethnic members (this includes nominal members)
> Ed - no sense of ethnic identity, identity forgotten or denied (this includes latent members)

Fig. 8.3 — Ethnocultural Identities

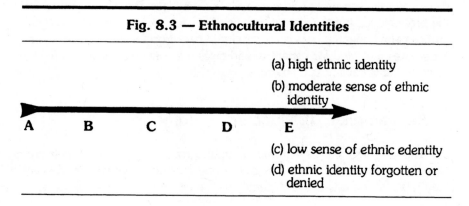

(a) high ethnic identity

(b) moderate sense of ethnic identity

A   B   C   D   E

(c) low sense of ethnic edentity

(d) ethnic identity forgotten or denied

SUMMARY

This completes the Benchmarks for the First Generation. The Framework points to the main dimensions of ethnic identity as it unfolds in a person's life after a major culture shift. Because these shifts are so portentous to Canada and meaningful to an individual's whole life—this is not a trip abroad for work or play—many frames of reference are needed to get the picture of the whole; a multicultural country is one where the essence of the national culture is to be diverse and for no one culture to have complete sway. In fact, the task is to keep allowing new groups to feel that they belong. This is a difficult process because it seems to be "human nature" to resist change, hang on to what one has gained and exclude the new and different, even when one has just been through this process oneself.

The Acculturative Framework: Part 3 — The Second Generation And Beyond

We now pick up the thread of ethnic identity in the second generation and follow it through into the Canadian mainstream. There are difficulties in doing this, however. First, Canadian-born people often seem reluctant to delve into their ethnic identity, beyond a superficial acknowledgement of it. As Canadians, we are not on easy terms with our varying backgrounds. We do not talk about our ethnic identities in a comfortable, familiar way. My impression is that the ethnic part of ourselves is not easily recognized. Later in this chapter, I will describe an exercise on ethnic root behaviour patterns that shows how our cultures of origin still affect us deeply though this effect may be invisible to us.

Another piece of evidence for our unease with our ethnic identity is that our vocabulary about ethno-identity is stunted and underdeveloped. For example, the words "ethnic" and "immigrant" can be used in many ways but we do not seem comfortable with their many meanings and able to thread our way among them.

My own experience with this issue comes from talking to students in Social Work classes about their ethnic identity. What I have found is that though students may have been together for one or two years in classes with a great deal of opportunity to know each other, they have no idea about each others' background till the subject is raised deliberately and people are asked to talk about themselves and their family background. Generally, students enjoy the process and are amazed to find so much variation amongst themselves in ethnicity. I believe that as long as we look the same racially, we assume we are the same.

Why bother to hunt for the "thread" of ethnic identity if Canadians have left the thread to be worn away by neglect and denial? As mentioned in Chapter 2, it is important for professionals for several reasons. Looking for the quality and form of ethnic identity is a way of being inclusive and even-handed about ethnicity and race so that some people are not obliged to experience negative stigma from their ethnoracial identity while others may ignore it. If it is important for some people then perhaps it is important to everyone. At least two analytical trails lead away from this idea.

First, in this chapter, the premise forwarded is that the values stemming from ethnicity have more long-term effects than most suspect. Generations after the first family members came, descendants exhibit patterns related to their ethnic origins at Benchmark A, even though they are unlabelled and often unrecognized as such by those who have the patterns. As well, the Canadian-born generations include those well conscious of a deeply held and practiced ethnic identity (Figure 9.1).

Second, in chapter 10, since ethnicity and race have different meanings and outcomes, the combinations of race and ethnicity have very different sequelae for each combination. These differing identities are discussed there in some detail.

BENCHMARK F: THE SECOND GENERATION

As ethnic identity was difficult to summarize at Benchmark E for immigrants, it is even more complex in the next generation. Individual people can remain very strongly identified with the ethnocultural group or seem to lose it all. For example, someone born in the very large Italo-Canadian community in Toronto could easily appear as "ethnic" as the parents. Yet, such a person would have gone through the Canadian school system and grown up in a Canadian neighbourhood. Thus, the underlying content of the "Italianness" of that person will be very different from that of their parents. Alongside this person, in that Canadian school, could have sat a student who believed she/he had no ethnic identity at all. Between these extreme types are all the variations and degrees of cultural loss, retention and assimilation that can be imagined.

The timeline continues on into the Second Generation:

Fig. 9.1 — The Second Generation

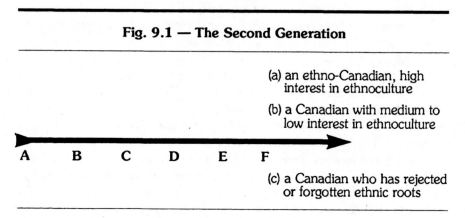

(a) an ethno-Canadian, high interest in ethnoculture

(b) a Canadian with medium to low interest in ethnoculture

A   B   C   D   E   F

(c) a Canadian who has rejected or forgotten ethnic roots

In his work on ethnic identity, Isajiw pointed out that ethnic identity loss is mainly experienced from the first generation to the second. This should not be confused with the loss that started at Benchmark B, when the first family members experienced the culture shift. In addition, the loss is differently experienced over different cultural attributes, and loss does not necessarily mean assimilation or the replacement of one pattern for another. For example, a person may lose much of their ethnic language capability, but not replace it fully with an English language capability.

The second generation is the pivotal generation; it has one foot in the immigrant culture and the other in the new culture. A child born into an immigrant home rushes out to play in a Canadian neighbourhood. There is no more effective socializing force in many instances than the neighbourhood gang in which a child must play. It is in this crucible that a child learns a particular local brand of Canadian culture. Perhaps it is one where the ethnic language is spoken or one where it is eschewed. Perhaps another ethnicity has the most power and the child who is different must win a place in it. Sometimes, a child must endure name-calling and other forms of bigotry. These "battles" are fought in school yards, on the streets and near home. There is no escaping them.

Some resultant modification of the original cultural forms is bound to take place. Parents will react, depending on how they see adjustment being made. Children may be ashamed of their parents, fearful of teachers who do not understand who they are, and hurt by the racial slurs of classmates. But many good things happen as well. Parents adjust and support their children, teachers try to show a special caring spirit, and classmates open up wonderful new worlds. Any combination of factors can occur and just what has been the experience of any one person or family can only be ascertained by asking about it. (This, in fact, can be an excellent way for a trainer to start students thinking about their own ethnic identity.)

Studies of second generation persons show this is a generation of higher incomes than the previous generation. It is also a generation of achievement in the English language. It appears also to be concurrent with ethnic language loss. Sometimes there is differential loss of language by the various adult family members. Perhaps one parent will learn English (French) and use every opportunity to excel in the new language. The other parent, though, may retreat into sole use of the ethnic language and reject English, or lack any opportunity to learn and use English. Children growing up in this milieu may speak English to one parent and the ethnic language to the other parent. Family dynamics can also reflect this polarized condition between the parents; the language issue may be cause or effect of parental tensions.

Professionals working with families must become aware of how language patterns change, or how changes in any other aspect of the original culture are involved in the family adjustment. Church membership, old country moral standards and even eating patterns can become the currency of family struggle (Sluzki, 1979). Thus, the second generation is a focal point for the struggle and tension between the immigrant and even old-world culture, and the adaptation required or learned in the Canadian context.

BENCHMARK G: THE THIRD GENERATION AND BEYOND

Into the home of the second generation, and especially in later family generations, comes the phenomenon called ethnocultural "returning," or "rediscovery." It is acknowledged as BENCHMARK G (b) on Fig.9.2. Often after a generation or two in which ethnicity appeared less important than "making it" in Canada, has come a rediscovery or return to the ethnic culture and perhaps the adoption of an ethnic identity. This can happen in a home where everyone seems very adapted to the Canadian scene. Studies show that the rates for returning vary by ethnic group, but it is a trend that has been found both in the United States (Herberg, 1960; Hansen, 1962), and in Canada (Reitz, 1980; Kalbach, 1981; Isajiw, 1981).

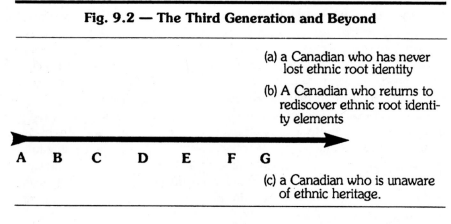

Fig. 9.2 — The Third Generation and Beyond

(a) a Canadian who has never lost ethnic root identity

(b) A Canadian who returns to rediscover ethnic root identity elements

A   B   C   D   E   F   G

(c) a Canadian who is unaware of ethnic heritage.

It is not the whole ethnic way of life that is rediscovered or returned to, of course, but some aspects of the culture of origin. It may be learning the ethnic language, attending the church of the homeland, learning the songs and dances, or reading history and literature from the old country. Reasons for this return vary widely. One principal influence for this in Canada over the last two decades has been the setting of Multiculturalism as official state policy in 1971, and the passage of the Multiculturalism Act in 1988; each furthered the legitimacy of all ethnic cultures and established the rule that there are no official minorities in this nation. For a family, the return may be a curiosity felt or a need to enrich a mass-culture lifestyle. Usually there is a strong need to connect with origins/cultural roots as a Canadian phenomenon.

ETHNIC ROOT BEHAVIOUR PATTERNS

(Much of what follows was originally published in the *International Journal of Intercultural Relations*, Herberg, 1982)

Following the Thread of the Culture of Origin: Discovering Ethnic Root Behaviour Patterns

This Acculturative Framework or chart can be amplified or reduced for different purposes. Some years ago, in an effort to make the transformation of culture more vivid, I developed a pictorial way of presenting this idea. I used the simple design of a flower to stand for a cultural pattern. By adding and deleting shapes that stood for a transformation in the Canadian environment, new, residual ethnic patterns result. The Benchmarks of the Acculturative Framework are roughly the same and are points in the transformation.

In Figure 9.3, "The Evolution of an Ethnic Behaviour Pattern," the "flower" that stands for a cultural pattern from a country of origin — Italy, Jamaica, Greece, etc. — is at Benchmark A. It is pictured rooted to the cultural soil of the home country at some past time. It is a dynamic, alive pattern that here can change and die and be replaced. The pattern can be abstracted, described and talked about, but the people who exhibit this pattern in this country are usually unaware of it. It is part of the life state — absolute, unnoticed and unquestioned. When the person emigrated, the pattern was carried in that person's mind and behaviour to the new country (at Benchmark C).

Fig. 9.3 The Evolution of an Ethnic Behaviour Pattern

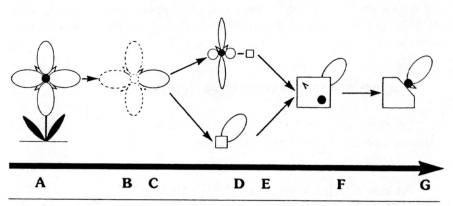

A   B   C   D   E   F   G

Source: Reprinted from Dorothy Herberg, "Discovering Ethnic Root Behaviours," Copyright © 1982,
           Pp. 153-168, with permission from Pergamon Press Ltd., Headington Hill Hall, Oxford   OX3
           0BW, UK.

The dotted lines of the flower petals and sepals represent that much of
the pattern at point C has become   only an idea reflected in someone's
behavioural repertoire. A little of the pattern may be concrete and can literally be carried to the new land — a costume, recipe, book, furniture, musical instrument. The solid petal and the one solid sepal symbolize these concrete possessions. The rootedness is gone because the pattern is no longer
part of its ongoing national culture. As the individual or group adapts, the
cultural idea becomes planted in Canadian soil and at Benchmarks D-E, a
new pattern evolves.

The recognizable, but different, flower at the top of Figure 9.3, symbolizes a full ethnic form of the pattern. It is accomplished in an institutionally
complete or highly sufficient ethnic community. The "small square"
attached by a hyphen acknowledges the Canadian part of the pattern that
links it to a real Canadian setting.

The pattern at the bottom, a larger square and one full petal, symbolizes a pattern that has been formed in mainstream conditions where few or
none of the like ethnicity are living. Much of the pattern has had to be
replaced by the (square) Canadian pattern — even if not fully replaced
(Isajiw, 1981: 1), but some parts of the cultural pattern will be maintained
even if done in isolation from other ethnic group members. Hence the
square and a petal symbolize a cultural life that is a unique mix of cultures.

It should be recognized, though, that we know very little about the families who keep their culture while isolated from others of their ethnicity-race-religion.

In between the two reduced flower patterns are many other intermediate versions. These have not been drawn to prevent the diagram from being cluttered. However, intermediate forms can be readily imagined.

The large square at Benchmark F is the acculturated Canadian. The remains of the flower appear disconnected and irregularly attached now as the tufts, loops and circles of the original flower. The second generation person can still be clearly connected to the fuller pattern at D-E, but the connection to the old ways will differ from those of the immigrant generation. Some patterns are maintained in a compulsive, repetitive way, important to the person's identity, but unlabelled as ethnic patterns. These residual patterns can be as widely different as domestic routines, family visiting and hospitality patterns, walking patterns, dream-analysis, and a variety of seemingly meaningless behaviours.

The origin of these residual, unlabelled patterns is, of course, Benchmark A, the Country of Origin. There, they were part of the larger national culture, but not noticeably separated out as they have become, generations later, in the new environment. It is hypothesized that these residual behaviour patterns carry within them the kernel of important values from the home culture. In their residual form they often symbolize these values to those who exhibit the patterns. Unfortunately, there often is little conscious awareness of the meaning of these behaviours and very often the original functions of the behaviours are not fulfilled in the new setting. One result is that one cannot predict completely what underlying values are represented by the behaviour pattern.

Finally, at Benchmark G, a piece of the "square Canadian" is consciously replaced with an ethnic pattern, here represented as a piece of the original flower, replacing a corner of the square. This pattern symbolizes the rediscoverer-returner, the one who rediscovers or consciously returns to a connection with those long-disjoined roots.

Exercise: Inducing an Ethnic Root Behaviour Pattern — A Process of Self-discovery

Summary of the exercise

First, look for a behaviour that is repeated over and over again. It is a behaviour that is often traceable back to childhood. The pattern once identified, can usually be found to be applied by the person compulsively and somewhat irrationally in context. Often there is a belief that other people (family, neighbours, clients) ought to follow this behaviour too. Even so, it is sometimes an uncomfortable pattern of behaviour, but still very important to the person possessing it. They believe they will always have that pattern: it is part of the self, the personal identity, and in this sense is exquisitely meaningful to the person. When this pattern is traced back to earlier patterns in the family, it can often be found rooted in the national culture of origin. This behaviour is called an ethnic root.

Steps of the Exercise

The process of ethnic root cultivation is usually a very instructive process for the person in their tracing back an important piece of behaviour to its source in the acculturative frame. The tracing back from one's own experience is called induction; this is the opposite of starting with a theoretical idea and looking for what that idea suggests. Ideas from induction are called operant values and those from deduction are called ideal values. It is discovering operant values that is the objective of the exercise.

The process of self-discovery can be aided by the keeping of a daily journal, which can be viewed after a week, or two or three, to see what is done repeatedly. For some people such a pattern is easily found, but for others it takes a long period of "looking" at one's personal behaviour to finally see what is "there." Usually, the pattern is so obvious that it is overlooked, is "invisible." As the pattern surfaces, examples of when it occurs are recorded in the journal and become the evidence for substantiating the existence of the pattern. As the reflective process continues, the meanings of the pattern should also be recorded; by this the value underlying the pattern becomes clear.

Doing all this, the person finds a personal connection to their own ethnicity and often becomes, thereby, more open to respecting and learning about other people's ethnicity. It is hypothesized that an openness to learning about ethnicity is an important element in the attitudinal set to accepting differences.

A Personal "Walking Root"

My own experience with the process started with discovering my own "walking" ethnic root. One winter day, when I was out walking I suddenly noticed that it was a very cold, windy day. There was no one else outside, but there was I, out walking for no purpose than to just "go for a walk." It suddenly struck me as strange, and I decided to inquire into this sometimes strange behaviour further. I discovered that "going for a walk" was a repeated behaviour — done at least three or four times a week, in a compulsive, even irrational manner. I felt the need to "go for a walk" often, but for no objective reason, and often in very uncomfortable circumstances — to wit — the extreme cold weather. I have gone for walks in blizzards, sometimes at considerable hazard. In addition to my own need to walk, I found also that I felt other people, especially my family, should also walk. I could feel quite disapproving of them for not wanting to walk and it was hard for me to understand that others close to me would not want to walk. The drive to get others to walk actually produced conflict on a repeated basis, when they felt no need to walk in and of itself.

These interactions with my family occurred many times before I connected those behaviours with my own compulsive walking. If I had been a practising social worker, I asked myself, would I have become angry with a client who asked for bus fare instead of walking to their destination? After pondering the matter for a long while, I realized that I had been heavily socialized into walking behaviour as a child. I was born in Kashmir when my parents were on a walking tour of the Himalayas, and walking was a regular activity when I was with them and later when I was with relatives. All my relatives had English origins one or two generations back. My father was born in Ontario and my mother in England where walking is a pronounced behaviour pattern, e.g., "walking trips by English holidayers in Scotland." It now was easy to connect England to my "walking root."

. My conclusions from this self-revealing process yielded a residual form of an ethnic pattern, and that I would keep the behaviour for myself. For me it is a meaningful activity, but I decided to abstain from insisting that other people engage in it, because although the walking root is a valuable piece of my personal identity property, when used in interaction with others, it can cause unnecessary friction.

Probably, the most important part of this exercise was my discovery of the values symbolized by the repeated behaviour. Why should walking have been so important to me? As I later reflected on the behaviour, I realized that, for me, the walking stood for the character traits of independence, self-reliance and assertiveness.

As I hypothesized further, I realized that these traits were highly valued by my parents and by Britons and Anglo-Canadians. I did not have the opportunity to discuss any of this with my parents and I am not sure that they would have fully agreed with my interpretation of this behaviour, although there is no question about these values having been a part of their own character. Nevertheless, on reflecting on my growing up, I speculate that they believed that if I had these traits, it would lead to security, good fortune and a moral life, outcomes that earnest, caring parents hope for their children. One could go on to suggest that the more earnest and caring the parents, the more intensely the behaviour pattern will be instilled. Thus, the values the parents care about are transmitted, even if the particular behavioural pattern was not used consciously by the parents for that purpose.

For the child there are mixed outcomes. The values underlying the ethnic root behaviour, although usually never verbally explicated, are nevertheless communicated. As well, the behaviour pattern itself, well and truly learned, becomes a compulsive pattern, probably only marginally effective in producing the original functional outcomes. Sometimes the pattern may even become dysfunctional but still adhered to. My walking pattern has, on the whole, been good for me, except when I might have endangered myself, as in walking out in a blizzard. The values that were communicated are certainly not only very important to me but also ones I could not change.

At this stage, my hypothesis is that for me, walking sort of operationalizes the Protestant Ethic, important aspects of which are independence and self-sufficiency in the production of something. However, I also know that walking is a pattern that comes from other places than England and that there are different meanings for this pattern. For example, some have reported that the walking root means freedom, and a feeling of "breaking out of the mould." For others it is clearly a health practice and mainly related to exercise. However, I would not count it an ethnic root behaviour unless the person was at least a generation away from the place of origin, it had the compulsive attributes and went back to childhood. Walking is a genuinely important behaviour to many people but it is not always a root pattern. When it is, I would surmise that it carries a strong underlying set of values that are even more important than the behaviour itself.

Other Examples of Ethnic Root Behaviours

Over the years, many patterns have emerged from this exercise conducted by social work students. A frequently occurring one has to do with saving leftover articles like string, pieces of aluminum foil, or plastic wrap, rubber bands, paper bags, and the like. Even though the accumulation of these can cause a lot of trouble for the collector, it seems impossible for them not to keep these materials. Conflict with others about the stuffed-full drawers, the brimming over baskets or boxes, cannot deter the rooted collector. The values that underlie this repeated pattern could be varied. Frequently the behaviour is rooted in a thrift value that has been passed down the generations from a British origin, and a Protestant Ethic sort of values; sometimes it appears to have come from the trauma of the Great Depression when their family's deprivation experience resulted in values emphasizing saving. The hoarding of small things, that would otherwise have to be thrown away, resulted. Often, it is an uncomfortable pattern because of the clutter generated by keeping many small things that usually are not needed. The urging of others to throw them away may be the source of repeated conflict, a hallmark of some patterns.

Another arena for repeated patterns is food, often rooted in proscribed or prescribed food practices. Food choice is related to ethnic identity and the preparation of food to observe religious rites, or the need to welcome guests with an overabundance of food is a commonly reported pattern.

Some examples of patterns that have appeared in my students' papers over the years are: punctuality, early rising, windows kept open at night regardless of the season, and tidying up and regular cleaning routines that seem unnecessarily stringent to others and obtrude on other activities are examples of Protestant Ethic values.

Various other behaviours include ones related to security needs such as repeated use of emblems, such as the "figa" used as a warding sign; dream analysis each morning before venturing out of the house; showing respect, for example, by always making the man sit at the head of the dining table; removing shoes at the front door, sometimes to show respect for the woman of the house.

Others are many kinds of repeated movements, such as tapping or rocking as well as humming and singing. Various repeated patterns relate to self-healing when ill or staying healthy.

Further Steps

After a pattern is identified, there should be a period for reflective introspection. Many reflective questions come to mind: what does it feel like; when does it occur; how long have I been doing this; why do I care about doing this; can I stop doing this; do I want to stop; is it hard to stop; what is the meaning of the behaviour in my own words? As the meanings emerge in the mind, they can then be expressed as a value and speculation undertaken to consider the origin of the pattern.

During this reflective process, the student is encouraged not to try to change the pattern but to acknowledge it, know it, appreciate it and generally deepen into the feelings about it, and affirm it as a part of their identity. This process is part of the more general process of integrating knowledge into one's self and into the professional repertoire.

The next stage involves a cognitive process of considering where the value comes from, given that the student has some grasp of their own ethnic background, from having constructed their own acculturative framework analysis. Even if there is not enough information to make a connection to past family history, the value stands in its own right as a part of the identity.

Finally, the student considers whether the value might interfere with their professional practice if it was imposed unwittingly on a client situation. There needs to be a beginning attempt, on the one hand, to start separating one's own values that are of use to oneself and, on the other hand, to consider how one's own values may become, inappropriately, part of the professional activity. This may occur because the values range around many subjects related to practice — family interaction, the showing of respect, attitudes toward work, concerns about saving and using one's time in proper ways, health and illness and many more. The student must begin to learn to separate their personal values from purely professional values, a skill essential in multicultural practice. Both the practitioner and the client thereby are respected.

Characteristics of Ethnic Root Patterns

One of the most marked characteristics of the process of inducing an ethnic pattern, is that what emerges is unpredictable. One cannot say, for example, that if one is of English extraction that there will be a walking pattern in one's repertoire. Sometimes a fellow national will not recognize the pattern at all, sometimes there may be recognition but no particular interest; and sometimes there is interest but it does not seem to carry any special values. Occasionally, there is a "rebellious" root, where the opposite of what the parents wanted is laid down in a compulsive fashion. What is important is the **process** of finding the pattern because self-discovery is encouraged. Usually, genuinely important values are unearthed that could be influential in practice situations. In Social Work, as in most professions, it is an explicit value to not impose values on a client. If values or beliefs are held that are not recognized openly, they can become an underlying dynamic in the practitioner-client relationship that the agency may not be able to monitor or modify, and may not even be consciously intended by the practitioner. Values about what the practitioner believes is proper about working, receiving help, the healing process and other matters can become embedded in the helping process, with the client, with lower power, caught in an unequal and, indeed, unethical struggle. Self-awareness from prior reflective introspection is the only safeguard in these interpersonal spaces.

Other characteristics of ethnic root patterns are that a person's root patterns seem to be done alone; even other members of the same family usually do not share the pattern though friends and family can often point out the pattern. Usually, the behaviours get attached to character traits, e.g., someone who eats a particular food, does not rise early in the morning, or sits at a desk to work instead of working with their hands, is seen to have a weak or poor character. Obviously, these attributions can be very damaging in a relationship. Repeated quarrelling is the result because the person with the rooted pattern cannot let go of the pattern, even though they recognize that it is causing damage.

For people with histories of severe political persecution, there are patterns that reflect the fearfulness or anger that was carried by the parents. Worries about security are reflected in repeated behaviours of checking and rechecking things in the house. Are the lights off? Did I lock the door? Did I turn off the iron? Greatly over-buying food and storing it up may reflect the prolonged fear of starving experienced by a grandparent.

For people who have only recently come to Canada, there has not been time for cultural patterns to be eroded and for the development of the residual, compulsively repeated form as in the case of earlier-generations people. However, it is possible to find repeated behaviour patterns but they are usually found in a more complete form, like the original pattern, and the person remembers the pattern from the place of origin.

THE HOST COMMUNITY

The Host Community and Practitioners

Thus far, the perspective has been from that of the unwinding, transforming culture as it is passed from generation to generation. Another equally important perspective is the one from the host culture. The community that accepts the new immigrant is called the host community. This large aggregate, that is comprised of everyone who has settled in Canada, tends to be silent about newcomers. Underlying that silence is often resentment, frustration and a sense of loss from changed surroundings. There is so much change to buildings, streets, and the configuration of the city, it feels as if one has left home.

Just as the new immigrant went through a culture shift (Benchmark B), the host community, which receives the immigrants and provides the settings for Benchmarks C and D, has a parallel adjustment to make. The adjustment is seldom addressed and politicians who make immigration decisions ignore the impact of unfamiliar cultures on unprepared neighbourhoods. Because preparing people for change has little short-term payoff for politicians, money and energy is not allocated to this function. In fact, like the messenger who got put to death because he bore bad news, politicians may be afraid of the same fate! They seem to prefer to let problems continue where they may, and duck out of sight, and act only when crises make it impossible not to act.

However, it is not completely fair to blame politicians for our own difficulty at facing change. It is the nature of multicultural countries to face a constant enlargement in membership from outside. For the most part, this process of incoming peoples brings the country great richness. Many newcomers are wealthy; most are talented. Given half a chance, most will repay many fold the investment of help given.

The host community is made up of everyone, but it is the earlier generations, the established peoples, who have to take on the role of adjusting to changes. This adaptation should be normatively required and acquired as part of professional training. This is not only a moral requirement, but it is in our own best interests, because well-adjusted people make good citizens and contribute to the common good.

Professional people of the second, third and earlier generations have a larger perspective on Canada than newcomers can possibly have. Even the well-educated newcomer must take a considerable time to understand what the country is like and what is needed. Thus, it is the service providers of earlier generations who must take cognizance of the kind of milieu in which they work and respond appropriately in seeing that truly multicultural work is possible in that milieu. For example, when training about multicultural work is required, it is the service providers that should be the ones to initiate and insist on such training. When information is needed to understand new cultural patterns, these workers should be the ones to ask for this information. Too often it is the newcomers themselves who are left to do all the training and all the adjusting.

In addition to abdicating responsibility for this adjustment, these later generations are often unaware of the cultural patterns that **they** exhibit. There is a "blind spot" about their own patterns, but these patterns are obvious to newcomers. Because of the norms that prevent talking about cultural patterns, and because they may feel alien and want "to belong" to the group, they do not bring forward their complaints. It is a difficult problem to resolve. To reap maximum benefit, it is an agency administration's responsibility to give legitimacy to bringing forward and discussing cross-cultural and cross-racial concerns in the workplace. This is where risk-taking can be seen as an important dimension of multicultural work. In the 1980s, several Toronto agencies took a deep, extensive look at their internal operations, planning exactly how they could become truly multicultural. They uncovered their own norms censuring discussion about race relations and each found ways to start the long process of training all their staff. Each step was a risk-taking venture, and was not always well understood, but both agencies have benefitted from their long process of self-discovery (Metropolitan Toronto Children's Aid Society, 1982) (YWCA, 1982).

The Host Community and Racially Visible Newcomers

For those who are racially visible, the path to integration in their society may be just as hard as for their parents, if their experience is one of continued rejection on the basis of race. For these people, the kind of ongoing social reactions will make a special difference. It is for these people that professionals, in whatever capacity—doctor, nurse, teacher, policeman, social worker — can play a special helping role. There is the need to firmly prohibit discriminatory rules or practises in the professional person's work milieu. Practitioners must learn special sensitivity for children who have been hurt by racial slurs, and to recognize how race can become a negative dynamic.

Da Costa (1976) has shown that the way parents and school personnel handle the issue of racial denigration of a child can have important repercussions for the child's identity. If the issue of race is constantly denied and not taken seriously when the child tries to talk about it, the child may become passive, daydream too much and fall behind in school work. But if it is treated only with reactive aggression and fighting, the child can develop "aggressive and disruptive" behaviour that causes problems in the school. Much can be done by parents and school personnel to make extreme behaviours — extremely passive or very aggressive behaviour — unnecessary. Of course, these situations also apply to adults.

Denial of racial problems is much more common than an aggressive reaction to it. For every racial fight or assault, there are many, many more cases of racial intolerance that are denied not just by the perpetrators but also by the victims. It is not surprising that in a society with strong norms against discussing ethnic and racial values, many people deny that painful ethno-racial events occur.

Part of the adjustment of the host community is to prepare for racial diversity. Some school systems have initiated programmes to help school personnel make this adjustment. A few have instituted penalties for staff who are actively intolerant. But all our institutions — hospitals, police stations, welfare agencies, government and business offices, factories, colleges and universities — should institute programmes to help staff "catch up" to the ethno-racially changing world around them. Where the staff themselves are the racially visible ones, particular attention must be paid to their work environment, including instances of rejection by patients, clients, students and even fellow staff.

In these few pages, only a few of the practical issues growing out of our multicultural/multiracial origins can be mentioned. They are only illustrative, but many studies available present depth analyses: Thomas and Novogrodsky, 1983; Thomas, 1987; MTCAS, 1982;, Pitman 1977; Toronto School Board, 1976; B.C. Task Force on Immigrant Women, 1982, among a great many others.

HUMAN SERVICES PRACTICE PRINCIPLES

It has been noted earlier in this book that academic studies can provide a useful backdrop to professional multicultural work. It would be ideal if Canadian ethnic studies literature formed part of the educational background of all helping workers. This branch of scholarly endeavour provides important concepts and directs one towards ways of enquiring about these concepts that would enable practitioners to develop their own knowledge base.

However, human service practice is action-oriented and must diverge in important respects from purely academic interests. First, it is often at the individual and family level that service intervention must occur and academic generalized information can only give rough guidelines for any individual case. Second, helping services personnel are often called on to assist those with the least ethnic cohesion and/or who are poorly integrated into Canadian society. Those who are **not** connected to networks stemming from place of origin and family are often those who need the most help.

Third, we must, of necessity, do much "talking about" ethnicity because, for the most part, ethnicity is expressed in behaviour and is therefore existential. Academic researchers must specifically spell out all their findings, but service providers have the option of doing and "behaving" as well. In fact, for many clients or patients a great deal of what is communicated will be communicated non-verbally. Chapters 5 and 6 have amplified this idea.

As pointed out earlier, the age, race and gender of the worker are the first "messages" one receives. Workers must know what messages they are communicating by their presence in a situation. In addition, what seems "cultural" to an observer cannot be dealt with explicitly in practise because many people are unaware of themselves as "cultural beings." An overview of the differences in cultural or ethnic awareness can be imagined. Using the Acculturative Framework as a rough set of points, it can be hypothesized that awareness of ethnicity/culture is low in the Settlement Phase (C), increases during the development of ethnic identity (D-E), and drops out of awareness in later generations (F) except for (G) where it is sometimes rediscovered or returns.

It is paradoxical that, even those whose ethnic identity is very high, may not perceive or understand it. In such cases, if the worker talks about, "programmes to retain ethnic identity," the programme must be explicitly and fully explained, e.g., "this is a programme, provided by the school board and given after school hours to teach children about their own cultural heritage." Ethnic identity in the abstract is for many newcomers too much an unconscious part of them to be perceived. Thus, it very much matters how ethnic identity is approached.

Ethno-specific community workers often are people with a high cultural awareness. If such personnel have worked through feelings of denial or of strong activism regarding their culture, then they can be more even-handed with clients or patients who have varying attachments to their culture. These workers can accept those who want to get away from their culture or depreciate it, as well as those who demand that high ethnic loyalty be shown at all times. For example, a Portuguese-Canadian worker told me, "They feel angry if I don't speak in Portuguese — as though I was being disloyal — but I'm not." Such workers have gained perspective on the adjustment process.

In contrast, for the second and third generations, ethnic identity awareness is usually very low or "forgotten." This is a different kind of low awareness than earlier in the process. Being aware of the very many ways in which ethnic identity can be structured leads to issues emerging from discussion of the Framework. For example, from Benchmark D, the Ethnic Community, a question arises about those who came to Canada and followed lives isolated from those of their own background (D_d in Figure 8.1). What happens to them? Do they move into Canadian life easily? What inner identity thinking do they have? Since losing one's culture does not mean that it is necessarily replaced by another cultural set, what deficits are they aware of? Are isolated people more affected by the loss of culture? Is the home atmosphere created by parents who feel or experience an extreme cultural loss, different from a mainstream home or one ensconced in a highly sufficient ethnic environment?

Also related to stages of the Acculturative Framework, very little is known about individuals' cultural adjustment over a long time period. Often literature and poetry are the best modes for communicating the complex feelings that the death-rebirth (immigration) experience must bring. Reports from my students suggest that the cultural conflict can be expected, and does not go away easily; for some, the conflict continues and is not resolved. For example, the issue of females retaining the values of chastity, modesty, docility and subservience to men is rigidly maintained in some families. Female students sometimes report compartmentalized lives: living according to one set of values in their parent's home, but a different set outside. Even after they have left home, the issue can continue via underlying guilt that never completely disappears. Such people appear well-adjusted and competent, but their inner life can be beset by doubts, fear or frustration. The first and second generation bear the burden of the potential conflicts in these acculturative changes.

Some people in an ethnic community do not ever seem to settle in. Their adjustment becomes a prolonged Benchmark C, Settlement period, experience. Danuta Mostwin (1976: 112) reported on a Polish immigrant saying "I feel like I am waiting for another train to get on." Such people are not numerous, but may be over-represented in caseloads of health or school personnel, or of social workers. Such people often still feel "temporary," and often still expect to return to the country of origin. They are unsatisfied with Canada, sometimes seeing it as a country of loose morals and no "culture" in comparison to their high context culture of origin. They may also experience repeated difficulties at work. Their children often are the ones seen by school social workers — the lack of adjustment in the parents is seen as child misbehaviour or under-achievement at school. Persons working with these chronic problem cases wistfully wish that better preparation prior to immigration were possible. They often think that the "$1,000 cure" of a visit to the place of origin, talked of earlier (Munro, 1981: 80) might be a helpful antidote.

In addition to those who never seem to adjust are other difficult situations, including those families with sequenced migration, sponsorship breakdowns, refugee trauma, and long-term language problems, such as an inability to master English/French even after long years in Canada (Herberg, 1985). Such people often had complicated cultural histories. For example, an East Indian from Guyana has a complex cultural mix by the time they reach Canada, because there may be a Hindu family structure from one or two generations back brought by a Hindu immigrant to Guyana, and superimposed on a West Indian society. Such a person already has adapted, in some unique way, to the blend of cultures. Once in Canada, the practitioner can have difficulty understanding this particular cultural blend. The individual themself may be unaware that this blend is perceived as unusual by the helping person. Such blended cultures are common.

Trinidadian society encompasses Christian, Muslim and Hindu backgrounds. Jamaica has East Indian, Chinese and Black and Anglo members. Sri Lanka has Moslem, Hindu, Malayasian and Christian elements and a Sri Lankan person could have been exposed to a blend of any or all of these elements. To the extent that Christianity was introduced in the place of origin, a "westernizing" influence would have started early in an apparently Asian setting. Often these influences meant cultural loss earlier in that person's family history. Adjustment in Canada, however, may thereby be easier, although the professional person may have trouble understanding the multiple cultural constituents of such persons.

A SUMMARY OF THE ACCULTURATIVE FRAMEWORK

In sum, this chapter has laid out the logical steps of the Framework for those who are acculturated to Canada because they, and in some cases their parents, were born in Canada. The second generation focussed on at Benchmark F, is the pivotal generation. From the experience of their parents they know about the "old country" origins and the immigration experience; from their own knowledge of the Canadian school system and growing up in Canadian neighbourhoods they know about Canada. This double knowledge can make second generation people particularly useful in multicultural helping work.

Benchmark G summarizes all the identities beyond the second generation. Special techniques are often needed to identify ethnic values that still operate but at a more subconscious level.

People at these later points in the Framework are often still proud of their origins although in many cases people are unaware of origins and identify simply as "Canadian." If training requirements are to be evenhanded, people of those generations will have to explore their origins in a deliberate and systematic way.

The Acculturative Framework is a systematic way of charting the many contributions to existential cultural behaviour. It is a way of recording sequences of events that can be considered as a person's immigrant career (Green, 1982: 225). The Framework follows this career beyond the immigrant phase, however, to include the adaptation to Canada of all citizens by extending the inspection of family histories for those who have been in Canada for generations. Simultaneously, it expresses our many cultural differences, our great diversity, and also enables us to see ourselves as one people. Every individual and ethno-racial group is covered, including Native Peoples, the two "charter groups" and all other contributing peoples. The Framework encourages a movement between "etic" and "emic" or general and specific concepts (Draguns, 1976: 2).

The Acculturative Framework deliberately uses visual imagery. The movement of people into Canada is projected as a wide river. On the banks of this river are Benchmarks that relate to this acculturative process, as well as making alternative tributaries along it. Everyone travels on this river. Some have just got on (new immigrants) and others have been on it all their lives. Some had parents who were born on this river, while others had parents who were born elsewhere and became parents after they got on the river. Many factors affect the acculturation process, but **when** you got on the river matters a great deal to the content of your identity as a Canadian. These ideas correspond to comments such as: "I am an immigrant to Canada" or "I came as a child to Canada" or "My family goes back generations in Canada." In each case there is an explicit recognition of one's place of origin and sense of where one is in relation to those origins. Sometimes, status distinctions are also made on the basis of how long one has been in Canada. In greatly simplified form, the Framework visually depicts the more readily identifiable benchmarks of this acculturative process.

The structure of the Framework is kept simple, and as abstract as possible. The time line does not apply to any specific date(s) and can be very long, as in the case of people who have been in Canada for many generations. There are more benchmarks within the immigrant generation than there are for Canadian-born, because it is culture change that is the focus here. The cultural changes are greater and faster at the beginning than after a culture shift has been adapted to. Also, one can convey an impression of entire lives that are in flux, rather than mere transitory detail. Detail can be added by the service provider to accommodate any one client situation. This Framework structure permits the "artistic" dimension that the helping practice requires: an accommodation to the variety, the detail, the flux that peoples' lives produce.

The Acculturative Framework is a conceptual tool for the helping services. It is not intended that the Framework chart be completely filled during an initial contact, nor is it necessary for all parts to be filled, even after many contacts. It is a graphic picture of the client's/family's progression into Canadian life. It provides a structure for collecting and organizing information that is necessary to understand the cultural frame of reference of clients or colleagues. The Framework thereby universalizes the consideration of issues about ethnicity and race, and is applicable to all ethno-racial groups. The Framework pinpoints important variables and organizes them in a logically sequential way. It draws attention to past generational changes that are part of any individual's existential identity, even if they are unaware of them. According to the Framework, a client's or colleague's frame of reference comes out of the events — biologic, social and cultural — implied in the chart.

The practitioner focusses on the parts of the Framework relevant to the client's present problem. As in any good practise methodology, the practitioner must recognize the degree of the person's awareness of the issues under study. There may be a large gap between what seems obvious to the practitioner and what is understood by the client. The gap is reduced by the service provider understanding the differences in frame of reference of self versus client, and reduced also if the collection of information is a process fully shared with clients. For both parties, it is a mutual learning experience, because the process of collecting the information is as important as the information itself. Problem-solving emerges as both worker and client become more aware of the client's cultural identity and, to some extent, the worker's own identity, in an in-depth way. This method contrasts sharply with a genealogical search for roots where the goal is to identify ancestors, conducted by an outside genealogical expert. This method also differs much from the method used if the worker wrongly assumes an information-gathering and treatment strategy is generic, applicable in an undifferentiated way to any and all, without having to vary techniques or concepts because of cultural differences.

Thus, the Framework provides the cognitive elements of a frame of cultural reference. Since a frame of reference is neither good nor bad but simply **is**, it becomes the place where helping starts. For health personnel, it locates the client's view of illness in the centre and makes health treatment relevant to the client's expectations and cultural identity. For penal institutions, rehabilitation must start with the prisoner's frame of reference. For example, if the incarcerated person is of Native origin, the Native perspective is essential before restoration of the person to the community can start. For each field of service practise, the Framework focusses on cultural perspectives essential for success.

The Framework is a set of materials with which to start the training of personnel. Awareness of one's own cultural roots and differing perspectives on ethnicity and race can be brought out. All of these points are well summarized by Edward Hall's own words:

Two things get in the way of understanding: the linearity of language and the deep biases and built-in blinders that every culture provides. Transcending either is a formidable task. In addition, the broad base on which culture rests was laid down millions of years ago, long before man appeared on this earth, and for better or worse it ties man forever to the rest of nature. This base is rooted in the old, mammalian brain — that part of the brain that treats things as wholes — which constantly synthesizes and comes up with solutions based on everything that happened in the past. Paradoxically, this old brain that can understand and integrate one's own culture on a pre-verbal level frequently gets in the way of understanding and integrating new cultural experiences.

This means that if one is to really understand a given behaviour, on the basic level I am referring to, one must know the entire history of the individual. It is never possible to understand completely any other human being; and no individual will every really understand himself — the complexity is too great and there is not the time to constantly take things apart and examine them. This is the beginning of wisdom in human relations. However, understanding oneself and understanding others are closely related processes. To do one, you must start with the other, and vice versa (Hall, 1976: 69).

Chapter 10

Race And Multicultural Work: Foundation For Anti-Racist Education

INTRODUCTION

A woman and a small child enter a restaurant, sit down and the child looks around. "Look at that chocolate man, Mummy!" he said, in a voice all could hear. Mother, deeply embarrassed, exclaims, "Ssh, it's not nice to speak like that about Black people!"

This episode reported by a social work student, who had been asked to describe some early memories about "race," captures the essence of the white Canadian attitude to racial difference. Several messages were conveyed at once and were never sorted out. First, it is impolite to talk aloud about people's racial appearance: second, there is something wrong with a 'chocolate man'; and third, strong emotional feelings are present that must be suppressed. Why should a situation, in which a child expresses a natural curiosity about something new to him, create such a repressed, emotional reaction?

As studies about race relations in Canada progress, some of the answers to this puzzling situation become clearer. Although it is with considerable resistance, we are gradually opening up the meanings of racial difference to ourselves. Some courageous social agencies are examining the climate and content of race relations within their own organizations; courageous because the agency is opened up to criticism and strong emotions. Many Boards of Education, often the earliest places to recognize the need for change, have race relations policies in place. In a few post-secondary programmes, beginnings are being made to understand how racism effects professional education and students in professional studies. What are the strong emotions that underlie this topic? Anger? Fear? Resentment? Hate? How do service providers need to think through the factor of "race" as it affects their multicultural work?

ANTI-RACIST EDUCATION

There are many parts to anti-racist education. This book is a contribution to this work. Throughout this discussion of multicultural work there has been an emphasis on including **everyone** in the language and method. This all-inclusion has been particularly directed at both client/patient and practitioner. The reasons for this are many but in particular is emphasized that culture is a two-way street; what is perceived or abstracted out as a cultural pattern in any moment-to-moment situation is done by a specific person and is relative to that specific transaction or exchange. The contribution of both parties is crucial to understanding what has happened.

As we move into anti-racism work, this dual approach is still very important. As we view racial interplays, and consider the power differentials that are at the bottom of the racial tensions, the perspective of both "white" and "non-white" groups must be taken into account; each has a different perspective. The patterning that underlies the behaviours of both groups is often invisible to the other. For example, the patterns of structural racism that give "white" people an advantage over "non-white" people is usually invisible to "whites." Making these advantages visible is part of anti-racism education. Conveying how "non-white" people feel about their position in society is also part of this process.

It is interesting to note who is considered "white." In an excellent treatise on racism, Michael Banton (1988) discusses on a world-wide basis how colour is perceived and links that idea to how these perceptions are used by those in power. In a handbook developed by the Metropolitan Toronto Board of Education (McCaskell, 1988) for a multicultural/multiracial children's camp, it is pointed out that at times people who are technically "white" are not regarded as "white." For example, in Toronto, in the 1960s, when there was a large wave of Italian immigration, Italians were not considered "white" by the host group; eating particular foods, low education and unwillingness to learn English were seen as traits that were "in the blood" i.e., a natural part of being Italian; Italians thus suffered much discrimination. As they became settled and their children went to school and they adapted to Canadian ways this view abated. Likewise, the Irish also were not considered "white" and suffered from religious discrimination for many years until this also abated and they adapted to Anglo ways. Now both Italians and Irish are both unequivocally "white" but both groups remember the discrimination accorded them and often it was called racism, although they were both "white."

Anti-racism work is complex and can only be understood by in-depth analysis of structural arrangements between people of perceived race. There are issues to do with identity and stereotypes; when and under what circumstances discrimination occurs; the structural elements of racism and its function in the society; its effects on everyone, and in terms particularly interesting to multicultural work, the outcomes on service delivery. Since any developmental change process, of the magnitude required for restructuring and re-establishing egalitarian values, that is required for the antiracist process, there will be resistance and strong emotion. A step-by-step path must be worked out. In this book, to start, we acknowledge that racism exists and that the goals of anti-racism work are accepted and worthy. Later, the three models developed in the book are used to illumine some of the in-depth issues that anti-racist work attends to.

ACKNOWLEDGING RACISM

Acknowledging racism is a revelatory process that each person, regardless of background, can profitably conduct. Theoretically, people in Canada can be placed on a continuum from those who already strongly acknowledge racism to the other extreme of those who strongly deny it exists in Canada. Since there is a strong emotional component to the process of acknowledgment, it cannot be only cognitive. In the following pages, ideas about race and helping work are added to the many excellent ones already published and in use (Thomas and Novogrodsky, 1983; Thomas, 1987; Christiensen, 1990) and many others. The ideas presented here build on the models introduced in this book — the Acculturative Framework, Contexting, and Non-verbal modes.

The first level of work in acknowledging race and racism in Canada is to establish one's own understanding of what is meant by racism and what one knows and feels about it. Many people would prefer, like the mother in the restaurant, not to talk about it and seldom allow the subject to cross their minds. Some people who have experienced racism would prefer to deny it because there is great pain involved. Thus both perpetrators and the victims of racism may deny its existence for different reasons.

Different reactions to racism can continue unchallenged even in human service organizations when pervasive norms exist that stifle overt discussion. For example, in a report on Metropolitan Toronto Children's Aid Society, (MTCAS, 1982), the visiting researchers commented extensively about a research finding that there was a sub-conscious but agency-wide acceptance of the norm to censure anyone who directly or indirectly raised the issue of racism. In other words, the "permission" to talk about racism and its many aspects was found to be "under cultural control" i.e., norms existed which inhibited discussion. These conditions were not seen as peculiar to this agency, which had, at least, courageously allowed a study of its organization to take place. Rather, it was suggested that these norms pervaded the society at large and that the agency, as part of the society, also reflected norms about race/racism.

Thus, acknowledging racism is not easy, but establishing the fact of Canadian racism is necessary, because there is no indisputable recognition of it. In contrast, the United States underwent a Civil Rights movement during the 1960s that publicly and in full national view identified the racism against American Blacks and pointed to its many manifestations such as segregation, poor living conditions and unequal opportunities in education and jobs.

Canadians watched this drama unfold nightly on their television sets and appear repeatedly in their newspapers and magazines. One reaction was to smugly deny that Canada was in any way the same. Another effect was that American vocabulary and ideas about racism subtly invaded the Canadian consciousness. Thus, often the idea of a "racial minority" became synonymous with "Black People" and race relations meant relationships between blacks and whites. This tendency blurred the fact that to achieve any understanding of race relations in Canada, it was necessary to include many races and ethno-racial groups, and realize that each group had a unique history and experience of discrimination in Canada. Some Canadians who started the process of reading these various histories found the truth unpleasant and painful. Few of these accounts had been present in the history books read in school. As more Canadians learn about these events, more will find their pride in Canada taking a beating; a painful experience.

However, the reverberations from those earlier injustices against, for instance, Native Peoples, Japanese, Chinese, Jews and Blacks, are still being felt, and the descendants of those early victims of racism will not allow the wrongs to be forgotten. Governments today are facing land claims for ancestral land snatched through false or unobserved treaties; apologizing to those wrongfully interned during war; considering restitution to those who paid a head tax to land in Canada; acknowledging the wrongful turning away of refugees at borders and sending them to their deaths; and many other acts that occurred because the people were non-white or Jewish.

The sooner we can as individuals, as a people and as a government, face up to the obligations we inherited, the sooner we can start to build a just society in the present and relieve the sense of being wronged that burdens many of our citizens.

ACKNOWLEDGING THE PAST

Colonization of Native Peoples

The most singular example of racism in Canadian history is the treatment accorded Native People from the first European contact four hundred years ago, continuously to the present. It was not just that the indigenous people were invaded, colonized, segregated, stolen from, culturally degraded and in numerous ways overwhelmed, but that pervading these aggressive actions was the belief that it was right to treat Native People badly because they were less than fully human, in fact, in a stage of barbarism, religiously pagan. Morgan, an anthropologist in this era, wrote a long treatise on the stages of evolution in human history (Morgan, 1877). He proposed that cultures could be classified on an evolutionary scale going from "savagery" through "barbarism" to "civilization." Obviously, European societies represented "civilization" and Native cultures, he said, had yet to go through the earlier stages of evolution that Europeans had already passed. Thus it was rationalized, Natives would not notice what was taken from them; moreover, it would be beneficial to them to be converted to Christianity; they were no better than children and therefore unaware of the value of their lands, animal pelts, minerals, etc. All in all, they would not feel deprivation or pain the way fully human people do. These beliefs were supported as late as the early 20th Century by reputable academics who were obsessed with classifying people on the basis of physical characteristics (Hughes and Kallen, 1974: 1-64).

White Supremacy Ideologies

Students reading such a book as Morgan's today, might view the effort as quaint and out-dated. However, the effects of such serious works in their time were to give credible foundations to the colonization of the "new world" by white European settlers; the rationale that was felt, if not always expressed, was the superiority of the white race. Although such early efforts to prove white racial superiority have been scientifically discredited, they nevertheless remain as cultural coin, in daily use. For example, in our own time, we have seen the consequences of overt "supremacy" ideologies in Europe. Such ideologies supported anti-Semitism and later justified the policy of genocide and the deaths of six million Jews, many Gypsies and others during World War II, (Hughes and Kallen, 1974: 80-82), and permitted Canadian leaders to deny Jewish refugees access to Canada (Abella and

Troper, 1982). In the 1990s we see a new form of discrimination in the atrocities called "ethnic cleansing" (*Refuge*, 1993). Countries in Europe and Asia have endured these events.

INFORMATION ABOUT RACISM

School Text Books

As the student moves on to more current events, other reports can be examined to ascertain how racist attitudes are maintained even today. An inventive study conducted in 1965 in Ontario, analysed school textbooks in order to remove material that was offensive to some of the people who make up Canadian society (McDiarmid and Pratt, 1971). It was not so much in obvious, explicit ways that the material was found to be biased but in more subtle indirect ways. They analysed the **kinds** of words and phrases used in apparently innocent statements about people of other races. The hidden, almost subliminal, messages conveyed negative values about Indians, Metis and immigrants. The kind of analyses made by McDiarmid and Pratt can increase awareness of how any media can manipulate public attitudes to people who are "different" — on racial, ethnic, religious or social class grounds. Studies on the media can be exemplified by one study on racism in the press that was conducted by Effie Ginzberg (1987).

Canadian Research on Racism

Other studies have also attempted to draw out hidden feelings, experiences, and attitudes. Pitman's (1978) study in Toronto attempted to uncover the kinds of racist attitudes experienced by some Asians, especially those from India and Pakistan. Physical assaults, racial slurs and discrimination from many sectors were investigated. Wilson Head studied the experience of discrimination by Black Canadians and found that about 15% had experienced overt discrimination. However, he reported that the experience of "polite" discrimination was widely recognized and felt most keenly.

Polite racism is difficult to prove and leads to accusations of being "too suspicious" by those who cannot see the intent. They evaluate the accused as "too sensitive," "thin-skinned," or overly ready to see racism in every act. For the victim, who is indeed sensitive if this has been a repeated experience, there can be a build-up of resentment, humiliation and anger. For some, a degree of self-hatred can develop and the progression to a healthy

Canadian identity is slowed. Service workers not only must be sure that they do not contribute to the accumulation of polite, discriminatory experiences of non-white Canadians, but also that they are able to help heal the negative effects of these experiences. Healing is helped by acknowledging what the client has experienced and allowing the pain to be expressed. Beyond that, advocacy help to get the needed resource or assistance that they deem has been denied should be given. For a sceptical service provider, to experience the intensity of reaction from the long-suppressed feelings of the colleague or client when the racial insult is finally acknowledged, there can be no doubt as to the reality of the experience and the destructiveness to those involved.

Use of Informants

Most non-white people, professional people included, have stories to tell about racial slurs they have encountered. Often these are told in a laughing manner. However, the laughter should not be taken at face value; the situation described was rarely funny, and in fact, may still be so painful that only by joking about it, can the event be related. If the listener is supportive, this experience may be retold with some of the original feelings unchanged. The person who has been hurt can be comforted by the experience of being heard, and those who are listening can learn about the effects of racist actions. Together, appropriate service responses to such experiences can be worked out. Workers can learn to confront those who commit racist acts, and how to listen to victims' experiences. They can communicate outrage at the occurrence and commiseration to the victim. In short, a full acknowledgement of the event should be accomplished. This kind of response is appropriate when a child or adult has experienced deep rejection of any sort, and a racial event is one of the worst kinds of rejection experiences.

Literature

There are many literature sources to learn about victims' perceptions and experiences with racism. Fore example, Austin Clarke and Bharati Mukerjee tell poignantly about the experiences of non-white immigrants in Canada in many of their writings. There are also novels about the immigrant experience which provide another way to learn. (Lee, 1990; Nasralloah, 1987; Vassanji, 1991; Vlassie, 1987).

THE EXPRESSION OF RACISM: AN EXAMPLE USING THE ACCULTURATIVE FRAMEWORK

The Erosion of High Context Culture Through Cultural Shifts in the Presence of Racism

For four hundred years, the cultures of aboriginal Peoples have been under siege from many sources. The result has been ongoing loss, erosion, and ruin of the fabric of previously rich and varied cultures. Today, these deeply impaired cultures are often unable to sustain the energy of the people who depend on them; the people are insufficiently sustained to participate fully and healthfully in their normal course of life. The purpose of the following sections is to show how aboriginal cultures have been destroyed by contact and colonialization. The idea of "culture shift" (Benchmark B) was introduced earlier in this book. This particular wording was chosen in order that the archetypal change, "death-rebirth," could be used to apply to many different situations faced by practitioners; it was particularly my concern that the case of Native Peoples be able to fit into the multicultural theme and be examined as part of the fabric of Canadian life. "They never left Canada but Canada left them" is one way of using the term, "culture shift." It is the numerous ways that "Canada left them" that are addressed. The discussion starts with a review of high context dimensions and goes on to show how repeated culture shifts with strong infusions of racism can destabilize and erode the way of life of a people who have thrived for scores of thousands of years. It is because of the racism present that the "rebirth" part of the archetypal cycle could not occur in a healthy way; i.e., with the ancient cultures integrating with the modern cultures in some way that would have sustained the people.

Benchmark A: The Original Culture

High Context Native Cultures

The dimensions of high context cultures discussed in Chapters 3 and 4 can be applied with strong concordance to Native cultures, which are ideal examples of very high context ways of life. Prior to contact with Europeans, aboriginal groups lived in self-sufficient societies, but in isolation from peoples elsewhere on the globe. Native life was formed almost entirely from the network of family and band ties. A person born into a Native culture learned from birth the highly interdependent norms and values of their family and clan. Not only did hierarchical and gender segregation values pertain but also the religious dimension was wholly integrated. The supernatural was involved in all aspects of Native life and each individual was connected to the spiritual life through patterned beliefs and life-long rituals. Their view of the world was an holistic one with animal and human beings interconnected with each other and with the rest of creation. Groups were deeply joined to "place"; each aspect of the environment was intertwined with the cyclical pacings of tribal life.

Before contact with European explorers and traders, this high context way of life sustained a huge variety of different native groups, all of whom lived with simple technology and sometimes with scarce food resources. However, European contact and colonialism with its attendant racism upset a large part of native existence and left most groups in peril of extinction. The more recent restitutive provisions of the federal government were often themselves causes of even further breakdown.

Although the issues to be raised here have been described many times, in numerous studies, what is done here is to connect each of the issues to one or more dimensions of high context culture to show how that dimension became undermined. Much of what has occurred has been more the destruction of the high context network than the gradual moving from high to low context in the way our modern policy of multiculturalism permits immigrating groups to do. It was the racism inherent in colonialization that extinguished native culture rather than allowing it to gradually move towards low context change.

Racism is operationalized for this historical period as, lack of respect for Native Peoples' way of life; a belief that Natives were "subhuman"; that their beliefs were paganistic and therefore to be eradicated; and a stereotyping of the Native person so that individuality and individual differences between people were not perceived. It has taken the work of scholars like Bruce Trigger (1976) and the type of royal commission by Justice Berger (1977) to show Native Peoples as human beings with individual histories and identities.

Benchmark B and C: Selected Culture Shifts and Their Impact on Dimensions of High Context Culture of Native Canadian Groups

(Much of the following data presented is deeply indebted to Krauter and Davis (1978)). During the 1600s, European invaders broke the isolation of these groups and the first historically recorded "culture shift" occurred for Indians and Inuit.

Health Shift

Although this could not have been foretold at the time, the health of Native groups was very adversely affected by the simple act of being forced into contact with peoples from Europe. Diseases such as smallpox, respiratory infections and the "social diseases" took a large toll on lives and depleted the numbers in a random, sometimes sweeping way. This kind of effect took place when Native and non-Native persons were at an interdependent stage, not yet segregated from each other but interacting in a state of primal technology and simple community. The effect on the Native high context culture can be construed as a depletion of the components of the high context network: people were no longer there to fulfil obligations of the interdependent web of relationships; functions could not be filled because significant others had died; in a high context culture no one can be replaced and, thus, new ways of meeting one's needs, unsanctioned by tribal mores, would have had to be found. This kind of substitution on a large scale could only be destructive to the culture.

Economic Shift

In addition to the health shift during this period, there was a beginning change in the relationships of Natives and Europeans. Europeans were taught to live in the Indians' land by Indians who believed they had entered equality relationships as they had with other Indian tribes. The trapping of animals, which was only one part of the indigenous life, became transformed into a dominant element: the fur trade; employee-employer (inferior-dominant) relationships emerged from the drive for furs and the riches to Europeans that these brought. This type of relationship was a new element in aboriginal life and undermined their traditional ways of production and commerce. Thus, in this period of interdependence between Native and non-Native, the fabric of high context culture underwent important changes. The period of colonization is marked from 1763 on. Settlers were recruited to come to the New World and land was given or sold to anyone who would take on the task of cutting down the trees and planting crops. For Native Peoples who had no conception of the land as private property, this period involved thinking of the land in an entirely alien way, a shift that is still being played out today in land claim battles.

Geographic Shift

From a high context position of the land as sacred, belonging to all, and over which all could move, there was a shift to the reserve system. This method of deploying people and curtailing movement was a massive encroachment on the traditional way of Indian life. It broke attachment to the intimate details of the land and its holdings such as waterways, hills, rocks, game, trees and trails. The integral part played by these elements in daily spiritual life was attenuated or destroyed. Instead, the reserve became a prison which trapped people within its borders and provided an arena for the dominant group to impose its religion and its ways of education. The authority of traditional tribal leaders was withdrawn by the colonizers and the focus of power was from the outside onto the vulnerable weakened people within. The forces were, in brief, assimilative and directed in such a way as to benefit the European. The opportunity to make low context shifts, as immigrants from high context cultures can do, was not available unless a Native person left the reserve. Thus, there was a destruction of high context ways and little to replace it.

Legal Shift

Before contact with Europeans, and until the Indian Act of 1876, there was no one set of laws covering all Native groups. With this Act, however, the British-Canadian government required Registration of those considered to be "Native"; anyone not registered at that time lost any legal claim to identity as a Native. Now there were "Native" and "non-Native" statuses of people who identified as Indian or Métis. These designations created havoc on reserves where people could be denied ancestral rights on the basis of this government designation. To this day, the restoration of identity as a Native band member remains a high priority for many people whose ancestors were not registered.

The government decided Indian women should lose their Indian status if they married a non-Native man. In addition to creating new statuses, the Act made the Government in charge of Indians' affairs. It also became possible to legislate behaviour for the Indian and as a result of new rules on reserves, Indians could be sent to jail for many newly-defined infractions, e.g., fishing without a licence or "out of season." Since this was a morality based on external norms, there was high incidence of Natives in jail. Thus, the Indian Act further destroyed the fabric of high context culture in terms of governance, male/female relationships, the nature of the family and what was moral. It was particularly destructive for matriarchal groups , such as the Mohawk, because a white, patriarchical system became imposed on them and undermined the traditional role of clan mothers. The Indian Act of 1885 removed Indians from their rights by denying them the vote as long as they maintained their reserve residence. Once again, a process open to immigrants was denied to Natives. And once again, a process that might have aided in the shift to low context culture was prevented.

Education Shifts

In preliterate societies, the young of the group are usually instructed according to the oral traditions and examples of the tribe. The young were taught by elders who used holistic means of teaching such as stories, rituals, dance and music. However, once the reserve system was in place, a "white-oriented," frequently church-oriented, education was instituted. Speaking the Native language was prohibited. The curriculum was irrelevant to the traditional ways of Native life and often demeaned what had been central to Native life for millennia past. With the increasing isolation of Natives from other Canadians, many myths and stereotypes about Indians flourished; these found their way into the consciousness of the non-Native population, even into the textbooks of school children where many decades later they still existed and were found by investigators like McDiarmid and Pratt (1971). It is interesting to note that the presence of these stereotypes in textbooks is both an act of racism and caused by racism. The unquestioning stance of those who wrote the books in the first place was an act of racism — and their approach was caused or influenced by the stereotypes held more generally by the members of the society.

Employment Shifts

From being self-sufficient and either agricultural or roving in their pursuits to gain subsistence, Native People were drawn into the money economy and often forced to become wage labourers. Their control over their own traditions/livelihood was taken away and they became reliant on the resources within the bounds of the reserve and on the largesse of the Department of Indian Affairs. Reserves were generally on too barren land to produce a living for the bands and too isolated to partake of opportunities existent in the wider society. The former interdependence of the family network as an economic unit, an interdependence that is at the heart of high context societies, was undermined and all but destroyed.

Housing Shifts

From housing that was adapted to the terrain, flexible for any conditions, available for normal pursuits of hunting, trapping or gathering, reserve housing relied on a meanly funded, modern technology which was either not understood by Native users or out of their range to modify. Consequently, their housing conditions have been very inadequate and often so inferior in construction that there is a lifelong effect on the health of tenants. It is easy to speculate on the damage to the family and its ability to solve problems and look after the welfare of its members — its *raison d'être* — when the basic conditions for living fell so far short.

Welfare Effects

Since traditional ways of meeting collective needs, especially those based on values of family interdependence, were disestablished, more and more reserve members became welfare recipients. As the sense of worth from being a functioning member of the kin network decreased, so family functioning became lowered. Alcoholism and other symptoms of despair reduced parental and tribal authority and energy; and often the results were high rates of children taken into the care of Children's Aid Societies. For a people to whom children were the most important joy in life, the sorrow and degradation of these acts were overwhelming.

New trends

There are many political, legal and economic initiatives such as the

James Bay Agreement, the acceptance of the Dene Nation demands, Native Child Welfare beginnings (Johnston, 1983: Chapter 6) and Schools of Native Social Work, e.g., at the Federated Indian Colleges of Saskatchewan, and at Laurentian University. Dalhousie Maritime School has been building responsive programmes for the Nova Scotia Black Community and for those of Micmac descent (Moore, 1991). At the University of British Columbia the First Nations House of Learning is developing holistic programmes. All these changes and many more indicate a move from dependency to regained dignity and self government. But there is long way to go yet.

RACE AND ETHNOCULTURE: DIFFERENTIAL CHANGE— APPLICATION OF THE ACCULTURATIVE FRAMEWORK TO HIGHLIGHT IDENTITY DIFFERENCES BETWEEN ETHNORACIAL GROUPS

Differential Change Between Cultural and Racial Identity

The first general point to be made is that, unlike cultural identity, physical racial identity will persist during a lifetime, and with little alteration from one generation to another if racial intermarriage does not occur. Thus, it is not possible to deduce a person's cultural identity from their racial appearance: cultural identity can evolve quite quickly but racial appearance will remain unaltered. This matters a great deal since so much stress is placed on visual attributes. As noted in Chapter 5, what the eyes "take in" has a dominant effect on our understanding of the world around us: we take in racial identity immediately from visual cues; it takes much longer to assess cultural identity.

Before comparing acculturative frames of different groups, it is an interesting aside to note that it is possible for a small amount of bodily physical change to take place over a lifetime. For example, what may change to a smaller or larger degree is the muscular, gestural aspect of the face. If, for instance, a person has learned to suppress emotion in a previous culture (Benchmark A), by the time of acquiring an identity at Benchmark E, emotion may be more fully expressed and this will include a more mobile facial expression. This mobility may alter the facial structure because the exercise of the muscles makes slight changes in shape, firmness and contour of the facial muscles and thereby slightly alters the appearance of the racial features. This alteration will be very gradual and may not be noticed in

Canada. However, if a person returns to the culture of Benchmark A, persons there may notice the change. For example, a second-generation Japanese woman, born in Canada, visited relatives in Japan and was told that she did not look Japanese.

Black People

The more important general point, though, is that people in the dominant culture equate Canadian identity with a "white" racial appearance. Even though there may be cultural assimilation in dress, accent, and other behavioural signs by Canadian non-whites, only their racial appearance is noticed by many people. The issue can be highlighted by an example. The case of a Black Jamaican immigrant child can be compared to that of a White Italian immigrant child. See Fig. 10.1.

To begin, it seems unnecessary to mention the race of the Italian child, but not superfluous to mention the race of the Jamaican child. This is one way of expressing the inequality of racial status between a "black" and a "white" child; we mention a person's non-white status but do not mention if a person is white. The situation of the two children can be compared more dramatically by using the Acculturative Framework.

The Framework identifies aspects of the acculturation process and suggests alternate paths to a Canadian identity. To this point in the book, the Framework has not explicitly included racial identity. However, when this component is added, it becomes necessary to consider other aspects that affect identity-formation. The solid black background of the Jamaican child's frame and the solid white background of the Italian child's frame symbolize that race remains unchanged throughout each person's life. That the black background encompasses the Jamaican child's time line symbolizes that this issue remains a **social** issue for this person throughout his/her life. That the background is white and blends in with the rest of the page for the Italian child symbolizes that being white is a non-issue, socially, for the Italian child throughout his/her life.

It is clear, therefore, that, to arrive at the identity of the Jamaican child more issues must be considered. At the Benchmark A stage (place of origin), with the ideas presented in Chapter 7, one would consider if the Jamaican child's parents had had the experience of being visible minority people or had been exposed to a multiracial society, especially one that is predominantly white. We know, that for a black family to experience this for the first time, can be a traumatic episode. The Italian family will not have to be concerned with this issue, since they are white.

Fig. 10.1 — Comparing A Jamaican Immigrant Child and An Italian Immigrant Child by Race in Canada

A	B	C	D	E
A Jamaican child, living in Jamaica, experiences a predominantly Black society.	emigration may be "sequenced", encounters suspicion by Immigration Officers.	Feels visibly different; his/her parents may experience discrimination in jobs and housing.	a) Jamaican-Canadian community institutionally incomplete. Very concerned with racial issues in the wider community. b) Isolated from other Jamaicans, highly visible, manages issues of race by him/herself.	a) A Canadian who is very conscious of and concerned with issues of race; has Black identity.

A	B	C	D	E
An Italian child, living in Italy, experiences a predominantly White society,	Emigrates with parents.	An Italian immigrant, a white person in a white society.	a) Italo-Canadian Community not concerned with racial issues; indistinguishable from white host community. b) Isolated from other Italians, blends in with the white community.	a) A Canadian who is unaware of his/her racial identity.

We also know that during the culture shift period, Benchmark B, the immigrating person may meet officials who are suspicious of that person's intentions and question their presence in the country. The Jamaican family will be more likely to experience suspicion than the Italian family because of their racial difference.

In addition, while settling into Canadian society, the first few years may be filled with experiences where one's race draws attention in a variety of ways; being new to a society one can make mistakes that are quite minor *faux pas* but if one is "visible," i.e., a racial minority, they are noticed more than if one is not visible and a connection may be made with one's race as a causative factor. A behaviour such as loudness of speech, or an awkward gesture or a different way of using one's eyes can become a major transgression that is believed to happen **because** one is of a particular race. Herein lies the potential for the error of stereotyping because all of these events are taken in by the eyes and the visual connection is made.

Many other experiences — not getting a job, not finding an apartment to rent, being slurred on the street — many of which have been documented in the reports cited earlier in this chapter, will be sustained where the basis of the interaction becomes linked to race.

Throughout this person's life lies the potential to attach the person to a racial identity rather than to the fact that one is a newcomer. These evaluations are felt by non-whites as signs of rejection and can hurt, and the memory of the hurt can linger a long time. It is by this time that black immigrants will start to identify themselves as a racial minority since their race always seems to intrude between them and some relationship or event. Since all these occurrences can also happen to the Italian family but not be attached to their **race,** they will not identify primarily as **white**.

The D Benchmark points to a variety of types of Jamaican-Canadian or Italo-Canadian communities that can exist in any locale; previously, in Chapter 8, attention was drawn to the institutional completeness of that community. There is high likelihood that the Italian community will be institutionally complete but almost no likelihood that the Jamaican one will be; for example; for example, an ethnic sub-economy will be largely lacking (Herberg, 1988: 228). Also, regardless of the size or complexity of the community of any visible minority, there is foremost a crucial question about the nature of the relationship between it and the larger community within which it is based, and the Jamaican family will be probably more aware of this factor than the Italian family. We know that if there are hostile or discriminatory practices on the basis of race, these are very regressive to adjustment, but that open and friendly relations will aid adjustment. For the example of the Jamaican and Italian families, the differences between them can be displayed, using a visual display of their circumstances: Chart 10.1 depicts the development of the two children, however, filling out Benchmarks D and E can only be done in approximation because of the many complexities of racial issues.

Here two children have been through the Canadian school system, lived in Canadian neighbourhoods and in general have been exposed to a myriad of Canadian experiences. As adults they both "feel Canadian." However, the responses to them through their life will be quite different. The adult person of Italian background cannot immediately be identified as "Italian" but the black person will frequently be asked "What island are you from?" or "When did you come to Canada?" merely because of their colour; their being "Canadian" will not be automatically assumed as it is with the white immigrant. (This is not to say that the Italian will not have experienced negative reactions to being Italian but this will not have been on the basis of **visible racial appearance**.) The stereotypical assumption that black people cannot be real Canadians is an experience that inhibits identification as a Canadian. It is an experience that follows many minority people of colour all their lives. In sum, we can make the point that the emphasis placed on visual (racial) information does not catch the important internal, identity information about ethno-culture; that a person **feels** Canadian is not as important as what he/she **looks** like. There is one hopeful possibility, and that is that the "culture" of how we perceive race will itself change; that we will start to pay only that attention to race that is appropriate.

A second general point is that people of the same racial appearance can have very different origins. This is true for people of all races including white people but for the latter it does not seem to influence their identity as much as with non-white people since white person's race is not an issue for gaining the status of a Canadian. The next section deals with this issue.

Black Canadians of Different Origins

The examples that follow focus on a few of the possible differences in origin for Black Canadians. In addition to the Jamaican origin displayed in the previous paragraphs there are many other origins that could be found. Three possibilities are displayed:

1. A Black American

A	B	C	D	E
born and raised in the United States	immigrates to Canada			a Black Canadian

In America, Blacks may live together on the basis of racial identity much more than is the case in Canada. A question that the framework suggests is whether or not Blacks from the U.S. have communal associations in Canada. If they are urban immigrants, they may expect to have few problems since urban life is familiar and they will not feel the need to live in close association with each other. Also, the American value of assimilating may be more powerful a value than keeping a black cultural community alive in Canada. Although the actual number of Blacks from the U.S. is low, like many other Black Canadians, race will be the main factor, and many White observers will not be aware of the background characteristics that make this person unique.

2. An African Black Immigrant

A	B	C	D	E
born in an African country	immigrates to Canada			a Black Canadian

Black people who emigrate from Africa will not fully comprehend the attitude towards racial identity held by people whose ancestors were brought in slavery to the New World, centuries ago. Their participation in Black communities and associations will depend on many factors beside racial congruence. In some cases they may not be as sympathetic to bonds based on race, but view culture and social class as more important.

3. A Canadian-born Black

A	B	C	D	G
born in Nova Scotia of 9th generation parents	migrates to Toronto			a Black Canadian of the 10th generation

The settlement of a Nova Scotian Black (Benchmark G, Beyond the Third generation) in Toronto will likely be as difficult a transition as for any other Maritimer. If this person comes from a rural, tight-knit community where segregation of Black people has long existed, the move to Toronto will be even more difficult. Again, settlement patterns of Blacks from other communities across Canada into the big cities need to be researched. The

Black identity at point G in example 3 is different from all other Black Canadian identities. If this person experiences in Toronto a lack of acceptance as a Canadian citizen, the frustration will be very great and a potential source of continued hurt. Again, although the cultural connection to Canada is of very long standing, the physical racial component, on what the observers base their remarks, remains largely unchanged.

There are many variations of the Black identities given above. In North America, there is a lineage of suffering, based on the original brutal culture shift of the slave trade that connects all Blacks. The cultures of origin underwent many of the same processes of high context culture erosion under conditions of racism presented previously on Native Peoples. However, several generations have elapsed since the Abolition of Slavery and Blacks in North America have dispersed widely and developed identities related to the communities in which they reside much as does every other immigrant. The lineage of suffering therefore is not accepted in the same way by all Blacks. However, like other "lineages" this one has "roots" and "lifetimes of changes and process" that constitute a body of knowledge. This very painful body of knowledge is one not all wish to claim. In Canada, the personal-cultural identity will vary greatly depending on culture of origin (Benchmark A), the recognition of him/her as Canadian, and the type of communal associations in a given locale or actively sought out or created. Very little is known about Black identity across Canada. The variables mentioned here are only some of the more obvious ones to which the Acculturative Framework would point.

That many white Canadians tend first to equate race in a physical sense with cultural identity, and second, to assume that a non-white person is not (and can never be?) Canadian goes back to points made at the beginning of this chapter. There can be a belief by whites of their racial superiority, and this issue of racial identity is handled by strong norms that prevent discussion about it. One of the consequences of these norms is that issues related to them do not get sorted out and information that would assist in their resolution is not passed along. For example, by this stage of our development in Canadian society, it should be common knowledge that non-aboriginal, visible minority people have been living in Canada for almost as long as the French and that people of different races and origins are quite different from each other and relate to creating and celebrating Canadian identity in as varied ways as do different white racial groups. However, reactions to visible minorities in Canada are still too stereotypical and too many people make assumptions about who is really "Canadian" (is Canadian-born, has Canadian citizenship, etc.). A comment like "what island do you come from?" is a verbal indicator of the trouble we still have with racial differences. The mother's embarrassment at the child's comment, "look at that chocolate man," is a non-verbal one.

THE FORMATION OF STEREOTYPES

Non-White Groups

One of the processes that has been addressed in the previous sections is known as stereotyping. Kallen's work on ethnicity and race is an important document on this subject. She describes stereotypes as overgeneralized, rigid, cognitive maps or pictures in our heads based on unsubstantiated beliefs about the members of another group (Kallen, 1982: 30). Stereotyping people on the basis of their race, likewise, means holding an unchanging image of people, one where all details become fixed and unchangeable. Thus a person who is non-white is always a "black" person or an "Indian" but not a Canadian, no matter how much their inner cultural life has changed; the only issue is the visible racial identity of the person. The Acculturative Framework was applied to make explicit the various cultural origins that can lie behind apparently similar racial facades, and that culture and race change at very different rates.

Contexting and Stereotypes

The analytical process of "Contexting" can also be used to understand stereotyping. Since contexting is a universalistic process and not relegated to any one group there is no reason to believe that non-white people are inherently more high context than white people. However it is quite possible that high context behaviour is **more noticed** when it is exhibited by non-white people than whites. Not only is the behaviour more noticed but also it may be more resented, challenged or discouraged by whites. The components for a stereotype can be: a high context behaviour, which is problematic for the low context person; a cross-racial situation; and concerning an issue of importance to service providers or society at large. Some examples follow:

1. **Child abuse** is a service and social issue that may be more noticeable when non-white parents are involved. The high context issue that is predominantly present is that of "hierarchy," i.e., the cultural value of giving parents life and death rights over a child.

Hierarchical power expressed in physical punishment is not greater for non-white people but when it is wielded, it often claims more attention from the public and from service helpers. The concern is often greater and retribution swifter for the non-white person. There is no statistical data to support this contention, but my informal discussions with non-white practitioners suggest that this reaction indeed occurs. The stereotype involved is that non-white persons are more abusive to their children and that this is "ingrained" or because of their race.

2. **Superstitious beliefs** and other "irrational" behaviours are viewed with contempt by both the public and practitioners. When non-white people appear to be superstitious it is more noticed than with whites. The high context dimension that is involved is the one related to the pervasive "religious" property of high context life. Again, non-white people are not more irrational than white people but some of the most vivid examples are from some Black cultures. For example Voodoo is a religion that immediately creates visions of shocking bloody rites occurring in very mysterious circumstances. The beliefs surrounding Voodoo are viewed as superstitious even though the beliefs about the supernatural powers of Voodoo are no more irrational than the beliefs in other religions. That it is Black people involved in voodoo makes the behaviour even more alien and shrouded in mystery for whites. The work of committed researchers such as Zora Neale Hurston (1978) and Henry Frank, a Haitian anthropologist, does much to increase the understanding as voodoo is portrayed in its real context.

3. **People who associate together** are often resented by the public at large and even by some service colleagues at work. Sometimes people of the same race will eat together in the lunch room or cafeteria of the office or company for which they work. The high context value related here is that of "interdependence." When interdependence is expressed by non-white people it is often seen negatively as being isolative. It implies that the members look out for each other at the expense of non-members. However if a subgroup feels fully accepted and liked by the larger group there will be less likelihood of them associating together as acculturative experiences recur and draw them into the larger society. Some high context people deliberately seek to isolate themselves to maintain their own way of life in Canada. Religion is usually a prime dynamic in this decision. However non-white people are not more prone to do

this than white people but their behaviour is more noticeable as "clannishness" and it may become part of their stereotype.

4. **Being late** is seen as a social problem by low context people whose values make time quantified and in a monochronic way. High context people who are still polychronic in time orientation do not see time as a commodity, and so may often be late. They do not intend to be thoughtless, but their minds are occupied differently; the passage of time is not a preoccupation. There are many derogatory expressions about this misdemeanour when non-whites are late: "Jamaican time" or "Indian (Native) time" are common expressions. The implication is that there is something inherently deficient in the non-white person who is not on time and this becomes part of the stereotype.

Non-verbal Modes and Stereotyping

Two of the main conceptual models of this book, the Acculturative Framework and Contexting, have been used to analyse stereotyping. The non-verbal modes can also be used to understand stereotyping.

5. **Loud-speaking, rude or aggressive sounding talk** has become associated with some ethnic groups. Gumperz has shown through sociolinguistic analysis how some voices could cause irritation and misunderstanding in the listeners who had different ways of speaking English. In his film, *Crosstalk*, discussed in Chapter 5, he showed how people with certain accents could come to be regarded as rude or pushy. When the sound of the accents became associated with the visual information of non-white identity, the stereotype was created. That is, the belief that people of a certain race were rude and aggressive became fixed and unalterable. He showed how becoming aware of the part played by accents and the meanings attached to the different emphases, pitch etc., might help to reduce racist or stereotypical thinking. (A Canadian version of this film, available in video is called *Crosstalk in the Workplace*).

6. **Unpleasant smells** can become associated with people who have different food and cleanliness routines. Although most white Canadians would not want to admit to a bias against non-white peoples on this basis, it nevertheless is a stereotype held by many that non-white people smell unpleasantly. In actual fact, non-white people in Canada probably are extra careful about cleanliness

because they are aware of this stereotype about them. It is true that some spicy foods do have an olfactory result in normal skin excretions and if this occurs in a cross-racial setting it may be more noticeable. Certainly, for many whites, the smell of curry and other spices is associated with brown-skinned people and, again, becomes a racial characteristic. That white people may have characteristic odours unpleasant to non-whites, or even other whites, is usually not contemplated!

7. **"Blacks have rhythm"** is a stereotype about Black people. All groups have their own timing and pacing that gives a particular flavour and that makes each culture unique. In particular, high context groups have always had their own music, dance and beat. For example, Scottish music and dance is undeniably "Scottish" but Scots are not stereotyped as being "rhythmic." Southern American Blacks, however, are very visible when they perform jazz or other music from that part of the world, and the rhythmic beat of jazz is associated with Black people. It is possible that out of the conditions of severe racial oppression in the Southern States that Black people used music as a mode of expression and catharsis because it could not be prohibited or censured. (Some sources report that spirituals were often covert ways of announcing secret meetings, e.g., "Steal away..." may not have had a prime religious intent at the beginning). Other music, like reggae developed as a nationalistic expression of a people, as did the various Latin American musical sounds and now has popular fame. However, that situation does not make those people more rhythmic than anyone else. The stereotype of "Blacks or Latinos having rhythm" may be a harmful one because there is the implication in it of people not being capable of being serious. It is a subtle, somewhat negative, somewhat positive comment, but, nevertheless a racial stereotype.

8. **"Inscrutable Orientals"** is a negative stereotype because it permits a distancing between people of oriental and non-oriental background. The non-verbal mode has to do with culturally proscribed facial expressions, a subset under the heading of gestures. It is true that in many oriental cultures the expression of emotion was likely to be considered immature because a mature person was master of their emotions. The combination of low facial mobility and the epicanthic fold over the eyes gives the "inscrutable" expression. However, "inscrutability" is not "in the genes." The epicanthic fold, however, will not change through time, just as skin colour will not.

ACKNOWLEDGING ONE'S OWN RACE

What can practitioners do about racism in Canada? There are many arenas for fighting racism. The legal foundation for racial equality is in Section 15 of the Canadian Constitution's Charter of Rights and Freedoms and the Federal and Provincial Human Rights Commissions that oversee the implementation of the law. Police forces and professional ethics committees also have their role to play. Several suggestions have been made here for practitioners. First to acknowledge that racism exists; second, to study the effects of racism through selected readings and the use of informants. The Acculturative Framework can be used to analyse any given racial identity issue. Having prepared ourselves to work in a society where racial identity is an important component of understanding the people with whom we work, how do we convey our concern? One way is to openly acknowledge that we **all** have a racial identity. It is not fair nor healthy for only non-white people to be burdened with a negative load from their racial appearance. White people do not have to consider their race; it is a non-issue for white Canadians. However, if white professionals acknowledged their own racial appearance whenever the issue of race arose, a new consciousness about the meaning of this dimension could develop. They might find such ideas emerging as "I don't want to have to think about my own race" or "my racial appearance is not something I feel from the inside of myself" or "my race has nothing to do with how I feel about an issue." This could create a role reversal effect and reveal the unfairness of racial stereotypes and our faulty thinking about race.

As pointed out in an earlier chapter, sometimes the race of the worker is one of the first messages that a client perceives. A white worker entering an Indian reservation, a white police officer entering a Black neighbourhood, a white teacher in a predominantly non-white school are all messages that can convey insensitivity and expressions of white racial superiority to those being served. Most white practitioners do not want to be associated with these values but unless active and positive steps are taken both by service providers themselves and more widely, the service agencies and society, these negative value positions will be ascendant by default. As anti-racist education goes forward, in all the complexities that have to be faced, these values will be taken for granted as natural and proper for all practitioners.

Chapter 11

Learning/Teaching and Applying Multicultural Skills by Human Service Practitioners

CULTURALLY AND RACIALLY SENSITIVE SKILLS REQUIRED FOR PROFESSIONAL COMPETENCE

Each practitioner must have an awareness of their *ethnic self*. They are aware of and appreciate their own age, race, culture and gender, and understand the effect of these personal characteristics on others. The sensitive practitioner needs to understand how his/her own statuses effect their assessment of others. They should be able to identify the role their own contexted values play in different situations, and identify the contexted values of others. They must recognize the distance that separates their own cultural values from those of others, and make the changes needed to reduce value conflict and allow the task to be completed with a minimum of discomfort and distortion. In this, they manifest a knowledge of what ethnicity **feels** like in their daily life and work.

Each type of awareness listed above has its personal or internal set of skills that must be developed.

1. A practitioner must become adept at identifying the part played by perception, and recognize that both the practitioner and the client have cultures. The practitioner's culture affects their perception of the client. Each practitioner becomes expert on how they learn and the part played by perception in learning. For example, this book employs visual and verbal imagery to capture the essence and origins of culture (patterning) in practice situations. It is important to become aware of how these conceptualizations, or others developed by students and teachers, facilitate learning and the step-by-step process that underlies the growth of a culturally sensitive person.

2. Introspection allows the practitioner to become skilled in the process required to objectively observe one's own self. For people

who are not already so introspective, it will have to be assiduously learned. This self-objectivity is best learned in an atmosphere of trust and openness. Each person learns to acknowledge their emotions and becomes aware of their feelings of physical tension that cue either values they had that are in conflict with others' values or that their own expectations are not being met. Learning occurs best when a meditative approach is used. Here one learns to allow the feelings to be present, to emerge and be consciously analysed by oneself, with an emphasis on conscious noticing, knowing about, and paying attention to them as the objective, not on punishing or berating the self, and yearning for something different. The practitioner needs to learn to avoid being defensive about their own values and needing to be "**right**," and to use the experience of self analysis to teach themselves what values and expectations exist in their cultural repertoire. One learns there is no need to be culturally competitive and that to be competitive is dysfunctional.

3. A culturally sensitive practitioner appreciates that values are often hidden from full conscious control and they therefore can place themselves into new, often uncertain situations to reveal and learn more about their values, ideas and beliefs i.e. under go mini-culture shock experiences. Many beliefs that are discovered through this have been laid down in the years of childhood socialization, and remained unchallenged in the person's behavioural repertoire. Insights gained through culture shock experiences can be very satisfying, even though sometimes be simultaneously painful.

4. Practitioners must learn to be comfortable with a wide range of people and to acknowledge that the others' values can be understood in relation to the culture with which these people identify. The practitioner learns to accept that there are no standards by which one can measure any culture's worth in absolute terms, and that they should express the value differences between cultures in conceptual ways, paying attention to the feelings that are engendered thereby. When differences in values exist, the practitioner must tolerate ambiguity, reduce any exclusionary language and ideas, and be able to risk entering new situations in which they are the person who is very visible and a minority person.

5. Part of the ability to be interculturally and interracially comfortable, is the skill to interact non-verbally when the norms of behaviour are unfamiliar. This comfort starts with an ability to analyse the six non-verbal modes, and pay attention to each separately.

Eventually, the practitioner will perceive that the separate modes intertwine and interact to enhance communication. Once they become skilled in interacting non-verbally, the multicultural practitioners realize they have new abilities: different behavioural norms no longer are disorienting, and there is less tendency to evaluate other people according to one's own norms. The practitioner becomes able to alter his/her own non-verbal behaviour to assist communication and to carry out the helping tasks, in part by interpreting people's non-verbal cues.

6. Another skill needed is the ability to face subject matter that is not commonly allowed to be discussed or that may even be taboo. Racial identity issues are often of this sort. In a situation when people feel threatened by the taboo on the topic of discussion, issues of power should be assumed to be interfering. When there is not freedom to talk about a subject, the practitioner needs to make an evaluation as to the extent that the vulnerable people involved can face up to this difficult issue, and when it might be appropriate to do so. The practitioner must learn the ability to risk doing an unpopular and difficult thing, in this case, acknowledging, confronting and objectifying the attitudes that exist. In addition, before they can work constructively with a group member as colleague or supervisor, the practitioner needs to unwrap their own feelings of guilt, jealousy, ignorance, anger and/or fear towards certain groups .

7. Relatedly, another ability of the practitioner who can self-objectify is to discover their own stereotypes. Stereotypes are often hidden from conscious knowledge and the uncovering of stereotypical thinking is an ongoing process. Because the mind tends to simplify events by using generalizations about instantly visible categories such as age, race and gender, the taboo nature of these and related characteristics makes it even more likely that they will not automatically be examined. An ability to tune in on one's stereotypical thinking, then, is a crucial skill for sensitive, multicultural service provision.

8. Being able to enter another person's cultural frame of reference means being able to move between *etic* and *emic* frames of explanation. This implies the ability to apply a generalizable model to any given situation and then to search in the person's past and in the present for the elements that make up a particular frame of reference. One must then continue to deepen their understanding about the cultural identity issues, and the ideas important to that

person. This may mean accepting new ideas or modifying one's own ideas on subjects about which one already feels knowledgeable. It may also mean helping people to enter the other's frame of reference with whom they must interact. In some cases, it may mean teaching low context skills to a high context person. Some of these low context skills are:

a.   being able to build contexts for themselves in each new situation;

b.   giving explicit explanations, when, before, meanings were **in the context**, i.e., learning to speak directly rather than indirectly;

c.   learning to self-objectify;

d.   being able to individualize;

e.   eschewing loyalties maintained merely because of tradition or precedents that are not appropriate to the situation;

f.   being analytical about problems and perceiving the components of a situation as well as the whole of it.

Entering another's frame of reference means being able to understand events, people and attitudes from the other's point of view. Both cognitive and affective information must be considered here. One particular issue of very great importance is appreciation of how difficult it is for someone to learn another language. Understanding this is important for all service providers.

9.   Many of the skills mentioned mean that the culturally sensitive person must be able to do at least two things at once. At the least, there is the dual perspective of oneself and of the other person, colleague or client, that must be maintained simultaneously. Also, the practitioner must be able to inspect the verbal and non-verbal output of both oneself and another and create effective communication in an optimum manner for both of you.

10. Sensitive practitioners should be articulate about cognitive and emotional concepts and thus be a resource about cultural and racial sensitivity to others.

11. A multicultural practitioner must be able to identify an ethnic community and analyse its major dimensions, such as its institutional components.

12. All of these previous skills depend on one central skill: being an

observer. This grows out of the foundation developed in self-awareness and being able to acknowledge one's self and senses in a spirit of compassion. These skills can be taught/learned only under conditions of openness, mutual acceptance and an atmosphere of trust.

MODELS OF CULTURAL CHANGE AND LEARNING MULTICULTURAL SENSITIVITY

Three models involving 21 variables have been discussed. These are building blocks in cultural and racial sensitivity training. Separately, or in different combinations, these variables enable an overview of the people to be served,and provide *entrée* to understanding the culture of any of these people. Examples have been presented with each variable, but teachers/learners should bring in issues of interest to their own workplace. Ideally, each workplace should develop its own expertise about the various cultures within its own locale. This completes the cycle from etic (generalized) to emic (specific) knowledge.

Cultural shifts are part of normal life and especially true of a world in which people are moving about more than ever before. Thus, a grasp of the factors in culture change is critical for all practitioners, and the Acculturative Framework inspected the major factors involved in the cultural changes that figure so greatly in rendering human services to peoples of many diverse cultures and races. The idea of contexting in this book concerns primarily people moving from high to low context situations. However, the future portends some limit to how "low" in context culture we can go. There already is some swing back to higher context dimensions, perhaps under political pressure, as the individualistic emphasis gives way to a renewed emphasis on a high context family, when the family looks after its own, rather than relying on the State, and when the family must make more decisions for its members than some mandated agency.

Even so, the return to a high context way can lead only to a quasi-family context, because, when the geographic mobility of its members divides the family, interdependence cannot be put back together again. Rather, services must be directed to build up quasi-family life: groups for living together and finding purpose and meaning in life. Whatever happens, there will be need to understand the cultures of those living and working together.

References

Abella, Irving and Harold Troper. 1982. *None is Too Many: Canada and the Jews of Europe 1933-1948.* Toronto: Lester, Arpen Dennys.

Anderson G.M. 1974. *Networks of Contact: The Portuguese and Toronto.* Waterloo, Ontario: Wilfrid Laurier Press.

Argyle Michael, and Mark Cook. 1976. *Gaze and Gaze Aversion.* Cambridge: Cambridge University Press.

Banton, Michael. 1988. *Racial Consciousness.* London and New York: Longman.

Bateson, Gregory. 1979. *Mind and Nature: A Necessary Unity,* New York: Bantam Books.

B.C. Task Force on Immigrant Women. 1982. *Immigrant Women in Canada: a Resource Handbook for Action.* Vancouver.

Berger, Mr. Justice Thomas R. 1977. *Northern Frontier Northern Homeland Vol. 1: The Report of the McKenzie Valley Pipeline Inquiry.* Toronto: James Lorimer and Co., and Publishing Centre, Supply and Services, Canada.

Birdwhistell, Raymond L. 1952. *Introduction to Kinesics.* Louisville: University of Louisville Press.

Breton, Raymond. 1964. "Institutional Completeness of Ethnic Communities and the Personal Relations of Immigrants," *American J. of Sociology,* 70, 2, (September 1964): 193-203.

Breton, Raymond. 1981. *The Ethnic Community as a Resource in Relation to Group Problems: Perceptions and Attitudes.* Toronto: Centre for Urban and Community Studies.

Bruneau, Thomas. 1983. "A Brief Introduction to Chronemics," presented at the Second International Conference on Non-Verbal Behaviour. Toronto, May 1983.

Campbell, Joseph. 1949. *The Hero with a Thousand Faces.* New York: Bollinger Series XVII Pantheon Books.

Canada: Employment and Immigration. 1981 and updated. *The Immigration Handbook.* Ottawa.

Capra, Fritjof. 1985. *The Tao of Physics: An Exploration of the*

Parallels Between Modern Physics and Eastern Mysticism, second edition, revised and updated. Boston: New Science Library, Shambala publications Inc.

Casse, Pierre. 1979. *Training for the Cross-Cultural Mind.* Washington D.C.: The Society for Intercultural Education Training and Research.

Christensen, C.P. 1990. "Toward a Framework for Social Work Education in a Multicultural and Multiracial Canada," In S. Yelaja, *Proceedings of the Settlement and Integration of New Immigrants to Canada Conference, Feb. 17-19, 1988.* Ontario: Faculty of Social Work and Centre for Social Welfare Studies, Wilfred Laurier University.

Coe, Ralph T. 1976. "Sacred Circles: The Indianness of North American Indian Art," in *Sacred Circles: Two Thousand Years of North American Indian Art..* Kansas City, Missouri: Nelson Gallery of Art - Atkins Museum of Fine Arts: 9-16.

Condon, William S. and Ogston W.D. 1971. "Speech and Body Motion Synchrony of Speaker-Hearer" in D.L. Horton and J.J. Jenkins eds. *Perception of Language.* Columbus Ohio: E. Merrill Press.

Condon, William S. 1978. "An Analysis of Behavioural Organization." *Sign Language Studies,* 13.

Conze, Edward. 1959. *Buddhist Scripture.* Penguin Books.

Da Costa, Granville. 1978. "Orphans and Outlaws: Some Impacts of Racism," *Multiculturalism* 2:1: 4-7.

Danziger, Kurt. 1971. *The Socialization of Immigrant Children Part 2.* Toronto: York University Ethnic-Research Programme, Institute for Behavioural Research.

Davis, Kingsley. 1951. *The Population of India and Pakistan.* Princeton, N.J.: Princeton University Press.

Disman, Milada. 1981. "Stranger's Homecoming: A Study of the Experience of Immigration." Unpublished doctoral dissertation. Department of Educational Theory, University of Toronto.

Draguns, Juris G. 1976. "Counselling Across Cultures: Common Themes and Distinct Approaches," in *Counselling Across Cultures.* eds. Paul Pedersen, Walter J. Lonner. Honolulu: East-West Center, The University Press of Hawaii. 1-16.

Erickson, Frederick. 1979. "Talking Down: Some Sources of Miscommunication in Interracial Interviews," in *Non-verbal Behaviour: Applications and Cultural Implications.* ed. Aaron Wolfgang.. New York: Academic Press. 99-126.

Forman, Frieda. 1985. "Reflections on the Feminization of Time," *J. of*

Canadian Women's Studies, 6:2, Spring: 27-31.

Germaine, Carol and Gittermen, Alex. 1980. *The Life Model of Social Work Practice.* New York: Columbia University Press.

Getzels, Jacob W., and Jackson, Philip W. 1962. *Creativity and Intelligence: Exploration with Gifted Students.* N.Y.: John Wiley. 13-14.

Gibbons, Boyd. 1986. "The Intimate Sense of Smell," *National Geographic,* 170, 3 September: 324-360.

Ginzberg, Effie. 1987. *Impact of the Media on Race Relations.* Toronto: Urban Alliance on Race Relations.

Green, James W. 1982. *Cultural Awareness in the Human Services.* Englewood Cliffs, New Jersey: Prentice-Hall Inc.

Guildford, J. Paul. 1959. *Personality.* N.Y.: McGraw-Hall.

Hall, Edward T. 1969. *The Hidden Dimension.* Garden City, New York: Anchor Press Doubleday.

Hall, Edward T. 1976a. "How Cultures Collide," *Psychology Today,* July: 67-74,97.

Hall, Edward T. 1976. *Beyond Culture.* Garden City, New York, Anchor Press Doubleday.

Hall, Edward T. 1984. *The Dance of Life: The Other Dimension of Time.* Garden City, New York: Anchor Press Doubleday.

Hansen, M.L. 1962. "The Third Generation in America," *Commentary* 14: 492-500.

Harney, Robert F. 1979. *Oral Testimony and Ethnic Studies.* Toronto: Multicultural History Society.

Head, Wilson. 1975. *The Black Presence in the Canadian Mosaic.* Ontario Human Rights Commission.

Henley, Nancy and Marianne LaFrance. 1984. "Gender as Culture: Difference and Dominance in Non-verbal Behaviour," in *Non-verbal Behaviour: Perspectives, Applications, Intercultural Insights.* ed. Aaron Wolfgang. Toronto: C.J. Hogrefe Inc.

Henry, Frances. 1978. *The Dynamics of Racism in Toronto.* Toronto: Secretary of State.

Henry, Frances and Effie Ginzberg. 1985. *Who Gets the Work? A Test of Racial Discrimination in Employment.* Toronto: The Urban Alliance on Race Relations and the Social Planning Council of Metropolitan Toronto.

Herberg, Dorothy Chave. 1978. "Child Care," in *The Work Incentive Experience.* eds. Charles D. Garvin, Audrey D. Smith and William J. Reid. New York: Allanheld, Osmun and Co. Universe Books.

Herberg, Dorothy Chave. 1982. "Discovering Ethnic Root Behaviours,"

International J. of Intercultural Relations 6: 153-168.

Herberg, Dorothy Chave. 1983. "Issues in Multicultural Child Welfare: Working with Families Originating in Traditional Societies," *Social Work Papers*, The School of Social Work, University of Southern California 17 (Summer): 45-57.

Herberg, Dorothy Chave. 1985. "Social Work with New Immigrants," in *An Introduction to Social Work Practice in Canada.* ed. Shankar A. Yelaja. Scarborough, Ontario: Prentice-Hall: 234-251.

Herberg, Dorothy Chave and E.N. Herberg. 1987. *Issues Concerning Agencies Serving Immigrants and Refugees*, submission to the Canadian Task Force on Mental Health Issues Affecting Immigrants and Refugees. Toronto, Ontario, May 6.

Herberg, Dorothy Chave. 1988. "An Adaptation Framework of Ethnic Communities," Chapter 11 in *Ethnic Groups in Canada: Adaptations and Transitions* by Edward Herberg. Toronto: Nelson Books.

Herberg, Edward N. 1988. *Ethnic Groups in Canada: Adaptations and Transitions.* Toronto: Nelson Books.

Herberg, Will. 1960 *Protestant-Catholic-Jew.* revised edition. Garden City, New York: Doubleday.

Howes, David. 1987. "Olfaction and Transition: An Essay on the Ritual Uses of Smell," *Canadian Review of Sociology and Anthropology* 24, 3: 398-416.

Hughes, David and Evelyn Kallen. 1974. *The Anatomy of Racism: Canadian Dimension.* Montreal: Harvest House.

Hurston, Zora Neale. 1978. *Mules and Men.* Bloomington, Indiana: Indian University Press.

Immigration and Refugee Board Documentation Centre. 1990. *Somalia: Country Profile.* Ottawa: Canada.

Isajiw, Wasevolod W. 1981. *Ethnic Identity Retention Toronto.* Toronto: Centre for Urban and Community Studies, University of Toronto.

Johnston, Patrick. 1983. *Native Children and the Child Welfare System.* Toronto: Canadian Council on Social Development in association with James Lorrimer & Co.

Kallen, Evelyn. 1982. *Ethnicity and Human Rights in Canada.* Toronto: Gage Publishing Ltd.

Kalbach, Warren E. 1981. *Ethnic Residential Segregation and its Significance for the Individual in an Urban Setting.* Toronto: Centre for Urban and Community Studies, University of Toronto.

Krauter, Joseph F. 1978. and Morris Davis, *Minority Canadians: Ethnic*

Groups. Toronto: Methuen.

Lee, Sky. 1990. *The Disappearing Moon Cafe.* Vancouver: Douglas and McIntyre.

Litwak, Eugene. 1965. "Extended Kin Relations in an Industrial Democratic Society," in *Social Structure and the Family: Generational Relations.* eds., Ethel Shanes and Gordon F. Streib. Englewood Cliffs, N.J.: Prentice-Hall

Maslow, Abraham. 1956. "Defense and Growth," *Merrill-Palmer Quarterly,* 3, 1: 37-38.

McCaskell, Tim. 1988. *Camp Facilitator's Handbook: Multicultural/ Multiracial Residential Camp for Secondary School Students.* Toronto: Toronto Board of Education, Office of the Advisor on Race Relations.

McDiarmid,Garnet and David Pratt. 1971. *Teaching Prejudice: A Content Analysis of Social Studies Textbooks Authorized for Use in Ontario.* Toronto: Ontario Institiute for Studies in Education.

McGoldrick, Monica, John K. Pearce, Joseph Giordano. 1982. *Ethnicity and Family Therapy.* New York: The Guildford Press.

Mead, George Herbert. 1934. *Mind, Self and Society.* Chicago: University of Chicago Press.

Metropolitan Toronto Children's Aid Society. 1982. *Task Force on Multicultural Programmes.* Toronto.

Montagu, Ashley. 1981. "Culture and Mental Illness," *Am. J. of Psychiatry,* 18, (July):15-23.

Montagu, Ashley. 1972. *Statement on Race: An Annotative Elaboration and Exposition on the Four Statements on Race Isssued by The United Nations Educational, Scientific and Cultural Organization.* Third Edition. New York: Oxford University Press.

Montagu, Ashley. 1986. *Touching: the Human Significance of the Skin.* third edition. New York: Harper and Row.

Moore, Dorothy E. 1991. "Recruitment and Admission of Minority Students to Schools of Social Work," *Canadian Social Work Review,* 8, 2, (Summer): 190-210.

Morgan, Lewis. 1877. *Ancient Society or Researches in the Lines of Human Progress from Savagery through Barbarism to Civilization.* Chicago: H. Kerr and Co. Co-operative.

Morris, Desmond. 1979 *Gestures, Their Origin and Distribution.* London: Jonathan Cape.

Mostwin, Danuta. 1976. "Uprootment and Anxiety," *International J. of Mental Health,* 5, 2:103-116.

Munro, Alistair. 1981. "Nostalgia," *Canadian Doctor.* March , 77-80.

Nasrallah, Emily. 1987. *Flight Against Time*. Charlottetown: Ragweed Press.

National Congress of Italians. 1979. *Study of Social Services*. Toronto.

Parkes, C. Murray. 1971. "Psycho-Social Transitions: A Field for Study," *Social Science and Medicine* 5 : 101-115.

Parry, Joan K.(ed.). 1990. *Social Work Practice With The Terminally Ill: The Transcultural Perspective*. Springfield, Illinois: Charles C. Thomas.

Pitman, W. 1977. *Now is Not Too Late*. Report submitted to the Council of Metropolitan Toronto by the Task Force on Human Relations.

Plaut, Gunther. 1975. *Refugee Determination in Canada*. Employment and Immigration, Minister of Supply and Service, Canada.

Poyatos, Fernando. 1984. "Linguistic Fluency and Verbal-Non-verbal Fluency," in *Non-verbal Behavior: Perspectives, Applications and Intercultural Insights*. Toronto: C.J. Hogrefe.

Reitz, Jeffrey G. 1980. *The Survival of Ethnic Groups*. Toronto: McGraw-Hill.

Reitz, Jeffrey G., Liviano Calzavara, and Donna Dasko. 1981. "*Ethnic Inequality and Segregation in Jobs*. Toronto: Centre for Urban and Community Studies.

Rosen, Aaron. 1982. "Barriers to Utilization of Research by Social Work Practitioners," Presented at the 25th Anniversary Conference of the Doctoral Program in Social Work and Social Science. Ann Arbor: University of Michigan, May 27-29.

Royal Commission on Bilingualism and Biculturalism. 1970. *Report: Book 4 — The Cultural Contribution of the Other Ethnic Groups* Ottawa: Information Canada.

Samuels, Mike M.D. and Nancy Samuels. 1975. *Seeing with the Mind's Eye: The History, Techniques and Uses of Visualization*. New York: Random House, Bookworks Book.

Sayadaw, Mahasi. 1977. "Insight Meditation: Basic and Progressive Stages," in *Living Buddhist Masters*. ed.Jack Kornfield, Boulder: Prajna Press: 51-81.

Scherer, Klaus. 1984. "State of the Art in Vocal Communication: A Partial View," in *Non-verbal Behaviour: Perspectives, Applications, Intercultural Insights*. ed. Aaron Wolfgang, Toronto: C.J. Hogrefe: 41-74.

Shweder, Richard A. 1991. *Thinking Through Cultures: Expeditions in Cultural Psychology*. Cambridge, Mass.: Harvard University Press.

Sikkema, Mildred and Agnes Niyekawa-Howard. 1977. *Cross-cultural Learning and Self-Growth*. New York: International Association of Schools of Social Work.

Sluzki, Carlos E. 1979. "Migration and Family Conflict," *Family Process,* 18, 4: 379-390.

Sokolov, Raymond. 1987. "Odd and Unusual Tastes," *Natural History,* Vol. 11, 104.

Special Issue on Central Eurasia and Eastern Europe.1983. *Refuge.* 12, 7, (February): entire issue.

Thomas, Barb and Charles Novogrodsky. 1983. *Combatting Racism in the Workplace: Readings Kit.* Toronto: Cross Cultural Communication Centre.

Thomas, Barb. 1987. *Multiculturalism at Work: A Guide to Organizational Change.* Toronto: YWCA of Metropolitan Toronto.

Toronto Board of Education. 1976. *Final Report of the Work Group on Multicultural Programs.* Toronto

Trigger, Bruce G. 1976. *The Children of Aataentsic: A History of the Huron People to 1600.* Montreal: McGill-Queen's University Press.

Vassanji, M.G. 1991. *No New Land.* Toronto: McClelland and Stewart, Inc.

Vlassie, Katherine. 1987. *Children of Byzantium.* Winnipeg: Cormorant Books.

Wallnofer, Henrich and Anna van Rottanscher. 1975. *Chinese Folk Medicine and Acupuncture.* London and Toronto: White Lion Publishers Ltd.

Watson, Graham. 1981. "The Reification of Ethnicity and its Consequences," *Canadian Review Sociology and Anthropology,* 18: 4: 453-469.

Waxer, Peter. 1984. "Non-verbal Aspects of Psychotherapy: Discrete Functions in the Intercultural Context," in *Non-verbal Behavior: Perspectives, Applications and Intercultural Insights.* ed. Aaron Wolfgang. Toronto: C.J. Hogrefe.

Weber, M. 1958. *The Protestant Ethic and the Spirit of Capitalism,* New York: Charles Scribners Sons.

Winks, Robin W. 1971. *The Blacks in Canada: A History.* Montreal: McGill-Queen's University Press.

Wolfgang, Aaron. ed., 1979. *Non-verbal Behavior: Applications and Cultural Implications.* New York: Academic Press.

Wolfgang, Aaron. 1984. *Non-verbal Behavior: Perspectives, Applications and Intercultural Insights.* Toronto: C.J. Hogrefe.

Wood, Marjorie Rodgers. 1984. *Social Service Agents and Indo-Canadian*

Immigrants in Vancouver. Ph.D. Thesis in Department of Anthropology, University of B.C.

YWCA of Metro Toronto. 1982. *Multicultural Development Programme.* Toronto.